JESUS AND HIS SACRIFICE

Books by Dr. Vincent Taylor

THE FORMATION OF THE GOSPEL
    TRADITION

FORGIVENESS AND RECONCILIATION:
    A STUDY IN NEW TESTAMENT
    THEOLOGY

THE GOSPEL ACCORDING TO ST. MARK
    The Greek Text with Introduction, Notes.
    and Indexes

THE LIFE AND MINISTRY OF JESUS

THE NAMES OF JESUS

THE CROSS OF CHRIST

THE PERSON OF CHRIST

Macmillan and Co Ltd

★

THE HISTORICAL EVIDENCE FOR THE
    VIRGIN BIRTH

BEHIND THE THIRD GOSPEL: A STUDY
    OF THE PROTO-LUKE HYPOTHESIS

Oxford University Press

★

THE FIRST DRAFT OF ST. LUKE'S
    GOSPEL

Society for Promoting Christian Knowledge

★

THE GOSPELS: A SHORT INTRODUC-
    TION

THE ATONEMENT IN NEW TESTAMENT
    TEACHING

THE DOCTRINE OF THE HOLY SPIRIT
    (in collaboration with H. Watkin-Jones,
    H. Roberts and N. H. Snaith)

The Epworth Press

JESUS AND HIS SACRIFICE

A STUDY OF THE PASSION-SAYINGS
IN THE GOSPELS

BY

VINCENT TAYLOR

Ph.D., D.D. (Lond.), Hon. D.D. (Leeds)

PRINCIPAL AND FERENS PROFESSOR OF NEW TESTAMENT LANGUAGE AND
LITERATURE AT WESLEY COLLEGE, HEADINGLEY, LEEDS

LONDON

MACMILLAN & CO LTD

NEW YORK · ST MARTIN'S PRESS

1959

First Edition 1937
Reprinted 1939, 1943, 1948, 1951, 1955, 1959

MACMILLAN AND COMPANY LIMITED
London Bombay Calcutta Madras Melbourne

THE MACMILLAN COMPANY OF CANADA LIMITED
Toronto

ST MARTIN'S PRESS INC
New York

PRINTED IN GREAT BRITAIN

TO

E. T. AND M. M. T.

PREFACE

AFTER devoting something like twenty-five years to the study of the problems of literary and historical criticism in connexion with the Gospels, and especially to the minutiæ of source criticism, I am conscious of a strong desire to investigate some more vital issue, arising out of these studies, which bears intimately upon Christian life and practice. For this reason during the last four years, in the intervals of a busy life spent in teaching and administration, I have endeavoured to make a careful investigation of the Passion-sayings, with a view to discovering how Jesus interpreted His suffering and death. The results of this inquiry are published in the present volume. Portions of the work were included in a course of Lectures given at University College, Bangor, in May, 1936, and I gladly take this opportunity of expressing my deep gratitude to Principal D. Emrys Evans and the members of the University Staff for the wonderful kindness I received during my visit to Wales. I also recall with the greatest pleasure the keen interest which is taken by Welsh ministers and students in theological studies.

The plan of the work is simple. In Part I, I have examined the outstanding Old Testament ideas which form a necessary background to the sayings of Jesus, and in the light of which alone they can be understood. Part II contains the critical investigation of the sayings themselves, in Mark, Luke, 1 Cor. xi. 23-5, and the Fourth Gospel. Here I have thought it well to give special attention to questions of genuineness, as well as of interpretation, in consequence of the most recent phase of Gospel research represented by Form-Criticism in Germany, Great

Britain, and the United States of America. Part III is constructive. It is devoted to an attempt to state the results to which the investigation leads. I am well aware that, in this section, my work reaches its most vulnerable point. Differences of opinion on these matters are inevitable, and I cannot expect that the views I have outlined will commend themselves to every reader. There is a not unnatural inclination on the part of many Gospel critics to avoid discussing ultimate questions. The critic comforts himself with the opinion that these are not his province; they are the responsibility of the theologian, whereas his own duty is to observe the wisdom of the proverb which warns us that the shoemaker must stick to his last. There can be no doubt at all that the observance of this principle has made possible a vast amount of learned research to which all students are indebted. It was, however, always a dangerous principle, since, in the limited province within which the expert must work, it is easy to see results out of focus. Many examples of this peril could easily be given, especially the attempts of the Liberal School to understand and explain the beginnings of Christianity. But, however hazardous it may have been, this method is doubly dangerous to-day, when the fortunes of the Christian religion in the world approach a kind of Armageddon in which its immense claims must finally be tried in the fires of conflict. The critic of to-day must live in two worlds, the academic region of his particular interests and the larger world of contemporary religion. At least once in his life he should be compelled to come out into the open and declare the bearing of his tentative results upon the larger problems of Christian belief and worship. Only in this way can he discover whether his work is worth while, or whether it is nothing more than academic trifling. It is in this persuasion that I have written Part III, and in particular the last chapter, in which I have sketched a theory of the Atonement in harmony with the conclusions reached in Parts I and II.

A sacrificial interpretation of the doctrine of the Atonement is regarded with hesitation by some theologians, in view of popular misconceptions about sacrifice, and the variety of opinion current among anthropologists as to its origins. I should therefore like to take the opportunity of saying that my discussion is not necessarily bound up with any one explanation, although I have not disguised my preference for the communion-theory of Robertson Smith rather than the gift-theory supported by G. Buchanan Gray. My argument, however, does not depend on a particular *rationale* of sacrifice, but is based rather on what is undoubtedly the highest expression of sacrificial worship as we find it in the Old Testament. I understand this to be the idea of an offering which man can make his own, and it is this conception which I have specially in mind when I speak of the sacrificial principle.

For the most part the references in footnotes will, I think, be sufficiently clear, but I ought perhaps to explain that when well-known commentaries are mentioned, I have simply given the page number after the author's name. A list of these commentaries is supplied on p. xiii.

It remains for me to express my deep sense of gratitude to my friends and colleagues who have so generously helped me by reading the typescript and proof sheets; to Dr. J. W. Lightley, formerly Principal of Wesley College, and to my present colleagues, Dr. H. Watkin-Jones, Dr. Harold Roberts, the Rev. N. H. Snaith, M.A., and the Rev. P. S. Watson, M.A. I am also very grateful for the help of one of my students, Mr. G. T. Roberts, M.A., who has compiled the Index of Proper Names and corrected the proof sheets. I desire also to thank the members of the firm of Robert MacLehose & Co., The University Press, Glasgow, for their patience, skill, and accuracy. The responsibility for any errors which may remain rests, of course, with myself. I send out this book in the hope that it may make some small contribution to the study of one of the most important doctrines of the Christian Faith.

VINCENT TAYLOR.

College House,
   Wesley College,
      Headingley, Leeds.
         Aug. 5th, 1937.

CONTENTS

CONTENTS

PART III: DOCTRINAL

ABBREVIATIONS

The following commentaries are cited by the page number after the author's name:

J. H. Bernard: *A Critical and Exegetical Commentary on the Gospel according to St. John.*

A. W. F. Blunt: *The Gospel according to St. Mark (The Clarendon Bible).*

A. E. Brooke: *A Critical and Exegetical Commentary on the Johannine Epistles.*

J. M. Creed: *The Gospel according to St. Luke.*

B. S. Easton: *The Gospel according to St. Luke.*

E. P. Gould: *A Critical and Exegetical Commentary on the Gospel according to St. Mark.*

E. Klostermann: *Das Matthäusevangelium; Das Markusevangelium; Das Lukasevangelium.*

P.-M. Lagrange: *Évangile selon saint Marc; Évangile selon saint Jean.*

H. K. Luce: *The Gospel according to St. Luke (Cambridge Greek Testament).*

H. A. W. Meyer: *Critical and Exegetical Commentary on the New Testament (The Epistles to the Corinthians).*

A. Plummer: *A Critical and Exegetical Commentary on the Gospel according to St. Luke.*

A. E. J. Rawlinson: *St. Mark (Westminster Commentaries).*

A. Robertson and A. Plummer: *A Critical and Exegetical Commentary on the First Epistle of St. Paul to the Corinthians.*

B. T. D. Smith: *The Gospel according to St. Matthew (Cambridge Greek Testament).*

H. B. Swete: *The Gospel according to St. Mark.*

H. G. Wood: *Mark (Peake's Commentary on the Bible).*

PART I
THE OLD TESTAMENT BACKGROUND

INTRODUCTION

A STUDY of the attitude of Jesus to His suffering and death naturally demands a close investigation of His sayings in the Gospels. It is, however, undesirable in the highest degree to proceed to the interpretation of these sayings without giving careful attention to the problems of sources, of language, and of text, to the history of exegesis, to the causes which led to the emergence of the Gospels, the conditions out of which they came and the ends they were intended to serve. It is necessary also to consider the relationship between the recorded words of Jesus and the things He actually taught and said. How far, for example, have later ideas and beliefs coloured the record, and with what qualifications can we depend upon its genuineness?

These are obviously complicated and difficult questions, but of their importance and necessity there can be no doubt. Their difficulty is enhanced by the fact that many of them involve still further inquiries. It is necessary, for example, to have regard to that which is taught concerning the Atonement in the rest of the New Testament, and to the history of the doctrine in the succeeding centuries down to the present day, for otherwise the distinctiveness of the sayings of Jesus cannot be justly appraised. Equally important is it to study the sayings against the background of thought and action found in the Old Testament. The thought of Jesus is steeped in that of the Old Testament and cannot be understood apart from it. It follows, therefore, that to attempt to understand His words without a preliminary study of such conceptions as the Kingdom of God, the Messianic Hope, the Son of Man, the Son, the Suffering Servant, and the idea of Sacrifice, is disastrous.

The importance of a study of the Old Testament is especially clear from the history of the attempts to interpret the life and thought of Jesus during the last fifty years. Many curious theories have gained a lively, if shortlived currency. Jesus has been represented as an Essene, or a Buddhist, or a Socialist, or as an Eastern mystic. It has even been questioned if He ever lived at all; and, where the extremer fashions have been successfully resisted, the tendency has been to modernize His figure, to dress Him in the clothes of a twentieth-century teacher, and to represent His teaching as a kind of genial morality suitable to the needs of an enlightened bourgeoisie. These pictures were shattered by the artillery of Albert Schweitzer who forced us to look upon a Jesus strange to our time.[1] Step by step we have been driven back, behind the Apocalyptic Literature, to the Old Testament itself, and compelled to see Jesus in its light. The New Testament scholar has shown that Aramaic tradition lies behind the Gospel record; the Old Testament scholar, with the added discipline of Comparative Religion, has continued to elucidate the ideas and practices of Hebrew religion; and the student of the Rabbinical Literature has expounded the ideas of later Judaism. In consequence, we have rediscovered the obvious: the Old Testament, we find, is of vital significance for our understanding of the mind and thought of Jesus. We perceive that, while we may be hampered by a limited acquaintance with the New Psychology, we are entirely disqualified for the investigation if we do not know the Law, the Prophets, and the Psalms.

It is in this persuasion that Part I of the present inquiry

[1] See *The Quest of the Historical Jesus*.

is devoted to the study of the Old Testament background of the thought of Jesus.   It is necessary, however, to emphasize the fact that this part of the investigation is only a preliminary stage.   We do not possess the key to the mind of Jesus when we know the relevant Old Testament concepts; all we have gained is the right to approach the door.   Such is His originality that it is never safe to assume that He simply appropriated whatever lay ready to hand.   He takes over traditional ideas and makes them His own.   If He is to speak at all, they are necessary to Him, but almost always they are an embarrassment; they clothe His thoughts, but need to be stretched, patched, and refashioned, because the life they hide is too strong.

I

THE KINGDOM OF GOD

THE first theme which claims attention is that of the Kingdom of God.

Although the expression 'Kingdom of God' is not found in the Old Testament, the idea is there, rooted in the concept of Yahweh as 'King'.[1] The *locus classicus* is Ex. xv. 18: 'The Lord shall reign for ever and ever.' This idea appears also in the prophetical literature: in Isaiah's vision of 'the King, the Lord of hosts' (vi. 5), and his proclamation: 'The Lord is our King' (xxxiii. 22); in Jeremiah's question: 'Is not the Lord in Zion? is not her King in her?' (viii. 19); and in the message of the Second Isaiah: 'I am the Lord, your Holy One, the Creator of Israel, your King' (xliii. 15).[2]

The term 'Kingdom', in relation to God, is found in later passages: in Psa. xxii. 28: 'For the kingdom is the Lord's'; Psa. xlv. 6: 'A sceptre of equity is the sceptre of thy kingdom'; Psa. ciii. 19: 'His kingdom ruleth over all'; Psa. cxlv. 13: 'Thy kingdom is an everlasting kingdom' (cf. Dan. iv. 3); and in 1 Chron. xxix. 11: 'Thine is the kingdom, O Lord, and thou art exalted as head above all'. In Dan. ii. 44 it is prophesied that 'the God of heaven'

[1] Cf. G. Gloege, *Reich Gottes und Kirche im Neuen Testament*, 6ff.; the article on βασιλεύς in Kittel's *Theologisches Wörterbuch*, i. 562ff.; H. M. Hughes, *The Kingdom of Heaven*, 13ff.; E. F. Scott, *The Kingdom of God*, 11ff.

[2] Cf. also Isa. xli. 21, xliv. 6; Psa. v. 2, lxxxiv. 3, lxxxix. 18. For a discussion of the 'Coronation Psalms' (xlvii., xciii., xcv.-c.) see Mowinckel, *Psalmenstudien*, ii.; N. H. Snaith, *Studies in the Psalter*, 88ff

shall 'set up a kingdom, which shall never be destroyed', and in Dan. vii. 27 it is said that 'the kingdom and the dominion, and the greatness of the kingdoms under the whole heaven, shall be given to the people of the saints of the Most High.' 'His kingdom,' it is declared, 'is an everlasting kingdom, and all dominions shall serve and obey him.'

The idea of the Kingdom is not limited to the passages in which the term actually appears; it is present in all the forecasts of a new order in which God's rule should be supreme.   No doubt bitter experiences of the monarchy fostered these hopes, but their core is always belief in God as King.   It lay in the nature of things that the idea should become eschatological, and it is not surprising that sometimes it is that of a restored and triumphant nation and sometimes that of a supernatural order established either directly by God Himself or mediately through the person of His Messiah.   More significant are the spiritual forecasts early and late as in Hos. xiv. and Zeph. iii. 20, and especially those which are universalistic in their range (cf. Isa. xlix. 6, Mic. iv. 1-5, Isa. ii. 2-4).   In the medley of dreams and hopes present in the Apocalyptic Literature Babylonian and Persian influences supplement religious beliefs derived from the Old Testament.   Sometimes the picture of the Age to Come follows that of a temporary Messianic Kingdom, and there is a marked tendency to calculate times and seasons and to depict in lurid colours a succession of events which include Messianic Woes, the Coming of the Son of Man, the Resurrection of the Dead, the Last Judgment, and the Final Restoration of all things.

For our special purpose it is not necessary to describe the hope of the Kingdom in greater detail; the more important question is the attitude of Jesus to this expectation.   Of its centrality in His teaching there can be no doubt; it dominates His thought both in relation to His person and with regard to His mission and work.

According to Mark, Jesus began His mission with the announcement: 'The time is fulfilled, and the kingdom of God is at hand: repent ye, and believe in the good news' (i. 15). What is this 'kingdom', and how did He conceive it?

The difficulty of translating βασιλεία is well known. At present there is a strong tendency, illustrated in the discussions of K. L. Schmidt, G. Gloege, and others, to render it by 'kingly rule' or 'reign' rather than by 'kingdom' or 'realm'.[1] This tendency is well justified. The idea of a community underlies the sayings of Jesus,[2] for the *Basileia* is not simply a spiritual experience, or a *summum bonum* reached by man's efforts; but the communal idea is secondary and derivative, since the 'kingly rule' necessarily implies and demands the association of those among whom it is exercised. It is a misinterpretation of the teaching of Jesus to speak of the Kingdom, with Ritschl, as 'the organisation of humanity through action inspired by love',[3] although, naturally, such a state of affairs would follow from the presence of the Kingdom.

Primarily, the *Basileia* is the Rule of God exercised among men and accepted by them.

If we examine the sixty[4] sayings and parables in which

[1]'Die wesentliche Bedeutung nicht *Reich*, sondern *Herrschaft* ist', K. L. Schmidt, *Theologisches Wörterbuch*, i. 582, *Theology*, May, 1927; G. Gloege, *op. cit.*, 49-58; R. N. Flew, *The Idea of Perfection in Christian Theology*, 8-40.

[2]In this lie the roots of the conception of the Church.

[3]*Justification and Reconciliation* (Eng. Tr.), 12. Cf. R. N. Flew, who instances Herrmann's definition: 'the universal moral community, the aspect under which humanity is included in God's purpose for Himself', *Expository Times*, xlvi. 214.

[4]Excluding parallel versions of the same saying.

Jesus speaks of the *Basileia*, we shall find that in less than a sixth of them is the thought of a community prominent or distinctive. Significantly enough five of the exceptions are sayings which, on other grounds, are widely believed to be spurious or corrupted in the course of transmission. Three of these sayings appear in the interpretation of the parable of the Tares (Mt. xiii. 38, 41, 43); a fourth is the saying: 'Whosoever therefore shall break one of these least commandments, and shall teach men so, shall be called least in the kingdom of heaven' (Mt. v. 19); the fifth is the difficult passage: 'I will give unto thee the keys of the kingdom of heaven' (Mt. xvi. 19).[1] Other sayings where the communal idea may be primary are: Mk. ix. 47; Lk. vii. 28, xvi. 16; Mt. vii. 21. In the overwhelming majority the thought is that of the Reign or Rule of God. Even in passages which speak of 'entering into' or 'sitting down' in the *Basileia* the thought is that of a fellowship in which God's Will is supreme.[2] If this is so, discussions as to whether the Kingdom is present or future are barren; it is obviously both. In several sayings the idea is definitely eschatological; it is that of the consummated Rule of God.[3] No saying, however, in which the *Basileia* is expressly mentioned, is apocalyptic.

The contrary opinion is due to various causes. Secondary passages, like Mt. xvi. 28,[4] which speaks of 'the Son of man coming in his kingdom', and sayings of doubtful authenticity, like Mt. xiii. 41, which describes the sending forth of the angels by the Son of Man to gather sinners out of His Kingdom to be cast into the furnace of fire, still

[1] Cf. B. H. Streeter, *The Four Gospels*, 258.

[2] Cf. Mk. x. 23-5; Lk. xiii. 28f., xxii. 30.

[3] Cf. Mk. xiv. 25; Lk. xi. 2, xiii. 28f., xxii. 16, 18, 30.

[4] Mk. ix. 1, on which Mt. xvi. 28 is based, reads: 'till they see the kingdom of God come with power'.

continue to haunt the mind. Or, it is assumed that the
ideas found in the Apocalyptic Literature and the preaching of the Baptist, somewhat modified and spiritualized,
are the ideas of Jesus. Or again, genuine sayings about
the coming of the Son of Man are connected in thought
with other sayings concerning the *Basileia*. Not one of
these assumptions is justified. Mt. xvi. 28 and xiii. 41
obscure rather than reveal the thought of Jesus. The
phantasies of Apocalyptic have no place in His sayings.
'Jesus', says Bultmann, 'rejects the whole content of apocalyptic speculation, as he rejects also the calculation of
time and the watching for signs'.[1] In His teaching there
is nothing corresponding to a passage like 4 Ezra v. 4-9
which speaks of the sun shining by night, trees dripping
blood, fire bursting forth, women bearing monsters, and
the like.[2] As for the sayings concerning the Son of Man,
it is a fact too little noticed that Jesus never refers to the
Kingdom when He mentions the Parousia, and never
associates either its emergence or its consummation with
His Coming. His teaching has certainly an eschatological element in it, but it is not an apocalyptic concept.

One important feature His teaching does share with
Apocalyptic: from first to last the *Basileia* is supernatural;
man does not strive for it or bring it into being. Our
modern idea of labouring for the coming of the Kingdom
is a noble conception, fully baptized into Christ and expressive of His spirit; but it is not His teaching regarding
the *Basileia*. He does indeed ask men to pray for its
coming (Lk. xi. 2), and it is likened to a merchant seeking
goodly pearls (Mt. xiii. 45f.), but always the coming is
sheer miracle (cf. Mk. iv. 26-9). It is God's gift (Lk.
xii. 32), and man's unexpected discovery, as when one
suddenly lights upon treasure hid in a field (Mt. xiii. 44).

[1] *Jesus and the Word*, 39.   [2] *Op. cit.*, 39f.

It does not come 'with observation' (Lk. xvii. 20), but is present already in the Messianic work and ministry of Jesus. 'If I by the finger of God cast out devils', He says, 'then is the kingdom of God come upon you' (Lk. xi. 20). Its fulfilment awaits the good pleasure of God (cf. Lk. xi. 2).

From what has been said it is plain that, while Jesus borrowed from the past, He remoulded the idea of the Kingdom and gave it a distinctive character.[1]   This is a fact which obviously cannot be ignored in thinking of His suffering and death.   Jesus lived and died contemplating and speaking of the Rule of God among men.   This ideal, and nothing less, is the constant assumption of His teaching and action.

[1] Cf. C. H. Dodd, *The Parables of the Kingdom*, 34-80.

II

THE MESSIANIC HOPE

THE attitude of Jesus to His suffering was of necessity deeply influenced by His estimate of His
Person, and, inasmuch as in the Gospels He is represented as, and as claiming to be, the Messiah of Jewish
expectation, it is necessary to describe the Messianic Hope
of Israel.

Like other Old Testament ideas that of the Messianic
Hope has a history.[1]   Its simplest beginnings are to be
seen in the use of the term 'anointed' which in various
ways is used to designate offices of divine appointment.
This description, for example, is used of kings.   Saul is
anointed to be prince over Israel (1 Sam. ix. 16), and when
David appears before Samuel the word of Yahweh to the
prophet is: 'Arise, anoint him: for this is he' (1 Sam. xvi.
12).   Even of a heathen king like Cyrus it is said: 'Thus
saith the Lord to his anointed, to Cyrus, whose right hand
I have holden' (Isa. xlv. 1).   In Psa. cv. 15 the patri-
archs are spoken of as 'mine anointed ones', and in Hab.
iii. 13 the same language is used of the people as a whole.[2]
These passages illustrate the wide uses of which the idea
which lies at the root of the term 'Messiah' was capable.
In course of time, however, it came to be applied in a
special sense in connexion with the expectation of the
Scion of David whom God would raise up for the rule and
deliverance of Israel.   This hope was based on the belief

[1]Cf. F. J. Foakes Jackson and Kirsopp Lake, *The Beginnings of
Christianity*, vol. i. part i. 346-68.

[2]Cf. also Psa. xxviii. 8, lxxxiv. 9, lxxxix. 38, 51.

in the permanency of David's dynasty which is expressed in 2 Sam. vii. 16, and which persisted in spite of the evil fortunes of his house and even after the monarchy ceased to exist. Its real foundation, however, was religious; it rested in the unwavering conviction regarding the faithfulness of God to His purpose of founding a Kingdom of righteousness of which Israel would be the expression and symbol.

Prophecies which originally may have had another application came to be read in the light of this hope. Isa. ix. 2-7, for example, speaks of the birth of a child for whom an almost semi-divine greatness is reserved, and Isa. xi. 1-9 describes the coming forth of 'a shoot out of the stock of Jesse' on whom 'the spirit of Yahweh' shall rest, and the dawn of a golden age when 'the wolf shall dwell with the lamb, and the leopard shall lie down with the kid'. 'The earth', it is said, 'shall be full of the knowledge of Yahweh, as the waters cover the sea'. These passages illustrate the close connexion between the Messiah and the Kingdom, and this is a characteristic of the Messianic Hope throughout its later history.

Jer. xxiii. 5f. expresses the hope, although here, it has been said, 'the idea has lost something of the glamour of its first inception' :[1] 'Behold, the days come, saith Yahweh, that I will raise unto David a righteous Branch, and he shall reign as king and deal wisely, and shall execute judgement and justice in the land. In his days Judah shall be saved, and Israel shall dwell safely: and this is his name whereby he shall be called, Yahweh our righteousness.'[2] A similar expectation appears in Ezek. xxxiv. 23f.: 'And I will set up one shepherd over them, and he shall feed them, even my servant David; he shall feed them, and he shall be their shepherd. And I, Yahweh, will be their God, and my servant David prince among

[1] J. Skinner, *Prophecy and Religion*, 319. [2] Cf. also Jer. xxxiii. 14ff.

them. I, Yahweh, have spoken it.'[1] Other passages of like tenor are Isa. lv. 3f., Psa. lxxviii. 70ff., lxxxix. 20-37. Psa. xviii. 50 illustrates the use of the term 'anointed': 'Great deliverance giveth he to his king; and sheweth loving-kindness to his anointed, to David and to his seed, for ever-more'. The same expression also appears in Psa. ii. 2, which, whatever its original application may have been, came to be interpreted in line with popular expectations.[2]

The hope of the Messianic Age was not killed by the bitter experiences of the Exile; indeed, it is to the post-Exilic period that much of the evidence for the belief belongs. A new form is given to the expectation in Zech. ix. 9f. which is of great interest because it is quoted in Mt. xxi. 5 and Jn. xii. 15 in connexion with the story of the Entry into Jerusalem. In this passage the unknown prophet portrays a Messiah-King who is 'lowly' or 'afflicted', who rides upon an ass and whose mission it is to bring universal peace:[3]

> 'Rejoice greatly, O daughter of Zion;
> Shout, O daughter of Jerusalem:
> Behold, thy king cometh unto thee:
>
> 'He is just, and having salvation;
> Lowly, and riding upon an ass,
> Even upon a colt the foal of an ass.
>
> 'And I will cut off the chariot from Ephraim,
> And the horse from Jerusalem,
> And the battle bow shall be cut off;

[1]Cf. also Ezek. xxxvii. 24.

[2]Cf. *The Beginnings of Christianity*, vol. i. part i. 353.

[3]'The prophecy may probably be dated shortly after May 23, 141, when the citadel of Jerusalem surrendered', R. H. Kennett, Peake's *Commentary*, 580. For the theory of a fourth century date see H. G. Mitchell, *I.C.C., Zechariah*, 253; J. E. McFadyen, *The Abingdon Bible Commentary*, 826. See also R. S. Cripps, *The Prophets and the Atonement*, 30.

'And he shall speak peace unto the nations:
And his dominion shall be from sea to sea,
And from the River to the ends of the earth.'

The Similitudes of Enoch and the Psalms of Solomon
show how the belief persisted in the century preceding the
birth of Jesus.   The teaching of the former, with reference to the Son of Man, must be considered in the next
chapter, but the descriptive passage in lxii. 2f. may with
advantage be quoted here:

'And the Lord of Spirits seated him on the throne of His glory,
And the spirit of righteousness was poured out upon him,
And the word of his mouth slays all the sinners,
And all the unrighteous are destroyed from before his face,
And there shall stand up in that day all the kings and the mighty,
And the exalted and those who hold the earth,
And they shall see and recognize
How he sits on the throne of his glory,
And righteousness is judged before him,
And no lying word is spoken before him.'

It is clear that in this description the Messianic idea has
passed from the historical to the supramundane sphere.
In the Psalms of Solomon, however, there is a closer ap-
proximation to earlier ideas under the influence of the
cruel times in which these poems were written.   In xvii.
23ff. prayer is made that God will raise up 'the Son of
David', and that he may be girded with strength 'that he
may shatter unrighteous rulers'.   His task is to destroy
the pride of the sinner 'as a potter's vessel', and to break
in pieces their substance 'with a rod of iron'.   A nobler
note is struck in xvii. 28f. where it is said:

'And he shall gather together a holy people, whom he shall lead in
     righteousness,
     And he shall judge the tribes of the people that has been sancti-
     fied by the Lord his God.

'And he shall not suffer unrighteousness to lodge any more in
   their midst,
Nor shall there dwell with them any man that knoweth
   wickedness,
For he shall know them, that they are all sons of their God.' [1]

The Gospels testify to the existence and strength of the
hope in the first half of the first century A.D. There must
have been many righteous and devout men like Simeon
'looking for the consolation of Israel' (Lk. ii. 25), and
many women like Anna who spoke 'to all them that were
looking for the redemption of Jerusalem' (Lk. ii. 38). The
expectation is further attested by the fact that Jesus (Mk.
xiv. 61) and John the Baptist (Jn. i. 19-28) were questioned as to their claims, and also in the confession of
Peter near Caesarea Philippi (Mk. viii. 29). In 4 Ezra
the Eagle Vision (xi-xii. 39)[2], and the Vision of the Man
rising from the Sea (xiii.)[3], show that the belief was current
at the end of the first century A.D.; and its persistence is
illustrated by the fact that Akiba recognized the Messiah
in Bar-Cochba, the ill-fated leader of the revolt against
Hadrian in 132-5 A.D.

It is not possible to reduce all the ideas which gather
round the figure of the Messiah to a single conception.
The outstanding portrait is that of an expected Scion of
David, a Prince of the Royal House, whose work it is to

[1] Cf. R. H. Charles, *Apocrypha and Pseudepigrapha*, ii. 649.

[2] The Lion which predicts the destruction of the Eagle (Rome) is described as 'the Messiah, whom the Most High has kept until the end of
days, who will spring from the race of David, and will come.' Cf. G. F.
Moore, *Judaism*, ii. 338.

[3] Before the Man rising from the sea everything quakes and his enemies
are burned to ashes by a fiery stream from his mouth. Afterwards he calls
to himself 'another multitude which was peaceable'. Cf. xiii. 12f.
W. O. E. Oesterley thinks that both visions represent a transcendental
Messiah, and that they are earlier than 4 Ezra itself. Cf. *An Introduction
to the Books of the Apocrypha*, 148-55.

restore the ancient glories of Israel, to execute justice on her heathen oppressors, and to inaugurate the reign of peace and of righteousness. Sometimes, however, the emphasis is so much on the Kingdom to be established that the figure of the Davidic King fades away into the background, and even, as for example in Isa. xlff., is not mentioned at all. When the Messiah is introduced into the picture, his work is that of an Agent; he is the divinely chosen instrument of God who Himself effects the deliverance. G. F. Moore, however, maintains that more frequently 'he appears on the scene only after the great deliverance has been wrought by God himself, as the ruler of a redeemed and regenerated Israel.'[1] In the later Apocalypses the Messianic Age is not final. In 4 Ezra, for example, it lasts four hundred years, and after a silence of seven days the Last Judgment follows (vii. 28-35). A conception similar in certain respects appears in the Christian Apocalypse of John (cf. xx).

In these Jewish forecasts the figure of the Messiah, however great in respect of his authority and power, remains essentially human, and his work is predominantly political and nationalistic. As we have seen, a very different conception appears in the Similitudes of Enoch in the portraiture of a Supernatural Being whose home is on high, and who waits the divinely appointed hour for his emergence in glory and in power upon the plane of human history. These two very different conceptions continued to exist side by side. The Fourth Gospel is only echoing current diversities of thought when it voices the opinion of those who held that the Christ would come from Bethlehem, 'the village where David was' (vii. 42) and the ideas of others who held that the Messiah would be of unknown and mysterious origin (vii. 27). It is abundantly manifest

[1] *Judaism*, ii. 330f.

B

that in the days of Jesus the way stood open for a Messianic claimant to select from among existing conceptions and, according to the degree of his insight, to make of them a symbol of redemptive activity at once old and new. Such an exercise of creative thinking is precisely what Jesus accomplished in connexion with the Messianic Hope of Israel as centred in Himself and in His ministry of suffering, death, and exaltation.

That Jesus claimed to be the Messiah has been repeatedly denied, and, in modern times, by no one more trenchantly than by W. Wrede in his *Das Messiasgeheimnis in den Evangelien* (1901; 2nd ed. 1913). His arguments have been answered by many scholars including Jülicher,[1] Schweitzer,[2] Sanday,[3] Peake,[4] and Rawlinson[5]; but they have been given a new importance by the leading Form-Critics, Dibelius[6] and Bultmann,[7] and by R. H. Lightfoot in his recent Bampton Lectures.[8]

In brief, Wrede's position is that Jesus did not claim to be the Messiah, that He was not recognized as such until after the Resurrection, and that in Mark's Gospel Messiahship is read back into the story of Jesus by means of the theory of 'the Messianic Secret'. Much is made of the injunctions to secrecy in Mark. Silence, we are reminded, is enjoined when the devils seek to make Jesus known (i. 23ff., 34, iii. 11f., v. 6f., ix. 20); after notable

[1] *Neue Linien in der Kritik der evangelischen Überlieferung.*

[2] *The Quest of the Historical Jesus,* 336-48.

[3] *The Life of Christ in Recent Research,* 69-76.

[4] *The Messiah and the Son of Man,* an essay printed from *The Bulletin of the John Rylands Library,* vol. 8, no. 1, Jan. 1924.

[5] *The Gospel according to St. Mark,* 258-62.

[6] *From Tradition to Gospel,* 55, 73f., 94, 223f., 229f., 260, 297.

[7] *Die Geschichte der synoptischen Tradition,* 371f.

[8] *History and Interpretation in the Gospels,* 16-22, 57-88, 220.

miracles (i. 44, v. 43, vii. 36, viii. 26); after Peter's Confession (viii. 30); and when Jesus speaks of His Messianic Mission (ix. 9).   Jesus also withdraws from the crowd on secret journeys (vii. 24, ix. 30), and gives private instruction to His disciples concerning the 'mystery of the kingdom', His Person, and destiny (iv. 10-3, 34, vii. 17-23, ix. 28f., xiii. 3ff.).   The purpose of this representation, it is argued, is to show why Jesus was not recognized as the Messiah during His earthly life.

It may be that, in points of detail, Mark has overpressed the idea of the Messianic Secret; but, in substance, Wrede's explanation is quite unconvincing. Everything is based on the effect of 'visions' of the Risen Christ; but it is in the highest degree improbable that such experiences would have taken place if Jesus had made no Messianic claims.   Moreover, belief in resurrection does not of necessity suggest Messiahship; it did not in the case of the Baptist (cf. Mk. vi. 14-6).   Again, the first Christians would not have created for themselves the most formidable of difficulties by preaching a Crucified Messiah, unless Jesus had been condemned as a Messianic pretender.   Further, as Schweitzer observes, 'a creative tradition would have carried out the theory of the Messianic secret in the life of Jesus much more boldly and logically, that is to say, at once more arbitrarily and more consistently.'[1]   Finally, the Markan representation is credibly explained as historical.   A record which begins with a story of revelation (i. 9-11) followed by temptation (i. 12f.), which describes efforts to conceal the secret from popular misconception, to reveal it to intimate followers, to express it, albeit in a veiled form, in the events of the Entry (xi. 1-11), and, finally, to confess it when the claim is extorted by the high priest's question (xiv. 61f.), has

[1]*Op. cit.*, 338.

every right to be accepted as trustworthy.   There can be
no reasonable doubt that Jesus believed He was, and
claimed to be, the Messiah.

But what Messiah?   The Gospels clearly show that to
Jesus Messiahship was a burden; no conception of it, current among His contemporaries, answered to His own.
It is highly doubtful if He ever used the term 'Christ' of
Himself, and it is significant that, according to Matthew
(xxvi. 63f.) and Luke (xxii. 70), His reply to the question
of Caiaphas is: '*You* say it', 'the word is yours'.[1]   It is as
if He were accepting a title under constraint.   How original and distinctive is the thought of Jesus is shown by
His preference for the term, 'Son of Man', and still more
by His bold reinterpretation of this title by the idea of the
Suffering Servant.

[1]Cf. J. H. Moulton, *Grammar of New Testament Greek*, i. 86.

III

THE SON OF MAN

THE frequency of this title in the sayings of Jesus, in respect of both the Parousia and the Passion, is in itself a sufficient justification for giving careful consideration to its meaning and usage.

The Jewish doctrine of the Son of Man begins with the book of Daniel (*c.* 165 B.C.), for while the term is used earlier, by Ezekiel (ii. 1, &c.) and in Psa. viii. 4, in these passages it is no more than a synonym for 'man'.

In Dan. vii., after the description of the four great beasts, the seer describes the coming of 'one like unto a son of man' with the clouds of heaven who is brought before 'the Ancient of Days', and continues: 'And there was given him dominion, and glory, and a kingdom, that all the peoples, nations, and languages should serve him: his dominion is an everlasting dominion, which shall not pass away, and his kingdom that which shall not be destroyed' (vii. 14). The seer makes it plain that this is not the description of an individual, for he remarks that the four beasts are four kings, and then says: 'But the saints of the Most High shall receive the kingdom, and possess the kingdom for ever, even for ever and ever' (vii. 18). Again, after a fuller description of the fourth beast, which represents the Greek Empire of Antiochus Epiphanes, he writes: 'And the kingdom and the dominion, and the greatness of the kingdoms under the whole heaven, shall be given to the people of the saints of the Most High' (vii. 27). It is clear that the 'one like unto a son of man' is a human figure which represents the purified Jewish race.

But, however definite the seer's meaning may be, it is equally apparent that, once his description is read apart from the framework in which it stands, and without the interpretation he gives, the portrait is capable of being presented as that of an individual of supernatural dignity and power. The rough print is discernible in vii. 13: 'I saw in the night visions, and, behold, there came with the clouds of heaven one like unto a son of man, and he came even to the ancient of days, and they brought him near before him.' It is a widely accepted opinion that the enlargement is to be found in the Similitudes of Enoch written in the first half of the first century B.C. In Daniel, R. H. Charles observes, 'the phrase ("Son of Man") seems merely symbolical of Israel, but in Enoch it denotes a supernatural person.'[1]

This view is so important that it is necessary to consider the most relevant passages in some detail.

The description in xlvi. 1 undoubtedly rests on Dan. vii. 9 and 13.

'And there I saw One, who had a head of days,
And His head was white like wool,
And with Him was another being whose countenance had the
    appearance of a man,
And his face was full of graciousness, like one of the holy angels.'

Enoch asks 'concerning that Son of Man, who he was, and whence he was, (and) why he went with the Head of Days', and receives the answer:

'This is the Son of Man who hath righteousness,
With whom dwelleth righteousness,
And who revealeth all the treasures of that which is hidden,

[1]*The Book of Enoch*, 307. For an exhaustive summary of critical opinion regarding the interpretation of Dan. vii. 13 see H. H. Rowley, *Darius the Mede and the Four World Empires in the Book of Daniel*, 62ff.

Because the Lord of Spirits hath chosen him,
And whose lot hath the pre-eminence before the Lord of Spirits
in uprightness for ever' (xlvi. 3).

In xlviii. 3 it is said that his name was before the Lord of
Spirits 'before the stars of the heaven were made', and in
verse 6 he is described as chosen and hidden before Him
'before the creation of the world and for evermore'. Of
him it is said:

'He shall be a staff to the righteous whereon to stay themselves
and not fall,
And he shall be a light of the Gentiles,
And the hope of those who are troubled of heart' (xlviii. 4).

Days are spoken of in which he will sit on God's throne,
and 'his mouth shall pour forth all the secrets of wisdom
and counsel' (li. 3). He is also described as 'the Elect
One' (li. 3). The same name is used in lxii. 1, and it is said:

'And the Lord of Spirits seated him on the throne of His glory,
And the spirit of righteousness was poured out upon him,
And the word of his mouth slays all the sinners,
And all the unrighteous are destroyed from before his face'
(lxii. 2).

The prophecy is made that the kings and the mighty and
all who possess the earth shall bless and glorify and extol
'him who rules over all, who was hidden' (lxii. 6).

'For from the beginning the Son of Man was hidden,
And the Most High preserved him in the presence of His might,
And revealed him to the elect' (lxii. 7).

Finally, he is given the power of universal judgment:

'And he sat on the throne of his glory,
And the sum of judgement was given unto the Son of Man,
And he caused the sinners to pass away and be destroyed from off
the face of the earth,
And those who have led the world astray

'With chains shall they be bound,
And in their assemblage-place of destruction shall they be im-
  prisoned,
And all their works vanish from the face of the earth.
And from henceforth there shall be nothing corruptible,

'For that Son of Man has appeared,
And has seated himself on the throne of his glory,
And all evil shall pass away before his face,
And the word of that Son of Man shall go forth
And be strong before the Lord of Spirits' (lxix. 27-9).

It can scarcely awaken surprise that one who sits on
God's throne, who is chosen before the creation, possesses
universal dominion, and has authority to judge all men,
should be looked upon by most students of the Similitudes
as a Supernatural Being. In the seer's Messianic Hope
the human Scion of David is replaced by the supramundane Son of Man.

This view has not passed without challenge. Its most
recent critic is T. W. Manson in his valuable book, *The
Teaching of Jesus* (1931). Manson reminds us that besides the terms 'the Elect one' and 'the Righteous one'
there are frequent references in the Book of Enoch to 'the
(my) Righteous ones' and 'the (my) Elect ones' in the
plural; and he suggests that 'it is at least arguable that the
singular term in these cases is the name for the body made
up by the individuals included in the plural term'. 'The
faithful Remnant', he says, 'may be personified as the
Elect one and the Righteous one or regarded as the community of the Elect and the Righteous.'[1] This suggestion is interesting, but it does not seem necessary to interpret in this way passages in which 'the Righteous' are
mentioned (cf. xxxviii. 2f., xxxix. 6f., lviii. 1f., lxi. 13,
lxii. 12f., 15). Indeed, in lxii. 13 f. they appear to be

[1] *The Teaching of Jesus*, 228.

expressly distinguished from the Son of Man in a way which emphasizes the personal character of the latter:

> 'And the righteous and the elect shall be saved on that day,
> And they shall never thenceforward see the face of the sinners and unrighteous.
> And the Lord of Spirits will abide over them,
> And with that Son of Man shall they eat
> And lie down and rise up for ever and ever.'

Manson further argues that even a title like 'the Anointed one' need not be construed of a personal Messiah; and that 'it is natural to take "Son of Man" in the same sense.'[1]   One must feel considerable hesitation about this suggestion.   No doubt there are many places in Jewish writings where what appears to be the portraiture of an individual is really the description of a community; but there must be limits to this possibility; otherwise, the power to describe an individual is lost.   And the description of the Son of Man in the Similitudes is so full, and the functions of judgment are such, that the personal interpretation is much the more probable view.   Manson also contends that his explanation 'would allow the reconciliation of Chapters lxx. and lxxi. with the rest of this part of Enoch', since in lxxi. 14 Enoch himself is identified with 'that Son of Man'.   R. H. Charles, however, has forcibly argued that the text is corrupt[2] and that the true reading must have been:

> 'And he (*i.e.* the angel) came to me and greeted me with His voice, and said unto me:

[1] *Op. cit.*, 228f.

[2] As it stands the text reads: 'Thou art the Son of Man who art born . . . thee . . . thee.'   Charles (*op. cit.*, 144-6) maintains that originally verse 13 spoke of the Son of Man as accompanying the Head of Days, and that the loss of this passage has led some scribe to change the text of 14 and 16 and

"*This is* the Son of Man who is born unto righteousness;
  And righteousness abides over *him*,
  And the righteousness of the Head of Days forsakes *him*
    not".'

This is a point on which certainty is not attainable, but it is not safe to interpret the figure of the Son of Man in Enoch xxxvii.-lxix. by the present text of lxxi. 14. For these reasons it is best to conclude that the Son of Man of the Similitudes is not the 'faithful Remnant' but a person of superhuman dignity and power.

How far Jesus was influenced by this conception is a difficult question. It has often been maintained that the Book of Enoch is the source from which He derived His use of the title 'Son of Man'. It may be doubted, however, if a close study of that Book encourages this theory, and all the more since, in reply to the high priest's question: 'Art thou the Christ, the Son of the Blessed?' (Mk. xiv. 61), Jesus quotes a passage with reference to the Son of Man, not from Enoch, but from Dan. vii. 13: 'I am: and ye shall see the Son of man sitting at the right hand of power, and coming with the clouds of heaven' (Mk. xiv. 62). In all His references to the Son of Man there is no certain trace of dependence upon the ideas of Enoch.

A very attractive suggestion to the contrary has recently been put forward by Rudolf Otto in his *Reich Gottes und Menschensohn* (1934). Otto draws attention to the fact that Enoch is first shown the Son of Man who has been hidden from the beginning (xlvi. 1), and that then, after a long interval, he is told, in lxxi. 14, by the angel that he himself is the Son of Man. This representation, he ar-

make it apply to Enoch. This suggestion, he points out, is supported by 17 where the scribe has 'forgotten to make the necessary changes':

'And so there shall be length of days with that Son of Man,
And the righteous shall have peace and an upright way,
In the name of the Lord of Spirits for ever and ever'.

gues, presents a remarkable parallel to the sayings in the Gospels regarding the Son of Man.[1] At first Jesus speaks objectively of the Son of Man; in due time the secret of His identity is revealed by God to Peter (cf. Mt. xvi. 17); and finally it is confessed by Jesus before the high priest (cf. Mk. xiv. 60-2).

The difficulty of this suggestion is that many scholars regard chapters lxx. and lxxi. as a later appendix to the Book of Enoch, while, as we have seen, Charles thinks that the text of lxxi. 14 is corrupt. Otto thinks otherwise, and, accepting the existing text, argues that it is only in these chapters that Enoch receives an answer to his question, asked in xlvi. 2, who and whence 'that Son of Man' was. This question is now answered in lxxi. 14: 'Thou art the Son of Man who is born unto righteousness'. 'This point', says Otto, 'is of quite decisive importance for the question whether Jesus' consciousness of a mission could have been, indeed must have been, itself determined Messianically.'[2]

It is too early to say whether Otto's fascinating suggestion will make any impression on the sobriety of critical opinion. In spite of all that he urges so persuasively, it may well be that Jesus independently took the term from Dan. vii. 13 and read into it His own meaning. In this case the Book of Enoch represents a different line of development. Other examples illustrate a similar process. As we have already seen, this is true of the Vision of the Man rising from the Sea (4 Ezra xiii.), whose glance strikes terror into all whom he beholds and whose fiery breath destroys his enemies. G. F. Moore has pointed out that at the beginning of the second century A.D. Akiba assigned one of the thrones mentioned in Dan. vii. 9 to the Messiah, and in the first half of the third century R.

---

[1] *Op. cit.*, 165, 181-7.   [2] *Op. cit.*, 165.

Joshua ben Levi harmonized the lowly figure of the Messiah in Zech. ix. 9 with the description of Dan. vii. 13.[1] A further Messianic interpretation of Dan. vii. 13 appears in the Sibylline Oracles (v. 414): 'There came from the wide heavenly spaces a blessed man, holding in his hands a sceptre which God put in his grasp, and he brought all into subjection'.[2] Both before and after the times of Jesus the tendency to ascribe supernatural functions to the Messiah is evident, and there is no reason why Jesus Himself should not have developed a conception gained from the Book of Daniel.

More important than the problem whence Jesus derived the title, 'Son of Man', is the question whether He used it of Himself, and with what meaning. The philological objections can no longer be said to be insuperable,[3] and the question turns on the interpretation we give to His sayings. In some cases the title is probably an editorial addition, and in others it has replaced, in the course of transmission, the personal pronoun 'I', but it is quite impossible to explain the majority of instances in this way.[4]

In the sayings which refer to the Parousia it often seems as if Jesus were speaking of some one other than Himself, as in Mk. viii. 38, where He says that the Son of Man, when he comes 'in the glory of his Father', will be ashamed of those who now are ashamed of Himself and His words. Even in this case, however, the inference is far from certain. The fact that Jesus is speaking of the Parousia

---

[1] *Judaism*, ii. 334ff.   [2] *Op. cit.*, 335.

[3] Cf. A. S. Peake, *The Messiah and the Son of Man*, 22-4; W. Bousset, *Kyrios Christos* [2], 10-3.

[4] Among doubtful passages of the kind are Mk. xiii. 26; Mt. x. 23, xiii. 37, 41, xxiv. 30, xxv. 31, xxvi. 2; Lk. vi. 22, xi. 30, xii. 8, 10, and perhaps Mk. ii. 10, 28.

makes it equally possible that He is describing Himself
as He will then be manifested.[1]

This view is strongly supported by His reply to the
high priest's question: 'Art thou the Christ?'. Jesus
gives an affirmative answer, and then says: 'And ye shall
see the Son of man sitting at the right hand of power, and
coming with the clouds of heaven' (Mk. xiv. 62). It is
extremely difficult to think that He is distinguishing the
Son of Man from Himself.

Similarly, in the Passion-sayings,[2] when Jesus declares
that 'the Son of man must suffer many things', He is
speaking of Himself. T. W. Manson's view, that in
these sayings, as in the Book of Enoch, the title describes
the faithful Remnant, 'the Kingdom of the saints of the
Most High',[3] does not seem to me to account for these
sayings. But it is the less necessary to discuss this interesting suggestion since Manson maintains that, in the
course of His prophetic ministry, Jesus came to restrict
the denotation of the title until it became a designation of
Himself. 'Finally', he says, 'when it becomes apparent
that not even the disciples are ready to rise to the demands
of the ideal, he stands alone, embodying in his own person
the perfect human response to the regal claims of God.'[4]

Besides the sayings which refer to the Parousia or to
the Passion, there are others of a more general character.
For example, Jesus speaks of the Son of Man who came
'eating and drinking' (Lk. vii. 34), who 'hath not where to
lay his head' (Lk. ix. 58), and whose mission it is 'to seek

---

[1] Cf. also Lk. xii. 40, xvii. 22, 24, 26, 30, xviii. 8b, xxi. 36, and Mt. xix. 28.

[2] Mk. viii. 31, ix. 12b, 31, x. 33f., 45, xiv. 21 (*bis*), 41, 62; Lk. xvii. 25,
xxii. 48, 69.

[3] *The Teaching of Jesus*, 227ff. This view may be true of Mk. ii. 28,
viii. 38 (and parallels), and perhaps Mt. x. 23.

[4] *Op. cit.*, 228.

and to save that which was lost' (Lk. xix. 10). Here again it is best to conclude that Jesus is speaking of Himself. In these sayings the title is not a simple equivalent of the pronoun 'I', or an editorial modification. In each case the point of the assertion is that it is made of One who is 'the Son of Man'; and in view of the fact that Jesus used the term in a distinctive but unfamiliar way, the indirect form of the sayings is natural upon His lips. This conclusion, both in respect of these more general sayings and those relating to the Passion, strengthens the probability that in the Parousia-sayings Jesus speaks of His own future manifestation as the Son of Man.

To these arguments more general considerations may be added. Outside the Gospels the title appears only once in the whole of the New Testament (Acts vii. 56). In the Gospels, it appears in all the principal sources laid bare by Criticism, and is employed by Jesus alone predominantly in the later part of His mission and in a striking and original manner. A title so employed has every right to be regarded as an authentic element in the tradition. Jesus certainly described Himself as the Son of Man, and the Messianic consciousness it expresses is the foundation of His estimate of His Person and Work.[1]

In view of this conclusion it is important to ask which use of the title stands at the centre in the thought of Jesus.[2] Not, I suggest, that of the Parousia-sayings; otherwise they would be more detailed. In these sayings the

---

[1]Cf. Ed. Meyer, *Ursprung und Anfänge des Christentums*, ii. 345; R. Reitzenstein, *Das Iranische Erlösungsmysterium*, 117ff. Even W. Bousset, who reduces the number of these sayings as far as possible, does not deny that Jesus ever used the title with reference to Himself. Cf. *Kyrios Christos* [2], 10f.

[2]I do not think that we can answer this question by counting passages or by dwelling on the fact that Passion-sayings about the Son of Man are not found in Q or M.

ideas emphasized are those of suddenness and glory. The Son of Man comes 'in an hour that ye think not' (Lk. xii. 40), 'in the glory of his father '(Mk. viii. 38), 'at the right hand of power' and 'with the clouds of heaven' (Mk. xiv. 62). His Coming is as a flash of lightning (Lk. xvii. 24), unexpected as the deluge (Lk. xvii. 26), swift as the destruction of Sodom (Lk. xvii. 30). We have only to compare these sayings with the commonplaces of Apocalyptic to be conscious of an enormous difference. Jesus does not say of the Son of Man, as in the Book of Enoch, that 'the word of his mouth slays all the sinners' (lxii. 2), or that 'all evil shall pass away before his face' (lxix. 29), and still less, as in the Vision of the Man from the Sea in the Ezra-Apocalypse, does He speak of 'a flaming breath' out of his lips whereby his adversaries are reduced to 'dust of ashes and smell of smoke' (xiii. 10f.). Indeed, He is surprisingly silent about His functions at the Parousia; and even the sayings which are open to the suspicion of contamination add little beyond conventional references to 'a great sound of a trumpet' and the gathering 'of his elect from the four winds' (Mt. xxiv. 31; cf. xiii. 41). The bareness of the genuine sayings suggests that, while Jesus foretold His Coming in power and glory, He did not ascribe to this event the place it had in contemporary Apocalyptic. His thought is nearer Dan. vii. 14 where the Son of Man receives 'dominion, and glory, and a kingdom'. The Parousia of which He thinks is not a coming for Judgment, the setting up of the Kingdom, and the Final Restoration of all things; it is rather entrance upon a kingship which is the Father's gift (cf. Lk. xxii. 29). It includes all that is meant by the Resurrection,[1] but is a more ultimate and inclusive concept.

The more immediate centre of interest, when Jesus

[1]Cf. C. J. Cadoux, *The Resurrection and Second Advent of Jesus*, 13-7.

speaks of Himself as the Son of Man, is the destiny of suffering and death He is to fulfil. The Parousia-sayings describe the culmination, when suffering is crowned with victory and death is lost in triumph. This is a complete transformation of the doctrine of the Son of Man, and is an entirely original conception of Jesus, based upon the Old Testament idea of the Suffering Servant.

IV

THE SON

AT this point, before considering the idea of the Suffering Servant, it will be of advantage to discuss the title 'the Son', which in the Old Testament[1] is used of Israel, of kings, and of the Messiah. The title rarely appears in the Passion-sayings,[2] but its use by Jesus elsewhere must of necessity, if the relevant sayings are genuine, throw light on His estimate of His Person, and, in consequence, on His view of His mission and destiny.

When Moses is sent to Pharaoh, he is commanded of God to say: 'Israel is my son, my firstborn: and I have said unto thee, Let my son go, that he may serve me' (Ex. iv. 22f.). Here, the term is used of the nation in its relation to God. The same usage appears in the well-known words of Hos. xi. 1:

> 'When Israel was a child, then I loved him,
> And called my son out of Egypt.'

Besides this use of the term it is also applied to individuals. This is done by implication in the case of David in Psa. lxxxix. 26f.:

> 'He shall cry unto me, Thou art my father,
> My God, and the rock of my salvation.
> I will also make him my firstborn,
> The highest of the kings of the earth,'

[1]The strange phrase, 'the sons of Elohim', in Gen. vi. 4 (cf. Job i. 6, xxxviii. 7) is used either of divinities or, in later times, of angels. Cf. *The Beginnings of Christianity*, vol. i. part 1, 392-403.

[2]Cf. Mk. xii. 6: 'He had yet one, a beloved son: he sent him last unto them, saying, They will reverence my son.' See later, p. 106ff.

and explicitly with reference to Solomon in 2 Sam. vii. 14:
'I will be his father, and he shall be my son'. In later
Jewish writings similar language is used to describe the
typically righteous man, as in Ecclus. iv. 10:

'Be as a father unto the fatherless,
And instead of a husband unto their mother:
So shalt thou be as a son of the Most High,
And he shall love thee more than thy mother doth',

and again in Psa. Sol. xvii. 30: 'For he shall know them,
that they are all sons of their God'.

The Messianic use of the title is both late and sporadic.
Psa. ii. 7 probably referred originally to an earthly king,
but already by the time of Jesus the words:

'I will tell of the decree:
The Lord said unto me, Thou art my son;
This day have I begotten thee',

had come to be interpreted Messianically.[1] Later, in
4 Ezra vii. 28f., the expression: 'My Son the Messiah,'
appears.[2] If Jesus spoke of Himself as 'the Son', He
may well have been influenced by Psa. ii. 7, just as He was
indebted for the phrase 'Son of Man' to Dan. vii. 13.

In Mark the term is used of Jesus in several passages,
of which the most important are the saying: 'But of that
day or that hour knoweth no one, not even the angels in
heaven, neither the Son, but the Father' (xiii. 32), and the
words of the heavenly voice in the stories of the Baptism
(i. 11) and the Transfiguration (ix. 7). The saying in
xiii. 32 is one of Schmiedel's nine 'foundation-pillars for a
truly scientific life of Jesus'.[3] Its genuineness has been

[1] Cf. J. A. Bewer, *The Literature of the Old Testament in its Historical Development*, 370.

[2] Cf. W. O. E. Oesterley, *2 Esdras*, 70.

[3] *Encycl. Biblica*, col. 1881.

contested by the Editors of *The Beginnings of Christianity*
who think that the phrase, 'neither the Son', may be a
scribal gloss, or may have replaced an original reference
to the Son of Man.[1]   Schmiedel's insight was truer, for
it is hardly likely that words which limit the knowledge of
Jesus would have been invented.   The saying is conclusive proof that Jesus spoke of Himself as 'the Son'.

In Q the same usage appears in the saying concerning
the Father and the Son in Lk. x. 21f. = Mt. xi. 25-7, and
the term 'Son of God' is used in the story of the Temptation (Lk. iv. 1-13 = Mt. iv. 1-11).   The opinion of
Albertz is that the Temptation story is the work of an
artist who 'is to be sought in Jesus Himself';[2] and, if
this is so, the story confirms the view that Jesus expressed His sense of vocation in the title 'Son of God'.
The former passage, however, is more important.   In its
Lukan form it is as follows:

'I thank thee, O Father, Lord of heaven and earth,
  That thou didst hide these things from the wise and understand-
    ing,
  And didst reveal them unto babes:
  Yea, Father; for so it was well-pleasing in thy sight.
'All things have been delivered unto me of my Father:
  And no one knoweth who the Son is, save the Father;
  And who the Father is, save the Son,
  And he to whomsoever the Son willeth to reveal him.'

The text and interpretation of this passage have often been
the subject of learned discussion.[3]   The attempts to ob-

[1] Vol. i., part 1, 396.

[2] *Die synoptischen Streitgespräche*, 48.

[3] Cf. Harnack, *The Sayings of Jesus*, 272-310; Dom Chapman, *The
Journal of Theological Studies*, x. 552-66; A. E. J. Rawlinson, *The New
Testament Doctrine of the Christ*, 251-64; T. W. Manson, *The Teaching
of Jesus*, 109-12; B. S. Easton, 164-7; J. M. Creed, 147-50; B. T. D.
Smith, 127-9; H. K. Luce, 202f; N. P. Williams, *Expository Times*, li.
182ff, 215ff.

tain a more original text,[1] by omitting either the second or
the third line in the second strophe, and by reading 'knew'
instead of 'knoweth', have not proved successful. The
reading 'knew', which appears in many quotations
of the early Fathers and in two Old Latin MSS.
(a and b), is probably due to assimilation to the preceding
aorists, while the case for omission is weakened by the
fact that it is exceedingly difficult to quote the saying
correctly.[2]

The genuineness of the saying is often questioned because of its similarity to the sayings in the Fourth Gospel,[3]
or because it is doubted that Jesus can have claimed to be
the sole revealer of the Father. Bousset, for example,
explains the passage as a word of Jesus which has been
transformed by the piety of Hellenistic-Christian circles,[4]
and he cites parallels from the Hermetic Literature of the
early Christian centuries. Probably, such doubts are
largely due to the habit of reading the saying in the light
of later Christological developments. The knowledge of
God implied is nearer to that which is described in the
Old Testament[5] than it is to the utterances of Hellenistic
piety. There is no real parallel, for example, in the
mystical prayer: 'I know thee, Hermes, and thou me. I
am Thou, and Thou I,' which is the first parallel cited by
Bousset;[6] and still less close are the examples in the extra-
canonical literature and the Odes of Solomon which are

[1] See the discussions of Harnack and Easton.

[2] As an experiment easily shows. In most cases clauses are quoted in the
wrong order or one of them is omitted.

[3] Compare the famous phrase of Hase: 'an aerolite from the Johannine
heaven', *Geschichte Jesu*, 527.

[4] *Kyrios Christos* [2], 50.

[5] Cf. Jer. xxxi. 34; Hos. iv. 1; Amos iii. 2.

[6] *Op. cit.*, 48.

quoted by Dibelius.[1]   If we allow for the influence of the
Old Testament, and perhaps also of Ecclesiasticus li,
upon the mind of Jesus, there is no adequate reason why
the genuineness of the saying should be doubted.[2]   The
words describe the intimate communion with the Father
which Jesus knew and which He was able to make known
to others; and the sense of Sonship which is revealed is
fundamentally ethical and religious.   Whether it is not
also metaphysical is a question which depends on our estimate of the Person of Jesus.   A metaphysical relationship
is not expressed in the saying, and there is no reason to
think that the mind of Jesus moved in such realms of
thought.   What is expressed is the consciousness of a
unique filial relationship to the Father, and it is in this relationship that we must find the foundation of His Messianic convictions.

This sense of Sonship is also expressed by the words
'my Father' in the saying (x. 22), and in many other sayings in which Jesus speaks of 'the Father', 'my Father',
and 'my heavenly Father'.   It lies behind the prayer:
'Abba, Father, all things are possible unto thee' (Mk. xiv.
36), and is implied in the words 'but the Father' which
follow the denial of the Son's knowledge in Mk. xiii. 32.
It also appears in several sayings in the M source in which
Jesus speaks of the Father.[3]   Some of these passages

[1]Cf. *From Tradition to Gospel*, 279-83.   Dibelius cites, for example, the
ninth Ode of Solomon: 'Open your ears and I will speak to you.   Give me
your souls that I also may give my soul to you.   The Word of the Lord
and His good pleasures, the holy thought that He has thought concerning
His Messiah. . . . Be enriched in God the Father, and receive the
intention of the Most High. . . .'

[2]Cf. W. F. Howard, *The Fourth Gospel in Recent Criticism and Interpretation*, 221; T. W. Manson, *op. cit.*, 110f. ; W. F. Lofthouse, *The Father
and the Son*, 29f; N. P. Williams, *op. cit.* 218ff.

[3]Cf. Mt. vii. 21, xv. 13, xvi. 17, xviii. 10, 19, 35, xxvi. 53.

could not be pressed if they stood alone, since Jesus also speaks, with reference to men, of 'your Father' and 'your heavenly Father'.[1]   If, however, we take the sayings of Jesus with reference to the Father as a whole, and relate them to those in which He speaks of Himself as 'the Son', a filial consciousness is revealed which, for the want of a better word, can only be described as unique.   If the term 'Son of Man' expresses a vocational consciousness closely related to the idea of the Reign of God, the title 'the Son' points to an intimate personal relationship to God out of which the sense of vocation springs.   It is because Jesus is the Son that He accepts the *rôle* of the Son of Man, and it is probably for the same reason that He recasts the form of the Son of Man in terms suggested by the figure of the Suffering Servant.   The ultimate truth about Jesus is that He is the Son of God.   The Synoptic Gospels do not tell us what that title means, and the best answers of Christian theology are incomplete.   What can be said with confidence is that a filial relationship with the Father, to which there is a parallel nowhere else, is the secret of the ministry and work of Jesus.

[1] Cf. Lk. vi. 36, xii. 32; Mt. v. 16, vi. 1, 14, 15, &c.

V

THE SERVANT OF YAHWEH

IN turning from the subject of the Messianic Hope to that of the Servant of Yahweh we enter a different world. In Jewish teaching the Servant is not identified with the Messiah,[1] and this identification is not the thought of the original writer. For our purpose it does not matter whether the Servant is an individual, or the nation,[2] the righteous element in the nation, or the ideal Israel, or whether, in line with the doctrine of corporate personality expounded by H. Wheeler Robinson, he is sometimes one and sometimes another of these entities.[3] The more important questions are the nature of the Servant-conception, the theology implicit in it, and its influence upon the mind of Jesus.

The Servant-passages include Isa. xlii. 1-4, xlix. 1-6, l. 4-9 and lii. 13–liii. 12. In these poems the Servant is the chosen messenger of God. In the third poem the indignities and the suffering he has endured in the course of his mission are mentioned, but it is in the fourth poem

[1] In the Targum on Isa. xlii. 1, the rendering is given: 'Behold my Servant the Anointed (Messiah), I will draw him near, my Chosen in whom my word delights; I will put my holy spirit upon him, and he shall reveal my judgment to the nations.' Cf. G. F. Moore, *Judaism*, ii. 327. See later, p. 45f.

[2] Cf. A. S. Peake, 'The Servant is not an ideal Israel, distinct from the empirical Israel, he is the empirical Israel regarded from an ideal point of view,' *The Servant of Yahweh*, 67.

[3] *The Cross of the Servant*, 32-7; W. L. Wardle, *London Quarterly and Holborn Review*, Oct., 1935, p. 437. Robinson argues that on this view of the Songs of the Servant 'we are able to explain the perplexing variety of interpretations offered by modern scholarship,' *op. cit.*, 36.

that this aspect of his work is presented fully. In lii. 13–liii. 12 the Servant's suffering is not only his experience, but the achievement in which his supreme task consists. In this poem the Servant's figure stands out with such solitary grandeur that one may easily miss some of the most important features in the representation as a whole. It is necessary, for example, to observe the peculiar relation which exists between the Servant and those for whom his service is rendered, and also the distinctive attitude of Yahweh to the Servant's work. The attitude of the onlookers is first presented as one of amazement. Astonished at the promised exaltation of the Servant, they explain their failure to recognize the true facts. They had received no revelation from God, and the appearance of the Servant had in no way suggested the nature of his work.[1]

> 'For he grew up as a sapling before us,
> And as a root out of a dry ground,
> He had no form that we should look upon him,
> No visage that we should desire him,
>
> 'Despised and forsaken of men,
> A man of pains and familiar with sickness,
> And as one from whom men hide the face,
> Despised, and we regarded him not.'

Nevertheless, illumination has now come to them; they see that the Servant has suffered for their own sins.

> 'But it was our sickness that he bore,
> And our pains, he carried them,
> While we regarded him as stricken,
> Smitten of God and afflicted.
>
> 'But he was pierced through our rebellions,
> Crushed through our sins,

[1] The translation followed is that of A. S. Peake, *The Problem of Suffering*, 51-9.

The chastisement to win our peace was upon him,
And by his stripes was healing wrought for us.

'We had all gone astray like sheep,
We had turned each his own way,
And Yahweh made to light on him
The sin of us all.'

This confession of sin and recognition of the redemptive character of the Servant's suffering is followed by a further description of his innocence and the indifference of his contemporaries. Then follows a statement concerning the judgment of Yahweh Himself:[1]

'But Yahweh was pleased to justify him,
And rescued his soul from trouble,
Caused him to see light and be satisfied,
A posterity that prolonged its life.'

Finally, Yahweh declares the future exaltation and glory of the Servant:

'Righteous shall my Servant appear to many,
Since he bears their iniquities;
Therefore shall he inherit among the many,
And with the strong he shall divide the spoil.

'Inasmuch as he poured out his soul unto death,
And was numbered with the rebellious,
Though he bore the sin of many,
And interceded for the rebellious.'

The theology implicit in this splendid conception is a

[1]Peake says that liii. 10f. are justly regarded by many scholars as almost incurably corrupt, *op. cit.*, 58. He omits the familiar phrase: 'when thou shalt make his soul an offering for sin.' The term '*Āshām* ('guilt-offering'), while post-Exilic, may have been current before the Exile, and, in any case, is implied in liii. 10 by the LXX. Cf. G. B. Gray, *Sacrifice in the Old Testament*, 67. If the text has been interpolated, the interpolation is pre-Christian. The term also appears in 1 Sam. vi. 3, 4, 8, 17, where the Philistines send a 'trespass-offering' of golden mice to compensate for the wrong done to the Ark. Cf. also 2 Sam. xiv. 13.

doctrine of representative suffering.   The ideas are not those of crude substitution; for it is not by the simple transference of punishment that healing comes to the recipients of divine grace.   There is, however, a substitutionary element in the delineation, in the sense that the Servant bears the consequences of the sins of others.   This view is implied, not only in the fact that he is pierced through the rebellions and crushed through the sins of others, but especially in the statement: 'Yahweh made to light on him the sins of us all,' and the declaration: 'He bore the sin of many.'   This representation, however, is only part of the poet's conception.   It is a point of cardinal importance to his view, not only that the Servant bears what others ought to suffer, but that these perceive this fact, and so recognize and confess their own sin.   In this sense, they participate in the Servant's oblation and make it their own, and it is the complete act, including the Servant's offering and the onlooker's response, which constitutes the sacrifice presented to God.   This inference is confirmed by the fact that it is only at the end, when both aspects have been described, that the poet declares that 'Yahweh was pleased to justify' His Servant, and puts into His mouth the cry: 'Righteous shall my Servant appear to many'.   The picture is clearly a poetical representation in which ancient Hebrew ideas of sacrifice are refined and sublimated.

It is obviously a question of first importance, how far Jesus was influenced by the Servant-conception and what effect it had upon His view of His suffering and death. Before, however, this question can be rightly answered, it is desirable to consider analogous ideas in the Old Testament and later Jewish Literature.

The story of the death of Achan (Jos. vii. 16-26) belongs to a different realm of ideas, for Achan dies for his

own sins, and the destruction of his family and his posses-
sions simply illustrates the solidarity of the Israelitish clan.
In the story of the sacrifice of the eldest son of the king of
Moab (2 Kings iii. 27) there is, for all its revolting features, at least the idea of an offering which avails for
others; but the predominant conception is that of averting
the wrath of Chemosh in order to bring about the destruction of Israel.   A nobler spirit breathes in the prayer of
Moses in Ex. xxxii. 31f.: 'Oh, this people have sinned a
great sin, and have made them gods of gold.   Yet now,
if thou wilt forgive their sin—; and if not, blot me, I pray
thee, out of thy book which thou hast written'; and also in
the words of David in 2 Sam. xxiv. 17: 'Lo, I have sinned,
and I have done perversely: but these sheep, what have
they done? let thine hand, I pray thee, be against me, and
against my father's house.'   But, great as they are, these
passages only illustrate the spirit of self-sacrifice which is
willing to bear the sins of others, and throw into relief the
solitary grandeur of the Servant's achievement.

The nearest parallel to the ideas of Isa. liii. is found in
the life and sufferings of Jeremiah.   It is possible that the
words: 'I was like a gentle lamb that is led to the slaughter'
(Jer. xi. 19), have suggested thoughts which are developed
in the description of the Servant, although the context
does not suggest vicarious suffering but the murderous in-
tentions of Jeremiah's enemies.   More to the point are
passages which express Jeremiah's sorrow for the sins of
his people and his self-identification with them in their
sin: 'For the hurt of the daughter of my people am I hurt:
I am black; astonishment hath taken hold on me. . . .   Oh
that my head were waters, and mine eyes a fountain of
tears, that I might weep day and night for the slain of the
daughter of my people!' (viii. 21–ix. 1).   There is good
reason to accept the claim of A. S. Peake that, while Jere-

miah is not to be identified with the Servant, 'some features in this delineation of Israel were drawn from his
career.'[1]

If anticipations of the Servant-conception are few, later
echoes are more surprisingly faint. Possible examples
are Psa. xxii, Zech. ix. 9f and xii. 9-14. Psa. xxii. contains the same contrast between suffering (vv. 1-21) and
exaltation (vv. 22-31), and there are parallel phrases in the
Psalmist's description of the sufferer as 'a reproach of
men, and despised of the people' (v. 6), and in his affirmation that Yahweh 'hath not despised nor abhorred the
affliction of the afflicted; neither hath he hid his face from
him' (v. 24). There are also verbal similarities in Zech.
xii. 10: 'And they shall look unto him whom they have
pierced: and they shall mourn for him. . . .'[2] But the
most interesting possibility is that the picture of the
Messianic King in Zech. ix. 9f. may have been influenced
in the use of the terms 'just' (or 'righteous'; cf. Isa. liii. 11)
and 'lowly' (or 'afflicted'), and in the description of the
'unostentatious royalty' of the King.[3] If this inference is
justified, we are afforded a pre-Christian example of the
modification of the traditional picture of the Messiah by
means of ideas derived from the Servant-conception. The
inference, however, is far from being certain, and in no
sense is the King a vicarious sufferer. There is more to
be said for the suggestion that Zech. ix. 9f. and Psa. xxii.
may have influenced the mind of Jesus in identifying
the Son of Man with the Suffering Servant.[4]

[1] *Jeremiah*, i. 28.

[2] Cf. R. S. Cripps, *The Prophets and the Atonement*, 29-32. Cripps
points out that the common reading, though strongly attested, can hardly
be correct, *op. cit.*, 31n.

[3] Cf. Cripps, *op. cit.*, 31.

[4] Cf. Mk. xi. 1-10, xv. 34.

In later Jewish thought the idea of the propitiatory value of the sufferings of the righteous appears. In 2 Macc. vii. 37f. the youngest of the martyr-brothers prays that with him and his brothers 'the wrath of the Almighty may cease', which, he says, 'has justly fallen upon our race'; and in 4 Macc. vi. 27-9 Eleazar prays that his blood may be a sacrifice for the purification of the people, and that his life may be taken 'as a substitute (ἀντίψυχον) for theirs'; while in 4 Macc. xvii. 22 the sufferings of the martyrs are characterized as a vicarious expiation.[1] The ideas of these passages transcend those of Isa. liii., inasmuch as they introduce the thought of a God whose wrath is appeased by suffering. This conception is absent from the Servant-poems; for the words: 'Yahweh made to light on him the sin of us all,' express no more than the characteristic Hebrew tendency to trace events to their ultimate cause in the purpose of God.

High ethical importance is ascribed to suffering in the teaching of Rabbinical Judaism, but in the time of Jesus no suffering Messiah was expected.[2] Suffering, it is held, leads men to repentance and is a means of expiation; it is the chastisement of love, intended to increase man's deserts and, in consequence, his reward. Where, in the case of the righteous, it is undeserved, it atones for the sin of the people. Billerbeck explains the fact that the Messiah is not thought of in this connexion by the expectation that the Messianic time would bring in complete blessedness.[3] The Messiah strikes down all the enemies

---

[1] Note what is said of the sacrifice of Isaac in the Jewish Prayers, some of which are ancient. Cf. Josephus, *Ant.*, i. xiii. 3.

[2] 'The old synagogue knows a suffering Messiah, to whom, however, death is not allotted; that is the Messiah ben David: and it knows a dying Messiah, but of whom no suffering is asserted; that is the Messiah ben Joseph,' Strack-Billerbeck, *Kommentar*, ii. 273f.

[3] *Op. cit.*, ii. 282.

of Israel with his word, brings all peoples under Israel's yoke, and from his throne rules the kings and powers of the earth. Such conceptions ruled out the thought of a suffering Messiah.[1] Only very gradually in later times did a few Rabbinical teachers pass over to the idea of bringing the Messiah into connexion with this and that suffering, and most teachers held fast to the older conceptions.[2] It is notable that, while the Targum Jonathan understands Isa. lii. 13–liii. Messianically, everything which could have relation to the suffering and death of the Messiah is artificially explained away. 'The idea that the Messiah bears the sin of the world, and so also that of non-Israelites, nowhere meets us in the old Rabbinical Literature.'[3]

From this summary survey of later Jewish thought, it is clear that a high ethical and religious conception of Messianic suffering lay waiting to be appropriated by any one who could approach the Servant-poems with insight and understanding, and with a mind free from the bondage of nationalistic and apocalyptic expectations. Such a mind was that of Jesus Himself. Antecedently, it is much more likely that it was He who first made use of the Servant-conception rather than the later Christian community. This opinion is contrary to that held by many modern New Testament critics who explain its presence in the Gospels by the beliefs of Hellenistic Christianity.[4] There is no doubt that Luke,[5] Matthew,[6] and the authors

[1]*Op. cit.*, II. 282.   [2]*Op. cit.*, II. 284.   [3]*Op. cit.*, II. 292.

[4]Cf. Bousset, *Kyrios Christos* [2], 69-72; Bultmann, *Die Geschichte der synoptischen Tradition*, 303f.; the Editors of *The Beginnings of Christianity*, i. 383f.; Burkitt, *Christian Beginnings*, 35-9. On the other side see Rawlinson, *St. Mark*, 255f., *The New Testament Doctrine of the Christ*, 238-41; Otto, *Reich Gottes und Menschensohn*, 203-14.

[5]Cf. Lk. xxiv. 26f.; Acts iii. 13, 26, iv. 27, 30, viii. 32-5.

[6]Cf. Mt. viii. 17, xii. 18-21.

of 1 Peter[1] and Hebrews[2] read the story of Jesus in the light of Isa. liii., and that the ideas of this chapter rarely appear in Paul's letters,[3] in the Fourth Gospel,[4] and in the Apocalypse of John.[5] It is this distribution of the evidence which led Burkitt to trace the application of the Servant-conception to the work of Gentile Christians.[6] Rawlinson, however, is better justified in describing the process as 'pre-Pauline', and in thinking that 'behind the ambiguous passages in the Acts there lurks an original Aramaic tradition (whether written or oral), in which the Messiah was described unambiguously as the "Servant" of the Lord'.[7]

The question turns in the end upon the opinion we form concerning several sayings of Jesus which, as they stand in the Gospels, reflect the ideas of the Servant-conception.   Only once, in Lk. xxii. 37, is Isa. liii. expressly quoted, but its echoes are unmistakable in the prophecies of suffering and death, in Mk. viii. 31, ix. 31, x. 33f.; in Mk. ix. 12b; in the 'ransom-passage', Mk. x. 45, and the prophecy of the Betrayal, Mk. xiv. 21. There are also traces of Isa. xlii. 1 in Mk. i. 11. With the exception of Mk. i. 11, all these passages are Passion-sayings, and they must be examined in detail in Part II. Such an examination, I believe, leads to a belief in their genuineness, and thus to the conclusion that Jesus was profoundly influenced by the Servant-conception. Apart from questions of detail, the broad fact that the passages are allu-

---

[1]Cf. 1 Pet. ii. 22. [2]Cf. Heb. ix. 28.

[3]But see Rom. iv. 25; 1 Cor. xv. 3, and Phil. ii. 5-8.

[4]Cf. Jn. i. 29, 36, xii. 38.

[5]Cf. Apoc. v. 6, xiii. 8, xiv. 5.

[6]*Christian Beginnings*, 38f.

[7]*The New Testament Doctrine of the Christ*, 241.

sions rather than quotations is significant. When later
writers read back their own ideas into an earlier time, they
are not, as a rule, content with echoes; and it is probable
that the Servant-conception would be much more obvious
in the Gospel tradition if it were not an authentic element
which goes back to Jesus Himself.

The conclusion that Jesus interpreted His suffering and
death in the light of the ideas of Isa. lii. 13–liii. is of the
utmost importance, and especially if the conception of
representative suffering which it contains is based ultimately on beliefs which are implicit in the Old Testament
sacrifices. If to our Western eyes this is the character of
the Servant-conception, how much more must its nature
have been evident to the mind of Jesus! The conclusion
is suggested that, if He reinterpreted the doctrine of the
Son of Man in terms of Isa. liii., and saw His own destiny
in the light of this perception, He must have thought of
His suffering as a sacrificial offering in which men might
participate. This is a conclusion of such moment, and
is exposed to so many misconceptions, that it is essential
to examine closely the Hebrew idea of sacrifice and the
the attitude of Jesus thereto.

VI

SACRIFICE

SACRIFICE as an idea and an institution is deeply rooted in Old Testament thought and has profoundly influenced the development of Christian beliefs and practices. Terms like 'blood', 'covenant', 'atonement', and 'expiation', which appear repeatedly in the New Testament and in later doctrinal discussions, are all related to sacrificial conceptions, and need to be examined against the background of Old Testament religion and worship.

Nowhere in the Old Testament is the rationale of sacrifice explained. The institution is taken for granted as a divine ordinance, and the only principle laid down is that 'the blood is the life'.[1] This attitude was maintained in Rabbinical Judaism,[2] and only in comparatively modern times have attempts been made to ascertain its underlying idea. Robertson Smith held that predominantly sacrifice is 'an act of social fellowship between the deity and his worshippers'; it is 'an act of communion, in which the god and his worshippers unite by partaking together of the flesh and blood of a sacred victim'.[3] The alternative view is that sacrifice is essentially a gift to God.[4]

[1] Gen. ix. 4; Lev. xvii. 10-2; Deut. xii. 23.

[2] Cf. *The Jewish Encyclopedia*, x. 628; G. F. Moore, Article on 'Sacrifice', *Encycl. Biblica*, col. 4226.

[3] *The Religion of the Semites*, (1927), 224, 226f.

[4] Cf. G. B. Gray: 'Whenever in later times the Jew sacrificed, he was consciously intending his sacrifice to be a gift to God', *Sacrifice in the Old Testament*, 20; G. F. Moore: 'The prevailing conception of sacrifice and offering in the O.T. is that of a gift or present to God', *Encycl. Biblica*. col. 4216.

It may be doubted whether these theories are mutually exclusive, and it is possible that a more vaguely defined purpose of establishing healthful relations with the gods represents the extent to which the original purpose of sacrifice can be defined.[1]

Popular misconceptions regarding the Old Testament sacrifices are still widespread. It is still widely believed, for example, that the sacrifice was a propitiatory offering intended to appease the anger of Yahweh. It cannot be denied that there are Old Testament stories which give ground for this opinion. An outstanding illustration appears in the words of David when pursued by Saul: 'If it be Yahweh that hath stirred thee up against me, let him smell an offering' (1 Sam. xxvi. 19). Here the implication is that the odour of burning flesh placates the wrath of God. The same idea is implicit in the story of Noah's sacrifice (Gen. viii. 21), and in the account of the numbering of the people by David (2 Sam. xxiv. 25). There was also a reversion to propitiatory human sacrifices in later times, as, for example, in the seventh century B.C. (cf. Jer. xix. 5). This evidence illustrates a persistent tendency in primitive worship, but it cannot be said to reveal the true nature of the Old Testament sacrifices.

The idea that the sacrifice is a substitutionary rite is largely due to a misunderstanding of the act of the worshipper in laying his hands on the head of the victim. This ritual act does not signify the transference of guilt, for the offering is still regarded as holy; it is the worshipper's acknowledgment that the offering is his own, and that he identifies himself with it.[2] Confusion has

---

[1] Among recent discussions see E. O. James, *Origins of Sacrifice*, 21ff., 255ff.; A. C. Welch, *Prophet and Priest in Old Israel*, 136ff.

[2] Cf. G. B. Stevens, *The Christian Doctrine of Salvation*, 12f.; W. F. Lofthouse, *Altar, Cross and Community*, 107, 113.

also arisen in connexion with the ritual of the scapegoat on the Day of Atonement (cf. Lev. xvi.). A long history lies behind the idea of transferring sins to an animal which bears them away into the wilderness.[1] The ideas are more primitive than those reflected in the Old Testament sacrifices, and it is important to observe that in the ceremonies of the Day of Atonement the scapegoat is not sacrificed.[2]

The distinctive character of the earlier Old Testament sacrifices, the *burnt-offering*, the *meal-offering*, and the *peace-offering*, is their tributary, eucharistic, and conciliatory nature; they are often an expression of joy as well as of contrition.[3] The *sin-offering* and the *guilt-offering* belong to the post-exilic period,[4] but so far from atoning for mortal sins, their scope was mainly ceremonial, the *sin-offering* covering inadvertent transgressions and acts of ritual defilement and the *guilt-offering* offences where restitution was not possible.[5] In general, the sacrifices are expiatory rather than propitiatory; they are appointed means whereby sin is *covered*, so that it no longer stands

[1]Cf. J. G. Frazer, *The Golden Bough*, ii. 3, vi.; G. B. Gray, *Sacrifice in the Old Testament*, 313-8; E. O. James, *Origins of Sacrifice*, 196-201.

[2]'And Aaron shall lay both his hands upon the head of the live goat, and confess over him all the iniquities of the children of Israel, and all their transgressions, even all their sins; and he shall put them upon the head of the goat, and shall send him away by the hand of a man that is in readiness into the wilderness: and the goat shall bear upon him all their iniquities unto a solitary land' (Lev. xvi. 21f.).

[3]Cf. G. B. Gray: 'Sacrifice was more often eucharistic than propitiatory, and it was more often offered with feelings of joy and security than in fear or contrition', *op. cit.*, 95.

[4]Cf. R. H. Kennett: 'There is no instance of this class of sacrifice in the older *strata* of the Pentateuchal legislation; not probably because such piacular sacrifices were never offered, but because the older *strata* deal with what is normal,' *The Church of Israel*, 111f.

[5]So far as the two can be distinguished. Cf. A. C. Welch, *Post-Exilic Judaism*, 292.

as an obstacle between the worshipper and God. This fact is illustrated by the many examples of the use of *kipper*, the Piel form of the verb *kaphar*, 'to cover' or 'to wipe away'.

The linguistic usage of *kipper* is one of great interest. In cases where it means 'to appease' or 'pacify', the reference is to man.[1] In other passages it is used of expiation for sin apart from sacrifice,[2] and where God is the subject the meaning is 'to forgive' or 'to purge away'.[3] The commonest use of the verb is in connexion with the sacrificial rites, and here the thought is that of covering ritual imperfections or of expiating sins. The illustrations of this usage are far too numerous to be given in full, and the following must serve as examples.

Lev. xvi. 33: 'And he shall make atonement for the holy sanctuary.'

Ezek. xliii. 26: 'Seven days shall they make atonement for the altar and purify it.'

Lev. i. 4: 'And he shall lay his hand upon the head of the burnt offering; and it shall be accepted for him to make atonement for him.'

Numb. xv. 25: 'And the priest shall make atonement for all the congregation of the children of Israel, and they shall be forgiven.'

2 Chron. xxix. 24: 'And they made a sin offering with their blood upon the altar to make atonement for all Israel.'

It would not be safe in all passages of this kind to press the root meanings of 'covering' or 'wiping away', for the verb comes to be used conventionally, like the English 'make atonement for'; but echoes of these ideas, especially

---

[1] Cf. Gen. xxxii. 20 and Prov. xvi. 14.

[2] Cf. Ex. xxxii. 30; Num. xvi. 46f., xxv. 13; 2 Sam. xxi. 3.

[3] Cf. Deut. xxi. 8, xxxii. 43; 2 Chron. xxx. 18; Psa. lxv. 3, lxxviii. 38, lxxix. 9; Jer. xviii. 23; Ezek. xvi. 63; Dan. ix. 24.

that of 'covering', can be found in most cases.[1] The idea
of 'cleansing' is expressed in Lev. xvi. 30: 'On this day
shall atonement be made for you, to cleanse you: from all
your sins shall ye be clean before the Lord.' In an invaluable study of ἱλάσκεσθαι and cognate words C. H.
Dodd has shown that 'the LXX translators did not regard
kipper (when used as a religious term) as conveying the
sense of propitiating the Deity, but the sense of perform-
ing an act whereby guilt or defilement is removed'.[2]
'Thus', he adds, 'Hellenistic Judaism, as represented by
the LXX, does not regard the cultus as a means of pacify-
ing the displeasure of the Deity, but as a means of delivering man from sin, and it looks in the last resort to God
himself to perform that deliverance, thus evolving a
meaning of ἱλάσκεσθαι strange to non-biblical Greek.'[3]

In addition to the indications supplied by the linguistic
usage, the representative and inclusive character of the
Old Testament sacrifices reveals the true nature of the
cultus as a means of maintaining or restoring fellowship
with God. The sacrifices are vehicles of self-expression;
they make possible religious activities with which the
worshipper can associate himself, and so in a very real
sense make his own. This aspect of the sacrifices is evident in the various elements which enter into the ritual.
Bishop Hicks[4] has distinguished six stages which may be
summarized briefly as follows: (1) The worshipper 'draws
near' with his offering; (2) He lays his hands (or leans or
rests them) on the victim's head; (3) He himself, and not

---

[1]'Underlying all these offerings there is the conception that the persons
offering are covered by that which is regarded as sufficient and satisfactory
by Yahweh', *Hebrew and English Lexicon of the Old Testament*, Brown,
Driver, Briggs, 498.

[2]*The Bible and the Greeks*, 93.   [3]*Ibid.*

[4]Cf. *The Fullness of Sacrifice*, 11-4.

the priest, slays the victim; (4) The priest presents the blood to God by pouring it upon, or dashing it against, the altar; (5) The flesh, or part of it, is burnt, and so is transformed in order that it may ascend to heaven, the dwelling-place of God; (6) A portion of the offering is eaten by the priests and the worshipper, except in the case of the burnt-offering, while the flesh of the sin-offering and the guilt-offering is reserved for the priests, except when atonement is made for their own sins.[1] This is, of course, a composite and idealized picture. We cannot suppose that the significance of the various stages was always present to the mind of the worshippers, since the tendency was to fulfil the prescribed rites because they were ordained by God. But the value of the description is that it shows how inclusive the rite was; it is not any one of the six stages which are distinguished; the whole is the sacrifice. Its representative character is also manifest; the worshipper identifies himself with his offering, and while it is presented to God, he participates in it himself.

From what has already been said it is apparent how erroneous it is to limit the idea of sacrifice to that of the death and destruction of a victim. This popular belief [2] isolates one element in the ritual and misconceives its purpose, for destruction is not the primary intention. The victim is slain in order that its life, in the form of blood, may be released, and its flesh is burnt in order that it may be transformed or etherialized; and in both cases the aim

---

[1]Cf. Lev. v. 13, x. 16-20.

[2]"The "man in the street", and many who are more familiar with theology than he, would still, if they were asked to describe a sacrifice, suggest an altar, with a living victim bound upon it, and a priest standing over it with a knife in his uplifted hand. Translated into the language of the Christian Sacrifice, that is the conception of Christ offering Himself upon the Altar of the Cross, of sacrifice as equivalent to, and completed in, death,' F. C. N. Hicks, *The Fullness of Sacrifice*, 327.

is to make it possible for life to be presented as an offering
to the Deity. More and more students of comparative
religion, and of Old Testament worship in particular, are
insisting that the bestowal of life is the fundamental idea
in sacrificial worship.[1]

At this point it will be useful to summarize the principal defects and advantages of the sacrificial system.

A marked weakness of the system was the passive character of the victim or offering. Its purity and innocence
were non-moral; the qualities of purity and innocence
were merely symbolized. In consequence, the worshipper could identify himself only with objects which
suggested ethical qualities; there could be no personal
bond between himself and his offering; the moral value of
his sacrifice was limited by its cost and by the degree to
which an external object could focus, discipline, and
direct his penitence Godwards. A second defect of the
system was its liability to abuse. It is always easy scru-
pulously to fulfil the external requirements of a cultus
without genuine repentance, and even to make costly
gifts a cover for extortion and wrong. The ritual may
evoke no spiritual response; it may foster unethical conceptions of God and of sin, and encourage unhealthy dependence upon a priesthood. The story of Israel and the
protests of the prophets show how serious these dangers
were. A third weakness of the sacrificial system was its
limited range. It had to do mainly with ritual trans-

[1]"The fundamental principle throughout is the same; the giving of life
to promote or preserve life, death being merely a means of liberating
vitality. Consequently, the destruction of the victim, to which many
writers have given a central position in the rite, assumes a position of
secondary importance in comparison with the transmission of the soul-
substance to the supernatural being to whom it is offered,' E. O. James,
Origins of Sacrifice, 256. 'Life—its recovery, uplifting, and communication—is the ruling conception of sacrifice: life as shared between God and
man, and between man and man . . .,' F. C. N. Hicks, *op. cit.*, 177.

gressions, with sins which the modern man would hardly regard as sins at all; whereas for sins done 'with a high hand' there was no provision save in the special rites of the Day of Atonement. The exception is significant; for, in adopting the ancient rite of the scapegoat, those who shaped the Levitical system departed from its basic principles. In admitting that sins could be put upon the head of an animal and borne away into the wilderness, they confessed the inadequacy of the existing system. Uneasiness with the system, as well as spiritual perception, is also revealed in the emphasis which the later Rabbis laid upon repentance as the *sine qua non* of sacrifice. It is noteworthy that it is the New Testament writer who more than all others has seized upon and utilized the sacrificial principle, the author of the Epistle to the Hebrews, who emphatically says: 'It is impossible that the blood of bulls and goats should take away sins' (x. 4). By its limitations the Old Testament system was driven into an impasse and failed where its help was needed most.

These defects are so obvious that it is easy to overlook the many excellent features in the cultus, but the merits are as certain as the defects and include elements which are of imperishable value to religion and to the practice of the devotional life.

The most notable advantage of the cultus was that it held out to the worshipper the possibility of fellowship with God. Its aim was to make that fellowship actual by overcoming the obstacles which prevented its attainment. Frequent failure cannot hide the greatness of the objective or obscure the fact that it was often realized. A further merit was that, within its limitations, the system sharpened the conscience of the worshipper. Sin was felt to be something which must be treated seriously; it could not be dismissed with a wave of the hand, but must be expiated before fellowship with God could be perfected. Again, the cultus gave real help in focussing and directing penitence towards God. Passive though the offering might be, it served to create a centre in the mind around which a strong and healthy sentiment of penitence might be established. The worshipper was not left to struggle alone with fugitive and fitful feelings of remorse. On the contrary, there was at his disposal a medium, material though it was, through which his contrition could be offered and his longing for better things could be expressed. Further, the cultus brought home to the mind the thought of reconciliation as a costly process. Doubtless there was a real danger that the worshipper might count the cost of his offering as a thing of merit, but at all events he was delivered from the easy belief that reconciliation can be taken for granted as an axiom of religious experience. More important still, the sacrificial system suggested that a surrendered and dedicated life was the basis of true fellowship with God. The writer of the Epistle to the Hebrews grasped this principle when he wrote: 'And according to the law, I may almost say, all things are cleansed with blood, and apart from shedding of blood there is no remission' (ix. 22). No doubt the shed blood might be regarded as if it were endowed with magical properties, but the instructed and thoughtful worshipper knew that it was the symbol of dedicated life and of a life with which he could identify himself. Thus, the way was prepared for richer applications of the sacrificial principle in Christianity. Finally, the system made possible a social, as well as an individual, approach to God. In the *sacra publica* the worshipper was reminded of common needs and communal sins in which he was involved as an individual within a clan, while in the sacred meal, which he celebrated with his family, his neighbours, and his guests, he enjoyed in common with others the sense of God's presence and favour.

In estimating the relative significance of these defects and advantages Old Testament scholars are divided. Much depends on whether the sacrificial system is regarded in the light of its origins, which to the modern man often appear revolting, or whether it is viewed from the standpoint of its religious possibilities. It is from the former point of view that G. B. Gray says: 'The truth is whatever is the root idea . . . that root idea belongs to a grossly material view of religion and of man's relation to God.'[1] It is from the latter standpoint that the same writer says that the real movement of Old Testament religion is upward towards a completely spiritual goal. 'It rises', he observes, 'to the conception that there is a gift which man can make to God, a gift of something that is his own and that God desires to receive; man can give himself; his will is his own, he can make it his present to God.'[2]

Each of the standpoints indicated is required if history is to be more than a summary of facts. Each, moreover, has its characteristic dangers. In recording facts the investigator will mark the gross beginnings of sacrifice, the different stages in the growth of the cultus, and the significance they appear to have borne for the ordinary worshipper. If, however, his study is to be complete, he must try to assign to sacrifice its real place in the story of man's religious development; and for this purpose he will need to examine the facts revealed by archaeology and ancient literature with insight and imagination. It is part of his task to note implications which may have been recognized by few in ancient times, but which are full of meaning for the story of later religious developments.

[1] *Sacrifice in the Old Testament*, 54.   [2] *Ibid.*

If this is the nature of a scientific investigation, those scholars are justified who insist that the most significant conception in sacrifice is that of life offered to God, with which the worshipper can associate himself through appropriate ritual acts. This conception unquestionably leads to an exalted estimate of the value of sacrificial worship, for, in the last analysis, it means that sin is expiated because, by the aid of a traditional cultus, the worshipper has presented to God in penitence and faith nothing less than himself.

It would be folly to pretend that this conception of sacrifice is taught in the Old Testament or was a theme of Rabbinical teaching. There are reasons for this. In part, the absence of explanation is due to the lack of an adequate religious and psychological terminology, but to a greater degree it is accounted for by the belief that sacrifice was a system of divine appointment. Such an idea does not encourage reflection; still less when it is associated with a strong belief in the sovereignty of God and the inscrutability of His will. These beliefs gave stability to the sacrificial system, but they discouraged speculation and threatened the ethical and spiritual development of the cultus. None the less, the evidence afforded by the Psalms proves that the barrier was not insurmountable. The significance of a ritual must be found in itself and in the religious spirit with which it is accompanied, and not merely in traditional explanations. If this is so, we are far from idealizing unduly the Old Testament sacrificial system if we assert that for many worshippers it was the vehicle of a truly spiritual approach to God and an opportunity for self-offering and surrender.

The use of a ritual does not preclude the possibility of a spiritual approach to God; it certainly was not so in the case of Old Testament religion. Far from being an unworthy substitute for self-surrender to God, the ritual provided at the time the only means whereby the idea could live in an ethical and spiritual form.   No Hebrew could think of offering himself as he was, frail and sinful to a holy and a righteous God,[1] while the idea of a purely spiritual offering would have seemed to him abstract and meaningless.   The life offered must be that of another, innocent and pure, free from all impurity and sin, and yet withal the symbol of an ideal life to which he aspired and with which he could identify himself.   It is because of this fundamental conviction that the idea of self-sacrifice is wanting, or is present only in germ, in the Old Testament.   Ideas, however, are often implicit in a ritual before they gain an independent existence.   In Old Testament worship the idea of self-sacrifice was waiting to be born, secured by its bonds from the cheap and attenuated expressions it has often suffered in later religious systems. The main obstacle to a healthy development was the passive character of the Levitical offering; the worshipper faced the demand of identifying himself with that which could neither will nor experience the glory of vicarious sacrifice.   If the system could have supplied this want, in a form which was at once both ethical and spiritual, it would have been able to furnish a perfect ritual of expiation, available not only for ceremonial defects, but also for desperate sins done 'with a high hand'.   To say this is only to make the just acknowledgment that underlying the Old Testament sacrificial system lay noble spiritual ideas, capable of being enlarged and purified, which belong to any doctrine of atonement worthy of the name.

Before examining the attitude of Jesus to the sacrificial principle it is necessary to consider the significance of the

[1]Cf. Isa. vi. 5-8.

prophetic reaction to the cultus.[1]   This inquiry is necessary because the two questions are closely related in current discussions; it is also required in view of the opinions
stated above.

While a study of the Old Testament reveals a noble idea
at the heart of sacrifice, it no less clearly shows how easily
sacrificial worship can be perverted and debased, so that it
becomes a moral opiate and a substitute for righteousness.
This danger is manifest from the protests of the prophets
of the seventh and eighth centuries B.C. which in some
cases are carried so far as to amount to a repudiation of the
cultus.   Amos declares that God will not accept the
burnt-offerings and sacrifices of the people, and indig-
nantly asks: 'Did ye bring unto me sacrifices and offerings
in the wilderness forty years, O house of Israel?' (v. 21-6).
'I desire mercy, and not sacrifice; and the knowledge of
God more than[2] burnt offerings' is the message of Hosea
(vi. 6).   Isaiah denounces the Temple treading of men
whose hands are full of blood, and cries: 'To what purpose
is the multitude of your sacrifices unto me? saith the Lord:
I am full of the burnt offerings of rams, and the fat of fed
beasts; and I delight not in the blood of bullocks, or of
lambs, or of he-goats' (i. 11).   In a well-known passage
Micah, or a later writer, asks whether Yahweh will be
pleased with thousands of rams or with ten thousands of
rivers of oil, and shows that what He requires is 'to do
justly, and to love mercy, and to walk humbly with thy
God' (vi. 7f.).   Similar views are expressed in some of the

[1]Among recent discussions see R. H. Kennett, *The Church of Israel*,
120-8; J. Skinner, *Prophecy and Religion*, 178ff; W. Eichrodt, *Theologie
des Alten Testaments*, i. 64-82; F. N. C. Hicks, *The Fullness of Sacrifice*,
55-91; W. L. Wardle, *History and Religion of Israel*, 180f.; C. R. North,
Expository Times, xlvii. 252f.; T. H. Robinson, *Hebrew Religion*, 201f.;
A. C. Welch, *Prophet and Priest in Old Israel*, 47f., 76-102.

[2]Or 'apart from'. Cf. J. Skinner, *Prophecy and Religion*, 179; R. H.
Kennett, *op. cit.*, 121n.

later Psalms, notably in Psa. xl. 6, l. 13, and li.16 f,[1] but
the most pronounced opposition to sacrifice is that voiced
by Jeremiah who sarcastically bids the people eat their
burnt-offerings as well as the flesh they are accustomed to
eat when offering sacrifice, and then roundly declares as
his message: 'For I spake not unto your fathers, nor commanded them in the day that I brought them out of the
land of Egypt, concerning burnt offerings or sacrifices:
but this thing I commanded them, saying, Hearken unto
my voice, and I will be your God, and ye shall be my
people: and walk ye in all the way that I command you,
that it may be well with you' (vii. 22f.).   In these words,[2]
and perhaps also in those of Amos,[3] the sacrificial system
is expressly rejected, and the demands of a purely spiritual
and ethical religion are set in its place.   All the prophets
place the ethical requirements of God in the foreground,
but in the case of Jeremiah they are made a substitute for
the cultus.   Thus, when he announces the new covenant
which Yahweh will make with the house of Israel, it is described in significant contrast with the covenant of Sinai.
It is 'not according to the covenant that I made with their
fathers in the day that I took them by the hand to bring
them out of the land of Egypt' (Jer. xxxi. 32).   Yahweh's
law will be put 'in their inward parts' and written 'in their
heart'.   No mention is made of sacrifices or of 'the blood

[1]But see the comments of C. A. Briggs, I.C.C., *The Book of Psalms*,
i. 354, 419, ii. 9.

[2]Cf. J. Skinner, *Prophecy and Religion*, 183; R. H. Kennett, *op. cit.*,
123f.; G. A. Smith, *Jeremiah*, 158f.

[3]Cf. E. A. Edghill, *The Book of Amos*, 57; R. S. Cripps, *The Book of
Amos*, 27.   Cripps points out that in the wilderness wanderings there was
little opportunity for sacrifice, and says that the words of Amos 'fall short
of the implication of those of Jeremiah,' *op. cit.*, 339.   See also W. O. E.
Oesterley and T. H. Robinson, *Hebrew Religion, its Origin and Development*: 'But that Amos contemplated the entire abrogation of the sacrificial
system at the time at which he lived . . . is difficult to believe,' p. 299.

of the covenant', as in Exodus xxiv. 8, and the forgiveness of God is promised directly. 'And they shall teach no more every man his neighbour, and every man his brother, saying, Know the Lord: for they shall all know me, from the least of them unto the greatest of them, saith the Lord: for I will forgive their iniquity, and their sin will I remember no more' (Jer. xxxi. 34).

The greatness of this conception and of the personality of Jeremiah are undoubted, and there is no need to speak of the blessings which have attended the 're-discovery of the prophets'. These things are plain to read for him who runs. In life, however, as it exists, advantages are not unaccompanied by corresponding disadvantages, and in return for its unbalanced appreciation of the teaching of Jeremiah modern theology has paid a heavy price. It is astonishing that it has been so little observed that Jeremiah makes impossible demands on human nature and too easily assumes that man can fulfil the demands of a holy God. Of the symbolism of sacrifice and its value for frail and erring men he has no appreciation, nor can he penetrate beneath pagan excesses to those underlying principles which find a sublimated expression in the figure of the Servant of Yahweh. The truth is that Jeremiah identified sacrifice with its abuses, and in this he displays the characteristic vice of an ardent reformer. His true greatness lies in his splendid affirmations and in his unsparing condemnation of magical practices; his failure is his inability to see the greatness of the system he condemns. It is not too much to say that his rough rejection of sacrifice, as endorsed by many commentators, has not a little to do with the widespread modern assumption that an objective Atonement is unnecessary, for, if his teaching is valid, the sole function of the Cross of Christ is that it gives a final revelation of the love of God.

With the exception of Jeremiah, and possibly also of Amos, the teaching of the pre-exilic prophets does not amount to a repudiation of the sacrificial system,[1] but is a vigorous and healthy protest against its patent abuses. This protest did not go unregarded, and in the post-exilic period every effort is made to establish and commend a purified system. Thus, Ezekiel who speaks of 'a new heart' which God will give to His people and 'a new spirit' which He will put within them (xxxvi. 26), puts sacrifice at the very centre of Jewish ritual in his picture of the worship of the restored Temple (cf. xl.-xlviii.); and Haggai and Zechariah urge upon the people the supreme necessity of the rebuilding of the Temple (Hag. i. 4-11; Zech. i. 16f.). This change of attitude is partly to be explained by the fact that the abuses against which Amos, Isaiah, and Jeremiah had thundered were now a thing of the past, but it is also due to growing conceptions of the divine holiness (cf. Ezek. i. 26-8). The later Psalms not only re-echo the teaching of the pre-exilic prophets, but also reveal the joy with which sacrifice was offered and the spiritual ideas with which it was associated. The writer of Psa. xxvi. desires to wash his hands in innocency and to compass Yahweh's altar, and says:

> 'Lord, I love the habitation of thy house,
> And the place where thy glory dwelleth.'

Psa. xxvii. speaks of offering in God's tabernacle 'sacrifices of joy' and of singing praises unto Yahweh (verse 6), and the same spirit appears in Psa. lxvi. 13-5:

> 'I will come into thy house with burnt offerings,
> I will pay thee my vows,
> Which my lips have uttered,

[1]See the important article of A. R. Johnson, 'The Prophet in Israelite Worship', *Expository Times*, xlvii. 312-9.

And my mouth hath spoken, when I was in distress.
I will offer unto thee burnt offerings of fatlings,
With the incense of rams;
I will offer bullocks with goats,'

and in Psa. cvii. 21f.:

'Oh that men would praise the Lord for his goodness,
And for his wonderful works to the children of men!
And let them offer the sacrifices of thanksgiving,
And declare his works with singing.'

In Ecclesiasticus the son of Sirach emphasizes the ethical demands of righteousness in the spirit of the earlier prophets, when he says (xxxiv. 18f.):

'He that sacrificeth of a thing wrongfully gotten,
His offering is made in mockery;
And the mockeries of wicked men are not well-pleasing.
The Most High hath no pleasure in the offerings of the ungodly;
Neither is he pacified for sins by the multitude of sacrifices,'

but he also exalts the priesthood of Aaron who was chosen,

'To offer sacrifice to the Lord,
Incense, and a sweet savour, for a memorial,
To make reconciliation for thy people' (xlv. 16),

and describes at length and with enthusiasm the glory of the high priest Simon, the son of Onias, the way in which he received the portions out of the priests' hands while his brethren were 'as a garland round about him', and how afterwards the sons of Aaron shouted and sounded trumpets of beaten work, while the people fell down upon the earth on their faces 'to worship their Lord, the Almighty, God Most High' (l. 1-21).

In the Rabbinical writings the importance of repentance as a necessary condition in sacrificial worship is stressed. In the Mishnah it is laid down that 'death and the Day of

E

Atonement effect atonement if there is repentance' (*Yoma*, 8). A man is not to presume on the possibility of expiation by saying 'I will sin and the Day of Atonement will effect atonement'; if he does so, 'then the Day of Atonement effects no atonement'. It is also said that 'for transgressions that are between a man and his fellow the Day of Atonement effects atonement only if he has appeased his fellow' (*Yoma*, 9).[1] The destruction of the Temple in A.D. 70 naturally raised the greatest problems in Jewish minds regarding sacrifice. A well-known story tells that when R. Joshua ben Hananiah saw the Temple in ruins, he said to his teacher, R. Johanan ben Zakkai, 'Woe to us, for the place where the iniquities of Israel were atoned for us is destroyed!' 'Do not grieve', was the reply of Johanan, 'for we have an atonement which is equal to it, namely, deeds of mercy, as the Scripture says, "For I desire mercy and not sacrifice".'[2] A saying of R. Nehemiah explains that sufferings 'are a better atonement than sacrifice, for sacrifices are of a man's property, sufferings in his person, and "all that a man hath will he give for his life" (Job ii. 4)'.[3] These noble sayings show how deeply the ethical teaching of the prophets had influenced the minds of Jewish thinkers in later times; it would be a mistake, however, to suppose that they came to repudiate the sacrificial cultus. In the '*amidah* the devout Jew prays: 'Mayest Thou bring back the sacrifice to Thy holy house, and the fire-offerings as well as their prayers receive with favour'[4], and in the additional '*amidah* for sabbaths, new moon, and festivals he asks that 'the prayers of our lips may be ac-

---

[1]Cf. H. Danby, *The Mishnah*, 172.

[2]Cf. G. F. Moore, *Judaism*, ii. 172.

[3]See Strack-Billerbeck, ii. 277.

[4]Cf. F. C. N. Hicks, *The Fullness of Sacrifice*, 107.

counted, accepted, and esteemed before Thee, as if we had offered the daily sacrifice at its appointed time, and had been represented by our delegation'.[1]

The question: What was the attitude of Jesus to the sacrificial system? must now be faced. This question is of great importance because it is bound up with the further question whether He thought of His suffering and death in terms of sacrifice.

The variety of critical opinion upon these questions is in itself a sufficient warning that the true answer is not easy to find. Our previous discussion of such themes as the Kingdom of God, Messiahship, and the Suffering Servant predisposes us to expect that His attitude to sacrifice will display the same originality and distinctiveness we have found elsewhere. This, in fact, proves to be the case.

On the one hand, an attitude of detachment from the cultus on the part of Jesus is visible in the Gospel records. It is remarkable that there is no evidence to show that He ever participated in the Temple sacrifices. Not even in the Fourth Gospel, where there are several references to 'feasts' at Jerusalem,[2] is it said that Jesus offered sacrifice or was present at the time of offering. The only evidence which might suggest that He did take part in the sacrifices is the story of Preparations for the Passover (Mk. xiv. 12-6) and the saying: 'With desire I have desired to eat this passover with you before I suffer' (Lk. xxii. 15). This evidence, however, is uncertain because, while the Passover counted as a sacrifice,[3] its character at the time was

---

[1] M. Gaster, *The Prayer Book and Order of Service* of the Spanish and Portuguese Jews, i. 11, cited by E. O. James, *Origins of Sacrifice*, 264.

[2] Cf. Jn. ii. 13, v. 1, vi. 4, vii. 2, 10, x. 22.

[3] Cf. G. B. Gray, *op. cit.*, 352.

mainly that of a memorial meal.[1]   Moreover, the offering
of the lamb is not mentioned. The argument from silence
always needs to be stated with care, and it may be accidental that no positive tradition has survived, but the probabilities are that Jesus stood apart from the Temple rites
without questioning their validity. This attitude is further illustrated in the story of the Cleansing of the Temple
(Mk. xi. 15-7).   It is probably too sweeping a conclusion
to infer, with R. H. Kennett,[2] that the story implies an
attack by Jesus upon the cultus, but there is in His action
an implicit condemnation of the traffic in victims insepar-
ably connected with the sacrifices, as well as a protest
against the greed and the secular spirit which turns 'a
house of prayer' into 'a den of robbers' (Mk. xi. 17).[3]

On the other hand there is no sufficient evidence to
show that Jesus shared the attitude of some of the pre-
exilic prophets in repudiating the sacrificial system. The
only passages which might seem to point in this direction
are Mt. ix. 13a, xii. 7 and Mk. xii. 33f.

Of these passages, the first two are quotations of Hos.
vi. 6: 'I desire mercy, and not sacrifice.' Both are
Matthaean insertions in Markan stories, Mt. ix. 13a in
the story about Eating with Publicans and Sinners (Mk.
ii. 16f.), and Mt. xii. 7 in the story of Cornfields on the
Sabbath Day (Mk. ii. 23-8). It would be a rash interpretation to say that in using this quotation Jesus was repudiating the cultus. The attitude implied is that of
Isaiah, Hosea, and other prophets who condemned unethical sacrificial practices. There is a bold assertion of
the superiority of moral claims over those of ritual, but
nothing parallel to the root and branch rejection charac-

[1]Cf. G. B. Gray, *op. cit.*, 376; R. H. Kennett, *op. cit.*, 135
[2]*Op. cit.*, 133.
[3]Cf. A. E. J. Rawlinson, *St. Mark*, 156.

teristic of Jeremiah.   This view is confirmed by the more
important passage in Mk. xii. 33f. where Jesus agrees
with the scribe who says concerning God: 'To love him
with all the heart, and with all the understanding, and with
all the strength, and to love his neighbour as himself, is
much more than all whole burnt offerings and sacrifices.'
Again, there is the same healthy recognition of the supre-
macy of the ethical over the ceremonial, shown by the
reply of Jesus: 'Thou art not far from the kingdom of
God.'   No one, however, would suppose that the scribe
meant his words as a rejection of the Old Testament sacrificial system, nor can the reply of Jesus be interpreted in
such a sense.   The point of view is bold and detached,
but it is not one of repudiation.

Far from rejecting the cultus, Jesus on occasion commanded its observance.   When He healed the leper, He
said: 'Go thy way, shew thyself to the priest, and offer for
thy cleansing the things which Moses commanded, for a
testimony unto them' (Mk. i. 44), and in the story of the
Ten Lepers He says: 'Go and shew yourselves unto the
priests' (Lk. xvii. 14).   The significance of these words is
seen only when it is remembered that the requirement of
the Levitical Law included the sacrifice of lambs and a
meal offering of fine flour mingled with oil (Lev. xiv. 10).
If it is said that only by fulfilling the commands of the Law
could lepers be certified as clean, it remains true that recourse to the cultus could never have been enjoined by one
who repudiated it, unless he had made it clear that his ad-
vice was merely in the interests of conventional prudence.
Of this attitude, however, there is no evidence in the records, and the suggestion is not in accord with the mind
and spirit of Jesus.

Even more significant is the saying recorded in Mt. v.
23f.: 'If therefore thou art offering thy gift at the altar,

and there rememberest that thy brother hath aught against thee, leave there thy gift before the altar, and go thy way, first be reconciled to thy brother, and then come and offer thy gift.' These would be strange words on the lips of one who rejected the sacrificial system! Not only is the spirit in which sacrifices are to be offered indicated, but a command or, at least, an invitation to 'come and offer' is given.

In view of these passages the conclusion must be drawn that, in relation to the sacrificial system, the attitude of Jesus was not that of an iconoclast, but rather that of one who, while alive to its limitations, recognized its place in the religious life of the nation. It may safely be said that, if Jesus had condemned the sacrificial system, early Christian tradition would not be as silent as it is, for the Gospels faithfully record His condemnation of scribal teaching in relation to the Sabbath, Korban, fasting, tithing, and ceremonial washings. But no word of His in opposition to that system can be cited, other than the inconclusive passages already examined, while, as we have seen, other sayings point in the opposite direction. It is therefore impossible to agree with the opinion of R. H. Kennett, that 'our Lord accepted and indeed "fulfilled" the teaching of the great pre-exilic prophets on the subject of sacrifice'.[1] Apart from the quotation from Hosea in Mt. ix. 13*a*, xii. 7, it is just the well-known anti-sacrificial Old Testament sayings which are so markedly wanting in the quotations of Jesus; and it is worth noting that, while He quotes the words of Isaiah freely,[2] His use of Jeremiah is sparing.[3]

---

[1] *Op. cit.*, 135.

[2] Cf. Mk. iv. 12, vii. 6f., ix. 48, xi. 17, xii. 1, xiii. 8, 24f.; Mt. v. 4, 35, vi. 6, xi. 5 (= Lk. vii. 22), xi. 23 (= Lk. x. 15); Lk. iv. 18f., xxii. 37.

[3] Cf. Mk. xi. 17 ('a den of robbers'); Mt. vii. 22 ('prophesy by thy name,') xxiii. 38 (= Lk. xiii. 35, 'Your house is left unto you desolate').

It is often said that, when Jesus spoke of a 'new covenant', He was referring to Jer. xxxi. 31. If, as is probable, this assertion is true, it must be inferred that He was correcting, or at least adding to, Jeremiah's teaching; for He spoke of 'the new covenant *in my blood*', or of '*the blood* of the covenant', an idea which is quite foreign to the prophet's forecast, and for which it is necessary to go to the account of the institution of the Covenant, with its accompanying sacrifices, described in Exodus xxiv. 8.[1]

The respect with which Jesus regarded the cultus is in harmony with His attitude to the Temple. While He foretold the destruction of the Temple (Mk. xiii. 1f.), it is clear from the evidence supplied by the Gospels, and especially the M source, that He held it in high esteem. He was often to be found teaching in the Temple-courts (Mk. xi. 27, xii. 35, xiv. 49; Lk. xix. 47, xxi. 37f.), and paid the annual tax of half a shekel for its support (Mt. xvii. 24). He spoke of the Temple as sanctifying the gold by which it was adorned (Mt. xxiii. 17), and of the altar as sanctifying the gift that was brought to it (Mt. xxiii. 19). The Temple was for Him the dwelling-place of God (Mt. xxiii. 21), and Jerusalem was 'the city of the great King' (Mt. v. 35). In consequence, it must be concluded that when He spoke of the doom of the Temple buildings, it was with the sorrow of a patriot rather than with the wrath of an iconoclast.[2]

The attitude of Jesus to the sacrificial system is entirely

---

[1]'And Moses took the blood, and sprinkled it on the people, and said, Behold the blood of the covenant, which the Lord hath made with you concerning all these words.' See further the discussion in Part II, p. 136f.

[2]Cf. B. H. Branscomb: 'Whatever the facts may be as to the charge that he threatened to destroy the Temple, we may be sure that he spoke of its coming destruction rather in the prophetic manner of a punishment to come upon the nation than as a divine judgment against the Temple itself,' *Jesus and the Law of Moses*, 114.

in keeping with His attitude to the Law of which that system formed part.   On the one hand, there is unmistakable evidence that His attitude to the Law, both oral and written, was singularly free and even revolutionary in its implications; on the other hand, it is equally clear that He reverenced the Torah and estimated its principles and its commands in the highest terms.   He subordinated the claims of the law of the Sabbath to the demands of compassion (cf. Mk. ii. 23-8, iii. 1-5); He reinterpreted the law of divorce (cf. Mk. x. 2-12; Lk. xvi. 18); He repudiated the growing demand that laymen should be ceremonially pure before partaking of food (cf. Mk. vii. 5-8); He condemned oaths which stood in the way of duties towards parents (cf. Mk. vii. 9-13); He roundly assailed the principle fundamental to taboos on food when He declared: 'There is nothing from without the man, that going into him can defile him: but the things which proceed out of the man are those that defile the man' (Mk. vii. 15).[1] In these passages the stage is set for those who would contend that Jesus rejected the Torah, but such a conclusion would be entirely erroneous, for both in Q and in M there are sayings of a totally different kind.   From Q comes the saying on tithing at the expense of judgment and the love of God, which ends with the words: 'But these ought ye to have done, and not to leave the other undone' (Lk. xi. 42; Mt. xxiii. 23); and the declaration: 'It is easier for heaven and earth to pass away, than for one tittle of the law to fall' (Lk. xvi. 17; cf. Mt. v. 18).[2]   Even more striking are the sayings taken from M—the claim of Jesus that He came, not to destroy, but to fulfil the law and the prophets (Mt. v. 17); the assertion that the man who breaks one of the least of these commandments, and teaches men so, shall be

---

[1] Mark adds to the similar saying in vii. 18f.: 'making all meats clean.'

[2] The Matthaean form of this saying may be derived from M.

called least in the kingdom of heaven (Mt. v. 19); the saying which sets the righteousness of the scribes and Pharisees as a standard to be exceeded if men are to enter into
the kingdom (Mt. v. 20); and, most remarkable of all, the
recognition that the scribes and the Pharisees 'sit on
Moses' seat', and the command: 'All things therefore
whatsoever they bid you, these do and observe: but do not
after their works; for they say, and do not' (Mt. xxiii. 2f.).
It is reasonable to urge that some of these sayings have
been sharpened in the course of transmission, and have
been given a definiteness which originally they did not
possess,[1] but it is in the highest degree unlikely that they
are inventions, without any historical basis in the actual
teaching of Jesus. The conflict between the more liberal
section in the primitive Church, represented by Paul, and
the more conservative party at Jerusalem, represented by
James, is inexplicable if both sides could not appeal to
sayings of Jesus which, taken in isolation, supported the
claims of each. It is impossible, therefore, to argue with
any justice that Jesus rejected the Torah; on the contrary, we must conclude, with B. H. Branscomb, that
while 'Paul stands out in a new and stronger light as an
interpreter and exponent of the teachings of Jesus', yet,
at the same time, 'Jesus had been no iconoclast', but 'had
spoken of the Torah in terms of deepest appreciation'.[2]

In the present argument it would be right to claim that
the greater includes the less, and that the attitude of Jesus
to the Law excludes the suggestion that He repudiated
the sacrificial system. Investigation, however, yields a
more positive result; it shows that in both cases His attitude was actually the same. Accordingly, we must con-

[1]Cf. B. H. Branscomb, *Jesus and the Law of Moses*, pp. 212, 231f.;
B. H. Streeter, *The Four Gospels*, 256f.

[2]*Op. cit.* 279f.

clude that, while perceiving the limitations of sacrificial worship, Jesus was no less conscious of its abiding religious values.

This conclusion raises a presumption in favour of the view that Jesus thought of His death in terms of sacrifice. The two passages which are usually cited in this connexion are Mk. x. 45: 'The Son of man came not to be ministered unto, but to minister, and to give his life a ransom for many' (λύτρον ἀντὶ πολλῶν), and Mk. xiv. 24: 'This is my blood of the covenant, which is shed for many.'[1]   These sayings must receive detailed consideration later.   Here it is sufficient to say that certainly the second, and probably also the first saying, indicates that, when Jesus spoke of His death, His thought was influenced by Old Testament teaching regarding sacrifice.   In the case of the first passage, this conclusion cannot be established on linguistic grounds, but depends on whether the phrase 'a ransom for many' reflects the influence of Isa. liii., and whether the idea of the Servant, as Jesus understood it, was a sacrificial concept.   In the second passage the sacrificial interpretation is inescapable. The term 'blood' does not simply indicate a violent death; its association with the idea of a 'covenant' in all the variant forms in which this saying appears fixes its meaning as blood poured out in sacrifice, and this interpretation is confirmed by the words 'which is shed for many'. Whatever explanation of the death of Jesus we may give to-day, there can be no doubt at all that Jesus Himself understood its meaning in terms of sacrifice.

Is it possible to express this broad conclusion more precisely?   It is quite improbable that Jesus thought of

---

[1]Matthew adds: 'unto remission of sins' (xxvi. 28).   In 1 Cor. xi. 25 the saying appears in the form: 'This cup is the new covenant in my blood.' Cf. Lk. xxii. 20.

His death as a higher substitute for any one of the Old Testament sacrifices, such as, for example, the sin-offering or the guilt-offering. This would be altogether too crude an explanation of His thought and would do justice neither to His detached attitude to the cultus nor to the character of these particular sacrifices. It is much more likely that the ideas implicit in sacrificial worship influenced His thinking, and, in particular, the idea of a representative offering to God in which men might share. Whether He entertained this belief depends on whether He thought of His death as representative and as mediatorial; and this question depends in turn upon the interpretation we give to His sayings and to the character of His mission and destiny as He saw them in the course of His ministry.

PART II

THE PASSION-SAYINGS IN THE GOSPELS

INTRODUCTION

AN ideal method of studying the sayings of Jesus with reference to His death would be to examine them in their historical context in the story of His life, to consider them in the light of events, and to relate them to any development it may be possible to trace in the progress of His thought concerning His mission and destiny. Unfortunately, our sources are such that only in part can we do this; some of the most important sayings have come down to us without any historical context, and the Markan order is itself a subject of controversy and debate. It is true that Form-criticism, which rightly emphasizes the fact that much of the earliest tradition circulated in the form of isolated units, has treated the Markan order in much too cavalier a fashion; but even when this criticism is admitted, the fact remains that it is no more than an outline in which many gaps are visible, and within which it is impossible to insert all the separate sayings in question. In these circumstances, it is better to study them in the order in which they appear in the sources.

Most of the sayings are found in Mark and in the L tradition which is peculiar to Luke; no Passion-saying can be traced to the M source, and probably the same is true of Q. This distribution of the evidence is not surprising if we have regard to the nature of M and Q. These sources are, in the main, collections of ethical and religious precepts bearing on life and conduct; and it is not in such collections that we should expect to find sayings of Jesus relative to His Passion. Sayings of this kind naturally appear in Pronouncement-stories, Passion-narratives, and

Stories about Jesus; and this means that we must find
them in Mark and in the tradition peculiar to Luke. Of
course, nearly all the Markan sayings have parallels in
Matthew and in Luke, and these too must be considered,
in order to see what changes have taken place in the course
of transmission; but primary consideration must obviously
be given to the sayings in Mark. Those peculiar to
Luke are fewer in number; some of them are parallel
versions of Markan sayings, others are new traditions of
great importance to the inquiry.

Besides the Synoptic sayings, those preserved in the
Pauline narrative of the Last Supper, in 1 Cor. xi. 23-5,
must be considered, for these are some of the most important utterances of Jesus relative to His Passion. The
Johannine sayings also call for investigation. Their
peculiar character is well known, but even as 'interpretations' and as utterances expressed in another 'idiom',
they cannot safely be neglected by any one who seeks to
know how Jesus viewed His death. We shall consider
then: (1) the Markan sayings; (2) the sayings in the L
tradition; (3) the sayings in 1 Cor. xi. 23-5; and (4) the
Johannine sayings.

One point regarding method is worthy of special notice.
It not infrequently happens that Passion-sayings appear in
two or more sources in a rudimentary narrative framework, and that a saying, or a portion of one, is found in
one source but is wanting in another. Very often this
fact is looked upon as a serious disqualification. Rashdall's treatment of the narratives of the Supper furnishes
a good example.[1] He points out that the phrase 'which
is for you', attached to the words: 'This is my body,' in
1 Cor. xi. 24, is wanting in Mk. xiv. 22 and in the shorter
text of Luke (cf. xxii. 14-9*a*). On this ground he rejects

[1] *The Idea of Atonement in Christian Theology*, 41, 43.

the phrase.   Similarly, he questions the words: 'which is shed for many' (Mk. xiv. 24), 'as these words are not found in St. Paul or in the shorter text of St. Luke'.   This was never a good argument, and the principles of Form-criticism ought to render it less cogent still, for it assumes that the narratives are reports and that only the common element is genuine.   If, however, as the new criticism is emphasizing, narratives owe their form to the special interests of those who shaped them, this assumption is baseless.   A phrase wanting in an original narrative may not be original, but this cannot immediately be assumed; it may fail to appear in a particular account simply because it does not lie on the high-road of the narrator's interest, or because its substance is taken for granted.   In other words, without neglecting 'omissions,' narratives must be judged mainly by what they contain, and not by what they omit.   Even if a peculiar phrase is an addition, it needs to be considered, whether it merely 'brings out' what is already implied, or whether it adds something alien to the meaning of the original saying.   A gloss may be a valuable comment which it is folly to ignore, and a textual variation indicates how the original was understood at an early time.   These considerations enhance the delicacy of Synoptic Criticism and are a salutary warning against the perils of doctrinaire assumptions.

I

THE MARKAN SAYINGS

THE Markan sayings relating to the Passion may be grouped as follows:

(1) The Saying about the Removal of the Bridegroom.
(2) The Sayings regarding the Suffering of the Son of Man.
(3) The Saying at the Descent from the Mount of Transfiguration.
(4) The Saying about the Cup and Baptism.
(5) The 'Ransom' Passage.
(6) The Parable of the Vineyard.
(7) The Saying in the Story of the Anointing.
(8) The Prophecy of the Betrayal.
(9) The Sayings at the Last Supper.
(10) Two Old Testament Quotations: The Stone, The Shepherd.
(11) The Gethsemane Sayings.
(12) The Cry from the Cross.

(1) THE STATEMENT ABOUT THE REMOVAL OF THE BRIDEGROOM (Mk. ii. 19f.; cf. Mt. ix. 15; Lk. v. 34f.).

19*a*. '*Can the sons of the bride-chamber fast, while the bridegroom is with them?*

19*b*. *As long as they have the bridegroom with them, they cannot fast.*

*20a. But the days will come, when the bridegroom shall be taken
away from them,*
20b. And then will they fast in that day.'

The agreement of Matthew and Luke with Mark is almost
verbatim, except that both Evangelists omit Mk. ii. 19*b*. The
omission of 19*b* by D W a b e &c. has probably no significance, and
may be an assimilation to the text of Mt. and Lk.

This saying of Jesus is of great interest since it is the
earliest recorded reference to His death in the Markan
story. It raises many difficulties just because it appears
so early in Mark, and also because it seems to reflect two
different attitudes to the question of fasting. On these
grounds many critics regard 19*b*, 20 as a later addition,
in which the Christian community justifies its existing
practice in respect of fasting.[1] The structure of the two
verses is against this view. 19*b* merely repeats the
thought of 19*a* in another form and the verse is a clear
example of Semitic parallelism. The parallelism, indeed,
is continued in 20, since there is an obvious contrast
between 19*a* and 20*a*, and between 19*b* and 20*b*. This
fact, so far as it goes, favours the originality of the entire
saying; as a later construction of the community, it is too
neat to be convincing. Again, the whole saying is naturally expressed; one thought leads to another. The idea
of the removal of the bridegroom in 20 is already implicit
in 19*b*, and indeed in 19*a*, in the words: 'while the bridegroom is with them.'[2] Thus, the section is a unity.
Further, there is no convincing reason why 19*b*, 20, as
well as 19*a*, should not come from the lips of Jesus. It is

[1]Cf. W. Bousset, *Kyrios Christos* [2], 40f.; R. Bultmann, *Die Geschichte
der synoptischen Tradition*, 17; M. Dibelius, *From Tradition to Gospel*, 65.
See the important note in C. H. Dodd's *The Parables of the Kingdom*, 116.

[2]It is perhaps a perception of this fact which led Bousset to recast 19*a*,
and to suggest that originally the question ran: 'Can wedding-guests fast?',
op. cit., 41.

unnecessary to assume that in 19*a* He is defending a mode
of life without fasting, and hence to infer that 20, which
contemplates fasting, cannot be genuine. What He
opposes is not fasting in general,[1] but fasting under the
special conditions of the Messianic time in which the
disciples are living in company with Himself. The absence of the bridegroom from the feast must obviously
make a difference to their joy, and it is to express this that
Jesus repeats the reference to fasting. The primary intention is not to prophesy the practice of fasting, but to
describe the change which the removal of the bridegroom
must bring. Now there is joy; then there will be sorrow!
The saying indicates that during the Galilean Ministry
Jesus faced the eventuality of death and its effect upon His
disciples.[2]

It is unfortunate that the saying cannot be dated with
any precision, since it belongs to a section (Mk. ii. 1–iii. 6)
which is arranged topically, and which probably existed
as a connected whole at the time when Mark wrote his
Gospel.[3]   Whether it really belongs to a point so early as
that suggested by the Markan outline, we cannot tell, but
the Evangelist is probably right in placing it well before
the account of Peter's Confession near Caesarea Philippi;
it obviously belongs to a time when the liberal spirit of
Jesus and His disciples was beginning to arouse comment
and opposition.   Its importance is great, not only because
it indicates that in the full tide of the Galilean Mission
Jesus faced the possibility of death, but also because it
shows that already He was confronted with the enigma

---

[1] Cf. Mt. vi. 16.

[2] A. E. J. Rawlinson thinks that the story is quite intelligible as it stands,
if we assume that the episode happened soon after the Baptist's death, *St.
Mark*, 31.

[3] Cf. *The Formation of the Gospel Tradition*, 16, 177.

present in the thought of the death of the Messiah. The term 'Bridegroom' is a descriptive title used with reference to the Messiah[1] in Mt. xxv. 1; Jn. iii. 28f., and recalls the ideas of Hos. ii. 19f., and its use by Jesus proves that He was alive to the problem which is solved by Him in the sayings of Mk. viii. 31, ix. 31, x. 33. These are the passages which speak of the suffering and rejection of the Son of Man.

(2) THE SAYINGS ON THE SUFFERING AND REJECTION OF THE SON OF MAN (Mk. viii. 31, ix. 31, x. 33f.).

(a) 'And he began to teach them, that the Son of man must suffer many things, and be rejected by the elders, and the chief priests, and the scribes, and be killed, and after three days rise again' (cf. Mt. xvi. 21; Lk. ix. 22).

(b) 'For he taught his disciples, and said unto them, *The Son of man is delivered up into the hands of men, and they shall kill him; and when he is killed, after three days he shall rise again*' (cf. Mt. xvii. 22f.; Lk. ix. 44).

(c) '*Behold, we go up to Jerusalem; and the Son of man shall be delivered unto the chief priests and the scribes; and they shall condemn him to death, and shall deliver him unto the Gentiles: and they shall mock him, and shall spit upon him, and shall scourge him, and shall kill him; and after three days he shall rise again*' (cf. Mt. xx. 18f.; Lk. xviii. 31-3).

Matthew and Luke reproduce these passages with very considerable fidelity. The changes are of minor importance, but are of much interest in connexion with the question of the genuineness of Mark's version. The alterations, made—it should be remembered—some fifteen or twenty years after Mark was written, may be summarized as follows:

[1]Cf. also Eph. v. 28ff. and Apoc. xix. 7, and see Strack-Billerbeck, *Kommentar zum Neuen Testament aus Talmud und Midrasch*, i. 517; E. Klostermann, *Das Markusevangelium*, 33.

The later Evangelists change 'after three days' into 'the third day' (Lk. omits the phrase in (b)). In (a) after 'must' Matthew inserts 'go unto Jerusalem', and omits 'rejected'; Luke turns the passage into direct speech. In (b) Matthew omits 'when he is killed'; Luke merely gives the first part of the saying, and omits the references to killing and rising again. In (c) Matthew deletes the phrase about spitting, and instead of 'kill' has 'crucify'; Luke summarizes the first part of the passage in the words: 'Behold, we go up to Jerusalem, and all the things that are written by the prophets shall be accomplished unto the Son of man,' and after 'mocked' adds 'and shamefully entreated'.

In the light of the use which Matthew and Luke have made of their source, the opinion that the Markan sayings are prophecies 'after the event' and products of early Christian reflection,[1] ought to be received with some degree of scepticism. After half a generation of further Christian experience, the sayings reappear in the later Gospels with less important alterations than might be expected. Most of the changes are omissions; there are few expansions; and the only alterations which are due to a knowledge of the Passion Story are the substitution of the phrase 'the third day' for 'after three days', the use by Matthew of the word 'crucify', and the reference by Luke to 'the prophets' and his employment of the words 'and shamefully entreated'. These changes are secondary modifications, introduced perhaps unconsciously because of a knowledge of what had happened. There does not seem to be adequate reason to suspect more in the case of the Markan sayings. Some modifications may well have been made in the course of transmission, but they are not

[1]Cf. Ed. Meyer, *Ursprung und Anfänge des Christentums*, i. 117f.; W; Bousset, *op. cit.*, 16; K. L. Schmidt, *Der Rahmen der Geschichte Jesu*, 218. M. Dibelius: 'What Mark reproduced therefore in these words is in brief the preaching of the Church about the Son of Man,' *From Tradition to Gospel*, 226; B. H. Branscomb, *The Gospel of Mark*, 157.

likely to have been such as to transform radically the meaning of the original announcement.

A very interesting attempt has recently been made by Rudolf Otto to trace the history of these sayings.[1] Otto finds the simplest and most original anticipations of suffering and death in such sayings as Lk. xii. 50: 'I have a baptism to be baptised with; and how am I straitened till it be accomplished!'; Mk. ix. 12: 'How is it written of the Son of man, that he should suffer many things and be set at nought?'; and Lk. xvii. 25: 'But first must he suffer many things and be rejected of this generation.' To this type belong the opening words of Mk. ix. 31: 'The Son of man is delivered up into the hands of men, and they shall kill him.' Here, observes Otto, nothing is said of being delivered into the hands of the Romans, nothing about details, nothing of crucifixion. Jesus, indeed, is probably thinking of stoning at the hands of a mob rather than crucifixion; and this may be suggested by His reference to Jerusalem which 'stoneth them that are sent to her' (Mt. xxiii. 37), and by His comparison, at the Supper, of His body with broken bread (Mk. xiv. 22). The doctrinal ideas of the community (*Gemeindedogmatik*) appear in the latter part of Mk. ix. 31, in the words: 'and when he is killed, after three days he shall rise again.' There is a further addition in Mk. viii. 31 in the reference to 'the elders, and the chief priests, and the scribes', and still more supplements in Mk. x. 33f., in the allusions to condemnation, delivering over to the Gentiles, mocking, spitting, scourging, and execution. Finally, the most complete form appears in Mt. xx. 19 where the word 'crucify' is expressly employed. While tracing this development, Otto argues that it points to the genuineness of the original forms (Lk. xii. 50, xvii, 25; Mk. ix. 12*b*, 31*a*),

[1] *Reich Gottes und Menschensohn*, 311-4.

since no one would have invented these at a later time. Jesus, therefore, actually foresaw His suffering; He possessed the charism of prophecy and exercised it in relation to Himself.[1]

There is undoubtedly much that is attractive in this critical reconstruction. Otto is not afraid of making concessions and can press them into the service of apologetics. He has a shorter line to defend and the citadel appears to be impregnable. Nevertheless, it should be considered whether the advantages are not purchased too dearly, whether the concessions are not made at the expense of history in the interests of a theoretical scheme. Is it necessary, for example, to dismiss the references to 'rising again'? By so doing, one escapes the severest strictures to which the sayings are exposed, for it has frequently been claimed that, since the disciples were completely overwhelmed by the events of the Passion and did not expect the Resurrection, these phrases cannot be authentic.[2] This argument cannot be said to be conclusive, if we have regard to the ideas of the disciples regarding Messiahship and remember how effectively attention to plain statements is limited by strong preconceptions. Moreover, if, as Otto powerfully contends,[3] Jesus was deeply influenced in His prophecies of suffering by Isa. liii., it is improbable that He would content Himself with dark allusions to suffering, and nothing more. Isa. liii. 12 definitely speaks of the triumph and exaltation of the Servant who 'poured out his soul unto death'. He is to 'see of the travail of his soul' (liii. 11) and to 'divide the spoil with the

[1] *Op. cit.*, 313f. Otto has already observed that it is a mark of the *Charismatiker* to prophesy his fate, and compares the case of Paul (cf. Acts xx. 22ff.), *op. cit.*, 310.

[2] Cf. K. L. Schmidt, *Der Rahmen der Geschichte Jeus*, 218.

[3] *Op. cit.*, 203-20.

strong' (liii. 12). It is reasonable, therefore, to believe that Jesus spoke, not only of His suffering and death, but also of His vindication and of His victory over death. Further, the phrase 'after three days', found in all the Markan passages, is worthy of note. Although C. H. Turner[1] has shown that in the Septuagint 'after three days' can be the equivalent of 'the third day', the fact that both Matthew and Luke independently alter their common source, suggests their uneasiness with the Markan expression and strengthens the possibility that, as used by Jesus, 'after three days' means a short undefined interval like the phrase 'on the third day' in Hos. vi. 2.[2] In this case the language is distinctive and is not likely to be a later addition.

The other points raised by Otto are opinions less open to close discussion. The suggestion that Jesus anticipated stoning is an interesting speculation, but one can hardly say more. There is no good reason why Jesus should not have referred to 'the elders, and the chief priests, and the scribes' (viii. 31), and the details mentioned in x. 33f. cannot be thought impossible in the mind of one who faced the certainty of suffering and rejection with any degree of imagination. At the same time the close agreement of the series—condemnation, surrender to the Gentiles, mocking, spitting, scourging, killing, and resurrection—with the events narrated in Mk. xiv. 53–xvi. 8, leaves room for hesitation, and it is in this saying, and still more in Mt. xx. 19 where crucifixion is mentioned, that there is most reason to infer the presence of modifications. As regards the sayings as a whole the opinion expressed at the beginning of this discussion seems well justified. In substance the sayings are not

[1] *St. Mark*, 40f. Turner refers to Gen. xlii. 17f. and 2 Chron. x. 5, 12.
[2] Cf. also Lk. xiii. 32, and see the discussion on p. 168.

vaticinia ex eventu, and such modifications as may have been made are not serious or important.[1]

The great importance of the sayings is beyond question.[2] The word 'must' (δεῖ) indicates that Jesus saw His suffering, death, and rising again as inward and divinely conditioned necessities. In Mk. ii. 19f. He contemplates the possibility of the 'taking away' of the Bridegroom; here He implies that this is no mere stroke of fate, but is an essential part of His mission. This conviction is announced as a new disclosure, but not as something of which Jesus thought for the first time after Peter's Confession. What is disclosed is a new interpretation of the mission and destiny of the Son of Man. Instead of the ideas of rule and dominion present in Dan. vii. 14, a *rôle* of rejection and suffering is assigned to him, and, although a time of conflict is described in Dan. vii. 21, 25, it is from Isa. liii. that the darker colours in the portraiture are derived. No reference, however, is made to any Old Testament passage, and this implies that before Caesarea Philippi Jesus had fused together diverse elements into the composite picture of the Suffering Son of Man in whose form He saw Himself. But this perception means that, besides facing the possibilities of rejection and death, Jesus had reached a solution. He did not see His death as a catastrophe, but as an essential part of His Messianic achievement. He had to suffer and to rise again; such was the Divine purpose He had made His own. Why rejection and death were necessary, and what purpose

---

[1]The opinion that the three Markan passages are variant forms of the same saying would, if true, strengthen its attestation, but this opinion (cf. A. T. Cadoux, *The Sources of the Second Gospel,* 25f.) has little in its favour and has difficulties of its own. Cf. Rawlinson, 143; Wood, 694.

[2]For an interesting and detailed account of the discussion which has arisen on the question, why Jesus went to Jerusalem, see Montefiore, *The Synoptic Gospels,* i. 190-3.

they would fulfil, the sayings do not explain; but it is certain that Jesus must have found in His sufferings profound ethical and spiritual meaning. Other sayings may throw light upon that meaning, but it is probable that its secret lies in the sense in which He interpreted His mission, and the relationship in which He believed Himself to stand both to God and to men.

(3) The Saying at the Descent from the Mount of Transfiguration (Mk. ix. 12*b*; Mt. xvii. 12*b*).

'And how is it written of the Son of man, that he should suffer many things and be set at nought?'

Luke does not make use of Mk. ix. 9-13; but cf. Lk. xvii. 25: 'But first must he suffer many things and be rejected of this generation.' Matthew alters the position of the saying and records it after the two references to Elijah in the form: 'Even so shall the Son of man also suffer of them.'

Like the sayings already examined, this passage speaks of the suffering of the Son of Man, but it differs from Mk. viii. 31, ix. 31, x. 33f. in that there is an explicit reference to Scripture, but no direct mention of death and resurrection. The critical questions which arise can be adequately treated only when the passage is studied in relation to its context. Only then can it be decided whether the words are a query of Jesus, a question of the disciples or of others, a statement of the Evangelist, or a community-saying. As they stand in Mk., the words are spoken by Jesus during the descent from the Mount of Transfiguration. Mark says that as they came down Jesus charged His disciples that they should tell no one of what they had seen 'save when the Son of man should have risen again from the dead'. He records that they kept the saying, 'questioning among themselves what the rising from the dead should mean,' and then continues:

11. 'And they asked him, saying, How is it that the scribes say
12a. that Elijah must first come? (R.V mg.). And he said unto them, Elijah indeed cometh first, and restoreth all things:
12b. *and how is it written of the Son of man, that he should suffer*
13. *many things and be set at nought?* But I say unto you, that Elijah is come, and they have done unto him whatsoever they listed, even as it is written of him.'

The difficulties raised by 12b are manifest: it does not appear to be related to the disciples' question; it separates the references to Elijah; and as a question put by Jesus it reads strangely. It is not surprising, therefore, that various transpositions have been suggested, and that in these reconstructions the complex 12a + 13 is a common feature. An attractive view, supported by Bousset,[1] Bultmann,[2] Klostermann,[3] and Sundwall,[4] is that originally, in whole or in part, 11-3 followed ix. 1, and that the connexion has been broken by Mark's insertion of the story of the Transfiguration (ix. 2-10). Bousset[5] solves the difficulties of 12b by cancelling it as a redactional addition,[6] but Sundwall transposes it with 12a, and in this way obtains the following rearrangement: 1, 11, 12b, 12a, 13. This suggestion furnishes little help. Two references to Elijah are brought together, but the diffi-

[1] *Kyrios Christos* [2], 61n 2; cf. Montefiore, *The Synoptic Gospels*, i. 208.

[2] *Die Geschichte der synoptischen Tradition*, 131f.

[3] *Das Markusevangelium*, 98, 101.

[4] *Die Zusammensetzung des Markusevangeliums*, 57.

[5] *Op. cit.*, 7.

[6] Bultmann explains the entire complex (ix. 1. 11-3) as a community-product: 'Its origin out of the theological debates of the community should be clear,' *op. cit.*, 131. The question of genuineness is discussed later.

culties of 12b are increased, since now the question is that of the bystanders, whereas, according to Mk. viii. 31, ix. 31, x. 33f., the teaching is given to the disciples alone.[1] A better reconstruction is the transposition suggested by C. H. Turner,[2] that 12b should follow 10. In this case, 12b is a statement of the Evangelist describing the disciples' perplexity; it assumes a question pondered, and perhaps asked, by them. This rearrangement has been received with much favour, and is perhaps the best of those which have been suggested.[3]

It may be doubted, however, if any transposition is likely to prove satisfactory; each solves some difficulties only to create others. The combination of 12a and 13, which is the common element in the various proposals, fatally obscures the remark about Elijah in 13: 'they have also done unto him whatsoever they listed, even as it is written of him,' which is prompted by the reference to the suffering of the Son of Man. Swete, therefore, is justified when he says that 'it is unnecessary to suppose that the order of Mark has here been disturbed, the true sequence being 11, 12b, 12a'.[4] If this is so, a fresh effort should be made to see if the existing order does not supply the best meaning.

The problem is the appearance of the question, 'How is it written of the Son of man, that he should suffer many things and be set at nought?' when the disciples have asked, 'How is it that the scribes say that Elijah must first come?' (Mk. ix. 11). Jesus concedes this scribal in-

---

[1] For Sundwall the question is only one of community-tradition.

[2] *The Study of the New Testament*, 61.

[3] K. L. Schmidt thinks that the question in 11 may have been asked by any one, or by the scribes and Pharisees. Cf. *Der Rahmen der Geschichte Jesu*, 226f. He takes Mk. ix. 11-3 as a self-contained unit.

[4] *St. Mark*, 194.

terpretation, which is based on Mal. iv. 5f.,[1] but He does
not believe that this is the only occurrence, still less the
principal event, preceding the Parousia. For Him, therefore, a bare agreement is not possible, and this is indicated
in the form of His reply: 'Elijah, it is true (μέν), cometh
first, and restoreth all things' (12a).[2] The situation is
one in which He found Himself not infrequently (cf. xii
14f., 19-23, xiv. 61f.), and, as elsewhere, He meets it by
asking a counter-question: 'And how is it written of the
Son of Man, that he should suffer many things and be set
at nought?' (12b).   For Him this is the decisive issue on
which the coming of the Kingdom waits.

It is not, of course, written anywhere that the Son of
Man should suffer. The question presupposes the
teaching given to the disciples in Mk. viii. 31, and implies
the identification in the mind of Jesus of the Son of Man
and the Suffering Servant of Isa. liii. The suggestion
that before the Parousia, not only must Elijah first come,
but also the Son of Man must suffer, is made allusively; it
is the protest of a teacher whose lesson has not been
learnt. The question asked by the disciples is not ignored.   It is answered again (ix. 13); but in such a manner that the idea of suffering is thrust into the foreground.
'Elijah has actually come; but consider how he fared!
They have also done unto him whatsoever they would, even
as it is written of him.'   Jesus is speaking of John the Baptist,[3] as Matthew records (xvii. 13), and the reference to

[1] 'Behold, I will send you Elijah the prophet before the great and terrible
day of the Lord come.   And he shall turn the heart of the fathers to the
children, and the heart of the children to their fathers; lest I come and
smite the earth with a curse.' Cf. Strack-Billerbeck, *Kommentar zum
Neuen Testament aus Talmud und Midrasch*, i. 597, 729, 753-8.

[2] Cf. Swete, 193.

[3] Cf. also Mt. xi. 14: 'And if ye are willing to receive it, this is Elijah,
which is to come.'

Scripture is to passages like 1 Kings xix. 2,[1] 10, and possibly to the traditions lying behind Apoc. xi. 3-13[2]; but
the unspoken suggestion is that what is true of John
(=Elijah) is true also of the Son of Man. Matthew
states this in so many words: 'Even so shall the Son of
man also suffer of them' (xvii. 12). In writing thus,
Matthew is recasting his source, but he correctly expresses what Jesus meant.

The kind of exegesis present in Mk. ix. 12f. is not that
of a scientific modern commentator. It is possibly this
fact which predisposes many critics to recast the section.
A relative amount of consistency is thereby imparted to it,
but at the cost of those marks of originality which are to
be found where Jesus uses the Old Testament. Jesus is
not a modern interpreter and cannot, without violence to
His words, be made modern. His methods are His own.
In His treatment of the Elijah-tradition, He follows precisely the method pursued in His treatment of the problem
of the Messianic sufferings of the Son of Man. Just as
He identifies the Son of Man and the Servant, so here He
identifies John and Elijah; and as He ascribes the suffering of the Servant to the Son of Man, so He applies what
is said of Elijah to the case of John. The difference is
that Isa. liii. 12 speaks of the death of the Servant whereas
the Old Testament does not mention the martyrdom of
Elijah. This difference, however, is not ignored by
Jesus; He restricts the parallelism in Mk. ix. 12*b* to the
thought of suffering: 'How is it written of the Son of man,
that he should *suffer* many things and *be set at nought*?'[3]

Those commentators are right who see in this saying a

[1]Cf. Swete, 194. John 'had found his Jezebel in Herodias'.

[2]Cf. Charles, i. 280-92.

[3]It is therefore beside the point when Montefiore asks: 'Where is the
martyrdom of *Elijah redivivus* predicted in Scriptures?', *op. cit.*, i. 209.

genuine utterance of Jesus.[1]   If we have correctly interpreted the meaning of the words, it is needless to consider
the suggestion that Mk. ix. 12*b* is a 'community-saying'.
That a community could so exactly reproduce the manner
of using the Old Testament characteristic of Jesus, and
could create the atmosphere which surrounds His mode of
interpretation, is not credible.   R. H. Lightfoot's suggestion that in Mk. ix. 11-3 'we may perhaps see the church
striving to construct some kind of a philosophy of history,
in the light of its convictions about the person and office
of its Master, and of his work and its results',[2] is not convincing.   Churches do not construct philosophies of history, although individuals under their influence may do
so; but, in this case, the result normally has a smoother
form, and lacks the note of reality characteristic of this
passage.   F. C. Burkitt shows a truer appreciation of its
nature when he says: 'The passage Mark ix. 9-13, so
abrupt, so unliterary, so obscure in detail, however clear
may be the general meaning, reads to me like reminiscences of a real conversation.'[3]

The saying is of the greatest importance.   It confirms
the view that Jesus believed He must suffer as the Son of
Man, and that He had taught this truth to His disciples.
Further, it is not open, as other passages are often said to
be, to the charge that its words reflect a knowledge of subsequent events.   A bare reference to suffering and being
set at nought is a disappointing *vaticinium post eventum*!
In one important respect the saying goes farther than the
other passages.   In these there is no express reference to

---

[1]Cf. Goguel, *Jean-Baptiste*, 59; Otto, *Reich Gottes und Menschensohn*,
209, 311.   Otto remarks: 'It is appropriate only in His own mouth, not
in the mouth of a later community,' *op. cit.*, 209.

[2]*History and Interpretation in the Gospels*, 92.

[3]*Christian Beginnings*, 33f.

Scripture: here it is definitely said that suffering 'is written of the Son of man'.   Moreover, the reference to Scripture appears naturally; it is occasioned by the question concerning Elijah.   Isa. liii. is not mentioned, but it is hypercriticism to doubt that this Scripture is in mind. Thus, a probable reference in Mk. viii. 31, ix. 31, x. 33f., is confirmed in Mk. ix. 12b.   Finally, by reason of its association with the question concerning Elijah, the saying shows that Jesus thought of His Messianic suffering in relation to the coming of the Kingdom.   He had faced the problem created by the expectation of the return of Elijah before the Parousia, and had solved it by identifying Elijah with John; but He had also faced a problem not contemplated in the thought of the time—the necessity of the suffering of the Son of Man before the perfecting of Rule of God.   This problem He had solved in the certainty of His own suffering and rejection.

(4) THE SAYING ON THE CUP AND THE BAPTISM (Mk. x. 38; cf. Mt. xx. 22).

'Are ye able to drink the cup that I drink? or to be baptized with the baptism that I am baptized with?'

Matthew has 'the cup that I am about to drink', and omits the reference to the baptism (xx. 22).   Luke does not make use of Mk. x. 35-41, but see the similar saying in Lk. xii. 50: 'But I have a baptism to be baptized with; and how am I straitened till it be accomplished!'   See pp. 165ff.

The figure of the cup of suffering is common in Old Testament usage (cf. Psa. lxxv. 8; Isa. li. 17ff.; Jer. xlix. 12; Lam. iv. 21; Ezek. xxiii. 31ff.).   The symbolism of baptism is not used in this sense, but the idea of water as a symbol of calamity appears in such passages as Psa. xlii. 7 ('All thy waves . . . are gone over me'), lxix. 2 ('I am come into deep waters'), 15 ('Let not the waterflood over-

G

whelm me'), Isa. xliii. 2 ('When thou passest through the waters . . .').[1] Moreover, there is good reason to think that in popular Greek βαπτίζεσθαι was used metaphorically in the sense of being 'flooded' or overwhelmed with calamities.[2] It is, therefore, unnecessary to think of the reference of baptism as the addition of any early transcriber[3] in a Hellenistic environment.[4] Matthew's omission of the clause is probably no more than an example of abbreviation, and Lk. xii. 50 furnishes independent testimony to the use of this imagery by Jesus.

The saying in the following verse, Mk. x. 39, 'The cup that I drink ye shall drink; and with the baptism that I am baptized withal shall ye be baptized,' is involved in the controversy regarding the 'alleged Papias tradition', that James and John suffered martyrdom at the hands of the Jews; and in consequence its genuineness is often questioned. It is impossible to discuss this problem here. I have treated it elsewhere, and can only repeat the conviction that the tradition 'ought unhesitatingly to be dismissed',[5] and with it the suspicions against Mk. x. 39. In any case, the problem does not affect Mk. x. 38, unless it is held to involve the entire narrative. There can be no reasonable doubt that Jesus did speak of a cup which He must drink and a baptism that He had to endure, and that, in particular, He was thinking of His Passion when He used these metaphors. It is wrong, however, to limit the

---

[1] Cf. also Psa. xviii. 16, cxxiv, 4f.

[2] Moulton and Milligan cite a use of the verb in this sense in a papyrus document c. 153 B.C., and say: 'That the word was already in use in this metaphorical sense (cf. Diod., i. 73. 6), even among uneducated people, strikingly illustrates our Lord's speaking of His Passion as a "baptism".' *The Vocabulary of the Greek Testament*, 102.

[3] Cf. B. W. Bacon, *The Beginnings of Gospel Story*, 148.

[4] Cf. A. Oepke, Kittel's *Theologisches Wörterbuch zum N.T.*, i. 536.

[5] Cf. *The Gospels: A Short Introduction*, 117.

reference in the saying to the thought of death.   In a true sense Jesus is already drinking the cup; it includes the whole of His Messianic sufferings of which death is the climax.

An additional suggestion calls for notice.   Jesus asks James and John if *they* are able to drink the cup and to endure the baptism; and, if x. 39 is accepted, He promises that they shall do so.   The implication is that there is a sense in which His disciples can share in His Messianic sufferings.   Martyrdom may be contemplated, but it is improbable that this is the only, or even the chief thought in the mind of Jesus.   Participation of a more spiritual kind is suggested.   The suggestion is that the destiny of James and John has a parallel in His own experience.   We cannot suppose, however, that Jesus interpreted His own Cup and Baptism only in terms of martyrdom; such an inference would be altogether too narrow an explanation of His thought.   But, if this be so, it is also too narrow an explanation of the promise to James and John.   Whatever the suffering and death of Jesus may be found to mean, some part in that experience is intended for them.   The nature of the sharing is not disclosed in the enigmatic words, but its reality is clear.   If the same conclusion is suggested by other sayings, it is a matter of first importance for our understanding of the manner in which Jesus viewed His suffering and death.

(5) THE 'RANSOM' PASSAGE (Mk. x. 45; cf. Mt. xx. 28).

'For verily the Son of man came not to be ministered unto, but to minister, and to give his life a ransom for many.'

Matthew reproduces the saying with a small stylistic alteration ('Even as the Son of man . . .').   Luke omits it probably because he regards xxii. 24-7 (True Greatness) as an equivalent.

If the genuineness of the passages already examined has often been contested, this is still more true of the present saying.[1] Its treatment has suffered gravely from the effects of doctrinal bias at the hands of both conservative and radical scholars. For this reason it is necessary to examine its meaning with great care and, as far as possible, apart from the theological implications which appear to be involved.

One of the most notable discussions in modern times is that of H. Rashdall in *The Idea of Atonement in Christian Theology*.[2] His view is that the words about a ransom are a 'doctrinally coloured insertion' and were probably 'never uttered by our Lord'. He argues that the passage is wanting in Q, is irrelevant to its context, and is paralleled by other examples of later ecclesiastical and dogmatic language in Mark. He does not deny, however, that the words 'possibly represent a genuine saying', and therefore inquires what the original meaning may have been. He thinks that there is something to be said for taking the words quite literally: 'in some way this death of His would save their lives—at least for the present.' Such a meaning, he says, would suit the context well. Rashdall, however, is not satisfied with this explanation. He admits that, if they are genuine, the words are an echo of Isa. liii. The thought is that the death would accomplish 'some kind of spiritual service' which would have 'a liberating, releasing effect'. Again, the idea may be that the death would benefit others 'just as the sufferings of other righteous men had done and might yet do', perhaps as F. C. Burkitt suggested, 'by causing the Lord of the Vineyard to hasten the judgement'; or, less definitely, that the death would procure benefits for many 'just as the prayers

[1] See the summary of critical opinion in Rashdall's *The Idea of Atonement*, 49-56.

[2] Pp. 29-37, 49-56.

and intercessions of the righteous might do'. The only doctrine of the Atonement, he says, which can trace itself back to Jesus Himself is 'the simple doctrine that His death, like His life, was a piece of service or self-sacrifice for His followers, such as they themselves might very well make for one another'.

It must be allowed, I think, that this exposition yields little satisfaction to any one who takes the passage seriously; it is an example of grasping at straws, at anything, in short, which renders the words as mild and inoffensive as possible. The assumption is that only a broad humanitarian interpretation, tinctured with a religious flavour, is historically conceivable. This assumption throws off all disguise in the assertion that the self-sacrifice of Jesus for His followers is 'such as they might very well make for one another'. There is nothing unique, or even distinctive, in the saying; it is a commonplace of religious experience! In sum, Rashdall's interpretation is that, either the words are not genuine, or else represent a passing reflection[1]; and it is to his credit that he preferred the former alternative. His views have been examined because *The Idea of Atonement* is one of the best known discussions of modern times. That, in his foundation chapter, he should have accorded such cavalier treatment to Mk. x. 45 is strange, and only stranger is the fact that his exposition has been so rarely challenged.

Whatever may be thought of Rashdall's interpretation, it has the merit of subjecting the Ransom-passage to detailed discussion. More commonly it is rejected, as a dogmatic insertion, almost without argument. The only scientific approach is to investigate the saying without prejudice to the question of genuineness.

There can be little doubt that the ideas which lie behind

[1] *Op. cit.*, 37.

the saying are those of Isa. liii.[1]   This is implied in the
declaration that 'the Son of man came . . . to *serve*'; it is
the same synthesis of ideas which appears in Mk. viii. 31
and parallel passages.   Further the words 'for *many*'
(ἀντὶ πολλῶν) are suggested by Isa. liii. 11f. where the
word 'many' is found no less than three times:

11. 'By his knowledge shall my righteous servant justify *many*',
12a. 'Therefore will I divide him a portion among *many*',[2]
12c. 'Yet he bare the sin of *many*'.

The phrase 'to give himself' and the use of the metaphor of a ransom are also probably suggested by the description of the Suffering Servant.   They describe a fate
like that which in the poem is characterized as that of being
'taken away' and 'cut off out of the land of the living' (cf.
Isa. liii. 8); and they interpret a service which entails bearing the griefs of others, carrying their sorrows, receiving
the stroke of God and the chastisement by which peace is
won (cf. Isa. liii. 4f.).   The service is costly; it demands
a ministry which the many cannot render for themselves;
and its effect is their deliverance.   As such, it is well described as one which provides 'a ransom for many'.   The
actual word 'ransom' is not found in Isa. liii., but it may
have been taken from Psa. xlix. 7f. by one who had
brooded on the nature of the Servant's task.[3]   The
Psalmist had said:

'None of them can by any means redeem his brother,
Nor give to God a ransom (*kopher*) for him:
For the redemption of their soul is costly,
And must be let alone for ever.'

[1]Cf. Swete, 240f.; Rawlinson, 146f.; R. Otto, *Reich Gottes und Menschensohn*, 207-19.   With reference to Mk. x. 45, Otto says: 'Wieder
haben wir hier die deutliche Synthese zwischen Menschensohn und
jesaianischem Gottesknecht', *op. cit.*, 210.

[2]The R.V., in view of the parallelism (cf. the reference to 'the strong'
in the next line), translates: 'the great'; but the same word is used in all
three cases in the Hebrew and the LXX.

[3]Cf. also Job xxxiii. 23f.

Jesus may well have reflected that this was to be the Servant's achievement, and that He, as the Suffering Son of Man, had come to effect the deliverance.

In seeking to understand the meaning of the saying it is necessary to examine its terminology, even if the problem cannot be settled in this way alone. The word rendered 'ransom' is λύτρον which, as Deissmann has shown, was used in the Greek world of the first century of 'the purchase-money for manumitting slaves'; it was also used of 'sacral manumission', a process whereby, in regaining his freedom, the slave became the property or *protégé* of some particular god.[1] *Kopher*, its commonest Hebrew equivalent, is also used of a 'payment' or 'requital'. Otto thinks that sacrificial ideas lie behind the word;[2] and, although in the Old Testament it is not used in connexion with the sacrifices, except perhaps in Ex. xxx. 12, its derivation, like that of *kaphar*, 'to cover' or 'to wipe away', supports this view. In any case, both the Greek and the Hebrew words describe something which is counted as an equivalent for purposes of deliverance or redemption. There is thus a definitely substitutionary idea in the terminology, although, of course, not one that is necessarily mechanical, or which demands a theory of vicarious punishment.

The meaning of λύτρον determines that of ἀντί in the phrase ἀντὶ πολλῶν ('for many'). This use of the rarer preposition, instead of what Moulton calls 'the more colourless ὑπέρ',[3] can hardly be accidental, and its commonest meaning 'instead of', rather than 'on behalf of', is probably required in this passage.[4] The 'ransom' is

---

[1] *Light from the Ancient East*, Revised ed., 327f.
[2] *Reich Gottes und Menschensohn*, 214-20.
[3] *Grammar of the New Testament*, i. 105.
[4] Cf. F. Büchsel in Kittel's *Theologisches Wörterbuch*, i. 373.

provided 'instead of' or 'in the place of' the 'many'. The word 'many', it need scarcely be said, does not exclude the meaning 'all', but is naturally used, as in Isa. liii. 11f., in contrast to the One who lays down His life for men.

It is wrong to conclude from this linguistic study that the saying must be interpreted in a crudely substitutionary sense. Undoubtedly, it contains a substitutionary idea, since something is done for the many which they cannot do for themselves. But the word 'ransom' is used as a metaphor, and ought not to be treated as if it were a fixed scientific term. Even if the language is metaphorical, it must not be explained away, as indicating some vague kind of spiritual service. After all, a metaphor is used in order to say something forcibly. At the least the saying means that, by the willing surrender of His life, Jesus, as the Son of Man, comes to provide a means of deliverance for men. It is difficult, however, to escape the conviction that Jesus regarded His death as in some way an act of requital. The activity is not on this account mechanical and external. Our knowledge of Jesus and of His teaching is enough to show that He can never have contemplated an act which should be operative of itself. If the thought is sacrificial, the offering of Jesus is to be appropriated actively by the spiritual participation which is an essential element in a true sacrifice. It should be frankly recognized, however, that, whether we find a sacrificial meaning in the saying depends ultimately upon other sayings of His, especially those connected with the Supper; it is also determined by our view of the relation of Jesus to the sacrificial principle.

The difficulty of the saying is that it stands apart among the recorded words of Jesus. It ought not to be dismissed on that account. Rather the question should be asked whether it is not organically related to His conceptions of

God, of sacrifice, and of the nature of His Messianic task.
It is in favour of the saying that its fundamental ideas are
those of Isa. liii.   Further, in spite of opinions to the contrary, it moves naturally to its climax.   A new idea is certainly introduced at the end in the thought of a 'ransom'
given by the Son of Man; but it cannot be described as
irrelevant in a context which speaks of service, or impossible as a word of Jesus.   Again, the idea that no act of
requital is due to a Holy God, or is needed by men, is a
modern notion which it would be a libel to attribute to the
ancient world; and to say that Jesus cannot have spoken
of His death in this way is to modernize His figure and
His thought.   Jesus is a stranger to the thought-world of
the twentieth century.   Finally, the restraint of the saying
is in its favour.   It is the duty of a dogmatic addition to be
reasonably explicit; but, as we have seen, the saying leaves
many important points open, and in no way characterizes
the need or condition of the 'many'.   As a 'community-
product', the saying is much too discreet; as an utterance
of Jesus, it has just that air of mystery, and the note of pro-
vocativeness, constantly found in His words.   For these
reasons it is better to conclude that Jesus has furnished a
theme for later Pauline developments rather than that
Mark has introduced a Pauline sentiment into the words
of Jesus.   This is the opinion of Lagrange,[1] and it is well
based.   The theologian has every reason to take the saying into serious consideration in his attempt to discover the
secret of the Cross.[2]

---

[1] *Évangile selon Saint Marc*, 5th ed., 283.

[2] Dibelius includes Mk. x. 35-45 among his 'Paradigms of a less pure
type'. Cf. *From Tradition to Gospel*, 43, 51. Bultmann also includes it
among his 'Apophthegmata', but regards vv. 41-5 as a Markan supplement. Cf. *Die Geschichte der synoptischen Tradition*, 23. For more recent
discussions see W. F · Howard, *The Expository Times*, l, 107-10; F.
Büchsel, *Theologisches Wörterbuch*, iv, 343-51.

(6) The Parable of the Vineyard (Mk. xii. 1-12; cf. Mt. xxi. 33-45; Lk. xx. 9-19).

> 6. '*He had yet one, a beloved son: he sent him last unto them, saying,*
> 7. *They will reverence my son.   But those husbandmen said among themselves, This is the heir; come, let us kill him, and the inheri-*
> 8. *tance shall be ours.   And they took him, and killed him, and cast him forth out of the vineyard.*'

Matthew and Luke reproduce these verses with but slight variations.   Both alter the order in 8.   Luke reads: 'And they cast him forth out of the vineyard, and killed him' (xx. 15; cf. Mt. xxi. 39). Luke's version of 6 is: 'And the lord of the vineyard said, What shall I do? I will send my beloved son: it may be they will reverence him' (xx. 13).

This parable is based on the allegory of the Vineyard in Isa. v. 1f.,[1] and has several peculiar features.   It is an allegory rather than a parable; it includes a direct allusion to the death of Christ; and some of its details, the sending of the son when the servants have been beaten and killed, and the argument that if the son is killed the vineyard will be the property of the husbandmen, seem artificial.   On these grounds objections have frequently been brought against its authenticity.   Since Jülicher wrote his *Die Gleichnisreden Jesu* (1899) it has frequently been held that Jesus did not use allegory, and that Mk. xii. 1-12 is a doctrinal construction of the Christian community.[2]   This view is not convincing.   While it is not the habit of Jesus to use allegory, we cannot be certain that He never did so. Moreover, the allegorical element in Mk. xii. 1-12 is partial; the lord of the vineyard is God, the husbandmen

---

[1] 'My wellbeloved had a vineyard in a very fruitful hill: and he made a trench about it, and gathered out the stones thereof, and planted it with the choicest vine, and built a tower in the midst of it, and also hewed out a winepress therein: and he looked that it should bring forth grapes, and it brought forth wild grapes.'

[2] Cf. Bultmann, *Die Geschichte der synoptischen Tradition*, 191.

are the Jewish leaders, the servants the prophets, and the heir Jesus; but there is no allegorical significance in the hedge, the pit, the winepress, and the tower, or in the departure to 'another country'. Further, Isa. v. 1f., the model on which Mk. xii. 1-12 is built, is allegorical and itself suggests the further use of allegory, while the use of this literary form is well adapted to the situation in which Jesus found Himself. Again, an early Christian writer would have been strongly tempted to bring the story into closer contact with the facts of history, by inserting a reference to the Resurrection,[1] or by mentioning the death after the casting from the vineyard,[2] in view of the idea that Christ suffered 'without the gate' (cf. Heb. xiii. 12). Finally, the alleged inconsistencies are permissible in a story, and indicate that the allegory is incomplete. One of them, the improbability that the heir would have been sent after the beating and killing of the servants, illustrates a point Jesus desires to make, the divine reluctance to believe that human obduracy can resist the supreme appeal of love: 'they will reverence my son'. With the eye of an artist Luke perceives this suggestion when he writes: '*it may be* they will reverence him.' The difficulties are real, but they are less than those of the theory of invention by the community; the design is new, but the workmanship bears its own signature.

No explanation of the purpose of the death of Jesus is given in the parable, but there are several implications of the greatest importance in forming an opinion upon this question: the position superior to the prophets which is quietly assumed by Jesus, the consciousness of a unique relationship of Sonship, the conviction that He has been

---

[1]Cf. F. C. Burkitt, *Transactions of the Third International Congress for the History of Religion*, ii. 321-8.

[2]So many commentators. See the Synoptic parallels.

sent by God as a final envoy to Israel, the recognition that
rejection and death await Him.   There is present also the
consciousness that the rejection involves the judgment of
Israel, which is voiced less as a menace than as a sorrowful
recognition of the inevitable course of history: 'What
therefore will the lord of the vineyard do? he will come
and destroy the husbandmen, and will give the vineyard
to others' (Mk. xii. 9).   The restraint of these words is
matched only by their poignant sadness.

(7) The Saying in the Story of the Anointing (Mk. xiv. 8; cf. Mt. xxvi. 12).

'She hath anointed my body aforehand for the burying.'

Matthew recasts the form of the saying, but does not alter its
meaning: 'For in that she poured this ointment upon my body, she
did it to prepare me for burial' (xxvi. 12).   Luke does not record
the Markan story in view of his similar narrative in vii. 36-50.

This saying, and still more the prophecy in the following verse, is widely interpreted as a subsequent expansion
of the story of the Anointing.   The addition, it is held, is
part of the editorial process by means of which the isolated
and self-contained story was fitted into the continuous
Passion-narrative.   This, for example, is the opinion of
Dibelius who classifies the story as a *Paradigm*,[1] and of
Bultmann who includes it among the *Biographical Apophthegmata*.[2]   These scholars argue that the story reaches
its climax in the words: 'Let her alone; why trouble ye
her? she hath wrought a good work on me.   For ye have
the poor always with you, and whensoever ye will ye can
do them good: but me ye have not always.   She hath

---

[1] Cf. *From Tradition to Gospel*, 43, 60, 178.

[2] Cf. *Die Geschichte der synoptischen Tradition*, 37, 59, 283; see also
Klostermann, *Das Markusevangelium*, 158ff.

done what she could' (xiv. 6-8*a*).   Its purpose is to show
that there are circumstances in which social duties must
give place to the claims of religion.

Bultmann is unusually sympathetic to the historical
value of the story as thus reconstructed.   He denies that
it is merely the symbolical clothing of the idea just mentioned,[1] and accepts the reference to Bethany (xiv. 3) as
original.[2]

The opinion of these scholars, that in the oral period
the story circulated as a self-contained narrative, must, I
think, be accepted; for it is complete in itself, and it gives
expression to a thought of practical importance in the life
of the primitive communities.   It is also possible, and
even probable, that the prophecy that the woman's deed
would be made known wherever 'the gospel' should be
preached 'for a memorial of her' (xiv. 9) is an addition; for
the words have a later ring, and, as it has frequently been
observed, the woman's name is not mentioned.   It is,
however, a much less convincing suggestion that the story
ended with the words: 'she hath done what she could.'
In this case, the only points in the narrative which make
it suitable for insertion in the Passion-narrative are the
reference to Bethany and the words: 'me ye have not
always.'   But once the story is read apart from its context, and the reference to anointing for burial is cancelled,
these words are less suggestive of death, although probably they imply it.[3]   A reason for including the story in
the framework of the Passion-narrative is obviously more
apparent if Jesus expressly said: 'she hath anointed my
body aforehand for the burying.'

[1]*Op. cit.*, 37.   [2]*Op. cit.*, 69.

[3]Klostermann observes that originally the words need not be a prophecy
of death, *op. cit.*, 158.   But this is not probable.   Cf. Montefiore, *The
Synoptic Gospels*, i. 317f.

The motive for the alleged expansion of the original story is variously explained. It is not, of course, of a doctrinal character; the intention is either to sharpen the allusion to death, or to suggest that the anointing which the three women failed to accomplish at the tomb (xvi. 1) had been done in Bethany by anticipation.[1] The latter suggestion seems unnecessarily subtle, and the former does not exclude the possibility that Jesus Himself sharpened the allusion to death. That Jesus spoke the words is the simplest and most convincing explanation. The manner in which the indignation of the guests is countered, and the woman's action is interpreted, has characteristics present in other stories about Jesus, as, for example, when He meets the question of the Pharisees by the request for a denarius (Mk. xii. 15), or suggests that John the Baptist is *Elijah-redivivus* (Mt. xi. 14). The objection of Montefiore, that nobody is astonished, is without foundation, for we do not know what effect it produced, and in any case Jesus often mystified His hearers.

For theology the saying under review has little importance, for it reveals nothing of the meaning which Jesus saw in His death, but for historical purposes the words are significant. They show how strongly the thought of death occupied His mind. Anointing is primarily a mark of courtesy,[2] and to anoint the head is in certain circumstances an act of kingly homage;[3] but neither of these associations is uppermost in the thought of Jesus. While recognizing the woman's reverence, He relates her action to His death. Only a dominating interest can account for this reference. In this respect the saying is impor-

---

[1] Cf. Montefiore, *op. cit.*, i. 318.
[2] Cf. Strack-Billerbeck, *op. cit.*, i. 427.
[3] Cf. 1 Sam. x. 1, xvi. 1, 13.

tant, and it bears on the question of the historical value of other sayings. If we are right in taking into account the interest of the primitive communities in Christ's death, we are no less bound to recognize its supreme significance for Jesus Himself. In the last days of His ministry it was the central point in His thinking and His words and actions were determined by it.

(8) THE PROPHECY OF THE BETRAYAL (Mk. xiv. 17-21).

17. 'And when it was evening, he cometh with the twelve.
18. And as they sat and were eating, Jesus said, *Verily I say unto you, One of you shall betray me, even he that eateth with me.*
19. They began to be sorrowful, and to say unto him one by one,
20. Is it I? And he said unto them, *It is one of the twelve,* he
21. *that dippeth with me in the dish. For the Son of man goeth, even as it is written of him: but woe unto that man through whom the Son of man is betrayed! good were it for that man if he had not been born.'*

In recording the sayings Matthew follows his source closely. In 18 he omits the quotation: 'even he that eateth with me' (cf. Psa. xli. 9). In 20 he omits 'it is one of the twelve', and adds *'the same* shall betray me'. After 21, which is repeated verbatim, he adds: 'And Judas, which betrayed him, answered and said, Is it I, Rabbi? He saith unto him, Thou has said' (Mt. xxvi. 20-5).

Luke's version in xxii. 21, 23, is probably independent.[1] In xxii. 22, which is based on Mk., he substitutes 'as it hath been determined' for 'even as it is written of him', and omits the words: 'good were it . . . not been born.'

In the corresponding Johannine story (Jn. xiii. 21-30), Mk. xiv. 18 reappears in the form: 'Verily, verily, I say unto you, that one of you shall betray me'. It is peculiar to this account that Jesus secretly indicates to the Beloved Disciple who the traitor is (xiii. 25f.). The suppositions of the disciples, when Judas goes out, are also mentioned (xiii. 28f.).

[1]Cf. *Behind the Third Gospel,* 40f.

Apart from such variations as are merely stylistic or editorial, the parallels are instructive.   If Lk. xxii. 21, 23 is independent of Mk., it is an additional authority for the incident.   Jn. xiii. 21-30 may also reflect an independent tradition which has been developed by the art of the Fourth Evangelist.   There is therefore good ground for believing the prophecy to be historical.

It will be seen that there is an increasing definiteness in the later narratives.   In Mt. xxvi. 25 Judas asks: 'Is it I, Rabbi?' and Jesus replies: 'Thou hast said'; while in Jn. xiii. 25-9 the traitor is secretly indicated and, when he departs, the surmises of the disciples are given.   These added details throw into relief the greater simplicity of the Markan story where Judas is neither named nor indicated. It is, however, a fair question whether even this narrative does not reflect a knowledge of subsequent events.   This, I think, is apparent in Mk. xiv. 20.   The words: 'It is one of the twelve,' may be the words of Mark, influenced by xiv. 17 ('with the twelve').   If this surmise is justified, the reply of Jesus to the question: 'Is it I?' was no more than a further allusion to Psa. xli. 9.[1]   It is highly improbable that He can have remained blind to the defection of Judas, and the narrative has characteristic notes of reserve and appeal.   The 'Woe' (Mk. xiv. 21) is not a curse[2] (cf. Mk. xiii. 17), but an expression of deep sadness and of warning.   The objection that Judas would not have returned after his visit to the authorities[3] is not convincing; it was essential to his plan that he should return and continue as before.[4]   Further, there is no force in the

---

[1]'Yea, mine own familiar friend, in whom I trusted, which did eat of my bread,

   Hath lifted up his heel against me.'

[2]Cf. Swete, 333; Rawlinson, 203.

[3]Cf. Montefiore, *The Synoptic Gospels*, i. 324.   [4]Cf. Rawlinson, 202f.

plea that no indication is given of how and when Judas made his exit from the Upper Room.[1] The Markan narrative is not a detailed report, and ought not to be treated as such. Moreover, as we have seen, in this narrative Jesus does not identify Judas as the traitor, but contents Himself with a veiled allusion, couched in the language of Scripture. All these considerations strengthen confidence in the story as a historical record.

The important saying in Mk. xiv. 21 occupies a natural place in such a context. The use of the term, 'Son of Man', and the belief of Jesus that His fate is the fulfilment of Divine purpose, are found in Mk. viii. 31, ix. 12b, 31, x. 33f., 45; and these points have been discussed in connexion with these passages. Mk. xiv. 21 resembles Mk. ix. 12b in that, while the Old Testament is referred to, no citation is made, or indeed is possible. It is perhaps a recognition of this which led Luke to modify his source in the phrase 'as it hath been determined' (xxii. 22). This is probably the sense in which Jesus used the words 'as it hath been written of him'. Behind this utterance lies His identification of the Son of Man with the Suffering Servant; it is so firmly established in His thought that He can say of the Son of Man what, so far as the text of Scripture is concerned, is true only of the Servant. Each successive example of this identification reveals how deep-rooted it is in the Markan tradition; it becomes more and more difficult to believe that, while it was an accepted idea in the earliest Christian communities, it was unknown to Jesus Himself.

The knowledge that He will be betrayed by one of the Twelve is an element in His Messianic sufferings. It is clear, however, that Jesus does not think of Judas as the

---

[1]Cf. B. W. Bacon, *The Beginnings of Gospel Story*, 202f.

blind instrument of fate; in that case the atmosphere of the story would be different, and there would be no occasion for the warning which He gives.   On the other hand, Jesus does not interpret His approaching death as simply the result of human action.   He is to be betrayed, and men will do their worst, but it is still true that He is fulfilling a Divine purpose with which He has completely identified Himself.   Herein is revealed the antinomy which appears whenever such a purpose is associated with human activity.   Jesus does not discuss the antinomy; it is not His method to deal with philosophical questions. He neither renounces the idea of a Divine destiny to be fulfilled through suffering and death, nor ignores human responsibility for evil deeds, although later He prays, 'Father, forgive them; for they know not what they do.'[1]   He will go 'as it hath been written of him', but alas! for men like Judas!   It is this tension which gives to the scene the 'solemnity and impressiveness' which Montefiore says 'cannot be denied'.[2]   Surely, we must add that it is the tension of historical realism, not the product of later invention.

(9) THE SAYINGS AT THE LAST SUPPER (Mk. xiv. 22-5; cf. Mt. xxvi. 26-9; Lk. xxii. 14-20; 1 Cor. xi. 23-5).

Since our main interest is in the Markan sayings, the complicated historical problems connected with the Supper need be discussed only in so far as they affect questions of exegesis.

The date of the Supper is a problem of very great difficulty.   The Synoptists appear to look on the Supper as

---

[1]For a discussion of the textual problem of Lk. xxiii. 34 see Streeter, *The Four Gospels*, 89, 123, 138.

[2]*Op. cit.*, i. 325.

the Passover Meal,[1] but the Fourth Evangelist implies that it was eaten before the Passover.[2]   Critics in general are rather evenly divided[3] in their attempts to solve this riddle, but in Great Britain it is perhaps the majority view to-day that the Supper preceded the Passover.   Among other arguments it is strongly maintained that this view is implied, not only in the Fourth Gospel, but also by statements in the Synoptic Gospels themselves such as Mk. xiv. 2 ('Not during the feast') and Lk. xxii. 15f.[4] and by such indications as the fact that the disciples bore arms (Mk. xiv. 47), and that Simon is described as 'coming from the country' (Mk. xv. 21).   Not all these arguments are equally cogent, and recently they have been keenly contested by Dalman[5] and by J. Jeremias[6] who identify the Supper with the Passover Meal.   The whole question calls for renewed examination and must be regarded as still *sub judice*.

Those scholars who think that the Supper preceded the Passover try to identify the meal in various ways.   G. H. Box[7] and others have argued that it was the *Sabbath-Kiddûsh*, or the sanctification of the Sabbath when wine was blessed and bread was broken; W. O. E. Oesterley,[8] G. H. C. Macgregor,[9] and others prefer to identify it with the *Passover-Kiddûsh*, or the ritual sanctification of the

---

[1]Cf. Mk. xiv. 12-6 and parallels.

[2]Cf. Jn. xviii. 28, xix. 14.

[3]A very full summary of critical opinion is given by J. Jeremias in *Die Abendmahlsworte Jesu*, 8-13.

[4]See pp. 180-3.

[5]*Jesus-Jeshua*, 86-106.

[6]*Op. cit.*, 5-39.

[7]*The Journal of Theological Studies*, iii. 357-69, x. 106f.

[8]*The Jewish Background of the Christian Liturgy*, 156-93.

[9]*Eucharistic Origins*, 37ff.

Passover.   Unfortunately, in neither of these cases was the meal in question eaten on a Thursday, and it is still necessary to assume that it was anticipated by a day.[1]   At the same time these suggestions are valuable as showing that, in addition to the Passover Meal, there existed in contemporary Judaism quasi-religious meals which, in certain respects, are not unlike the Last Supper.   The same may also perhaps be said of the theory of H. Lietzmann,[2] R. Otto,[3] and others, who see in the *Habûrôth*, or groups of associates who assembled in order to celebrate religious meals, a type to which the Supper conforms.[4] Otto, indeed, maintains that the Supper was not a new invention, but that, on the contrary, Jesus was repeating familiar table-rites to which He gave a special significance, in the circumstances in which He found Himself, by means of the words which He spoke over the bread and the wine.[5]   It may well be that, if the Supper preceded the Passover, no precise identification is necessary, and that it was a hurried anticipation of the Passover Meal to which Jesus had looked forward so eagerly (cf. Lk. xxii. 15f.).

These questions are obviously of great interest and importance, but their significance can be exaggerated. Whether the Supper was the Passover Meal or not, Paschal ideas and associations must have occupied the mind of

---

[1]F. C. Burkitt pointed out that 'Kiddûsh immediately precedes the actual celebration of the day, *e.g.* kiddûsh for Sabbath is done on what we call Friday evening, not twenty-four hours earlier,' *The Journal of Theological Studies*, xvii. 294.

[2]*Messe und Herrenmahl*, 210.

[3]*Reich Gottes und Menschensohn*, 234-41.   Otto ascribes a sacramental character to these meals.

[4]This suggestion, and Otto's views in particular, are strongly criticised by Jeremias, *op. cit.*, 20.

[5]*Op. cit.*, 241.

Jesus on this occasion; and this is the important fact to remember in studying both the narratives and the sayings.

A second question to which preliminary consideration must be given is whether the stories of the Supper are 'cult-narratives'. This question is partly a matter of terminology. If by 'cult-narratives' are meant stories freely invented to explain or justify an existing rule, none of the stories can justly be so described; they are too restrained in statement, too limited in detail, to be of this character. Moreover, such a usage leaves the cult itself unexplained. For its explanation it is necessary, either to postulate a tradition very much like that found in the existing narratives, or to have recourse to inferences suggested by the Mystery-religions, which break down when they are subjected to close examination. If, however, by a 'cult-narrative' is meant a story influenced by the practice of worship, it is probable that all the stories of the Supper are of this character. Nothing is more natural than that it should be so. Even in the Lukan story liturgical interests may lie behind the statement that Jesus received the cup and gave thanks (xxii. 17); they are more evident in the Markan narrative in the great detail of the story and the words: 'and they all drank of it' (Mk. xiv. 23); and most of all are they to be seen in the Matthaean account where the commands to eat and to drink are explicit (Mt. xxvi. 26f.). Naturally, the question arises whether such influences have corrupted the original tradition, and this point must be considered especially in connexion with 'the words of institution'. In general, I believe it is true to say that, while liturgical interests may have determined what is told or emphasized in the Gospel narratives, unhistorical elements have not been imposed upon the primitive tradition in any important degree.

The sayings in the Markan narrative are three in number and relate to (*a*) the bread, (*b*) the wine, and (*c*) the future Messianic Feast. These sayings must now be examined.

(*a*) '*Take ye: this is my body*' (Mk. xiv. 22).

Matthew has: '*Take eat.*' Paul adds: '*which is for you*'. The interpolation in Lk. xxii. 19*b* has: '*which is given for you.*'

The words: 'This is my body,' can be understood only in the light of the statement that 'as they were eating, he took bread, and when he had blessed, he brake it, and gave to them, and said' (xiv. 22).

The fraction of the loaf is symbolic and recalls the practice of the Old Testament prophets who sometimes in similar ways dramatized their words. Isaiah walks naked and barefoot (xx. 2), and gives to his son a significant name (viii. 3). Jeremiah is commanded to break a potter's bottle (xix. 10), and wears a yoke (xxviii. 10). Ezekiel takes a tile and uses it to depict a besieged city as 'a sign to the house of Israel' (iv. 3). In the New Testament Agabus binds his feet and hands with Paul's girdle, and declares that so the Jews will bind its owner at Jerusalem (Acts xxi. 11). The action of Jesus at the Supper is of the same character. The intention is to suggest that, as the loaf is broken, so His body will be broken in the near future. The words are interpretative and invest the fraction with dramatic significance.

This explanation, however, is only partial, and it may be that prophetic action provides a further parallel. It is now recognized that often the actions have more than a symbolic meaning; they are 'effective representations' for bringing about that which is depicted. The prophet believes that by wearing the yoke the Babylonian conquest is made inevitable, and when his rival breaks the yoke he imagines that he is rendering it ineffective (cf. Jer. xxvii., xxviii.). 'When Zedekiah equips himself with horns of iron (1 Kings xxii. 11), and thrusts with them like an angry bull, he is doing something that will help to achieve the thrusting of the Syrians which he predicts.'[1] 'The spoken word in the thought of the Hebrews has a real power and energy which fulfils itself. . . . And if a mere word can bring about its own fulfilment, how much more certainly will an *acted* parable ensure the coming about of what it symbolizes!'[2]

Otto's recent treatment of the significance of the Supper is of great interest in this connexion.[3]   He thinks that the action of Jesus is not only a prophecy of impending death, but is also an 'effective representation' for the purpose of imparting a share in that which is represented. This corresponds, he says, to the ancient view, that through the use of a representation one can carry over and appropriate the nature, the power, the influence, the individuality, the curse or the blessing, which belongs to a thing or an event, in consequence of the will of him who makes the representation.   He admits that this idea can be the basis of magical manipulation, but holds that it can rise into the religious sphere when it is the foundation of the 'sacrament', and it can be 'completely spiritualized', as in the action of Christ; 'then it is the foundation of the significant, symbolic act'.   Otto traces the presence of this conception in Israel, in the story of Isaiah whose lips are cleansed by the touch of a live coal from off the altar (Isa. vi. 6f.), and in the Old Testament belief that the altar itself represents the *numen* as 'effective' (cf. Mt. xxiii. 19). The action of Jesus at the Supper is in line with these ancient

[1]W. L. Wardle, *History and Religion of Israel*, 178.   Cf. Otto, *Reich Gottes und Menschensohn*, 253ff.

[2]Wardle, *ibid*.   [3]*Op. cit.*, 255ff.

ideas; 'it is the gift of a share (*Anteilgabe*) in the power of that which is represented, namely, the expiatory power of the broken Christ.'[1]   This interpretation does not mean that there is any change in the substance of the bread; such ideas, Otto maintains, lie wholly distant from this gift and experience of sharing.[2]   The thought is that of Psa. xvi. 4f., where the Psalmist speaks of Yahweh as 'the portion' of his 'cup,'[3] and it is expressed in the ancient Hebrew custom of 'eating before God' (cf. Ex. xviii. 12). St. Paul, therefore, is not under Hellenistic influences when he speaks of the bread and of the cup as 'a communion of the body' and 'of the blood of Christ' (1 Cor. x. 16), or when he asks concerning 'Israel after the flesh': 'Have not they which eat the sacrifices communion with the altar?' (1 Cor. x. 18).[4]

These extremely interesting suggestions take us beyond the question of the significance of the fraction, and emphasize the necessity of examining closely the words by which it is accompanied.   In point of fact, in the Old Testament examples of symbolic action it is the prophet's word which determines the significance and force of what is represented. We turn, then, to the words: 'Take ye: this is my body.'

The word, 'this', undoubtedly refers to the bread, and not to Christ Himself.[5]   The predicate, 'my body', does not mean Christ's flesh, still less the Church, but the body

[1]*Op. cit.*, 257.

[2]Cf. Dalman: 'There is no suggestion of a mystic food for the soul in the words of the Institution, and the connexion with Judaism is perfectly clear. The latter offered the usage which our Lord Himself, when He ate with His disciples, always observed,' *Jesus-Jeshua*, 144.

[3]Cf. Psa. xi. 6, where fire and brimstone and burning wind are spoken of as 'the portion' of the 'cup' of the wicked; also Psa. cxvi. 13: 'I will take the cup of salvation.'

[4]'They are in fellowship with the altar, and therefore with the unseen God, whose altar it is,' Robertson and Plummer, 215.

[5]Cf. Lagrange, *Évangile selon saint Marc*, 378.

which is surrendered to death for men.   In a true sense
the phrase describes Christ Himself; but this explanation
may prove misleading unless it is understood as meaning
Christ offering Himself in death.[1]   The term, 'body', is
used partly because the fraction easily suggests a body
dissolved in death, and partly because it is a natural cor-
relative to the term, 'blood', used in connexion with the
wine.   But there is probably a deeper reason.   The use
of the word is better explained if Jesus has sacrificial practice in mind.   In reading His words it is difficult not to
think of the sacred meal which normally was the final
stage in the Old Testament sacrifices, when the worshipper participated in that which he offered or in that
which was offered on his behalf.   If these are the associations of the saying—and our views upon this matter are
inevitably coloured by our estimate of the attitude of
Jesus to sacrifice—we must infer that Jesus uses the term
'body' because He looks upon His Passion as an offering
for men in which they are invited to share.

   This interpretation, which is in line with that of Otto,
raises the question of the copula which defines the relation
between 'this' and 'my body'.   It is not easy to find an

---

[1]Dalman gives as the Aramaic equivalent of τοῦτό ἐστιν τὸ σῶμά μου,
the phrase *dēn hū gūphī*.   Cf. *Jesus-Jeshua*, 141.   Otto renders this:
Dies bin ich selber (*op. cit.*, 250, 253).   See also Rashdall, *op. cit.*, 42.
While, however, Dalman admits that *gūph* can express the idea of 'self', he
thinks that the early Christians did not take it with this meaning, especially
in view of the similar reference to the blood, and he prefers the familiar
rendering: 'This is my body.'   At the same time he brings the words into
the closest relation with the person of Jesus.   To give the body for some-
one, he says, naturally means to die; in the Semitic idiom—to give one's
soul; it was 'because of the bread, in this case the yet unbroken loaf, our
Lord spoke of the Body instead of the Soul.'   Among other references he
mentions the description of Jassa bar Halputa (*Pirke Aboth*, 42c) as one
who 'gave his soul for circumcision,' and to Isa. liii. 12, 'where the Servant
of God is promised a reward when he gives up his soul unto death'.   *Op.
cit.*, 145f.

exact English equivalent for the Greek ἐστίν. In the Aramaic form of the saying there would be no copula, but, of course, one is implied, and the question is whether it is best rendered by 'is', or by some such word as 'represents', 'signifies', or 'means'.[1]

The translation 'is' suggests a relationship of identity which can, it is true, be interpreted spiritually, but is only too easily conceived materially. The saying is explained with reference to Christ's 'risen and ascended body',[2] or, in refined forms of the doctrine of Transubstantiation, it is urged that Catholic Doctrine leaves 'substance' unde-fined,[3] but in popular belief the materialistic interpretation becomes common. If such ideas are avoided, there is much to be said for the rendering: 'This *is* my body,' inas-much as it indicates a vital relationship between the bread and the offering of Christ.

On the other hand, such renderings as 'represents', 'signifies', 'symbolizes', suggest an almost casual and ex-ternal relationship between the bread and the body. Usually, they are defended by citing passages in which the copula indicates 'parabolic or symbolic parallelism', as, for example, Gen. xli. 26; Ezek. v. 5; Dan. vii. 17; Lk. viii. 11; Mt. xiii. 38, xvi. 18; Gal. iv. 24; 1 Cor. x. 4; Apoc. i. 20.[4] These passages show that the copula can have the meanings mentioned, but it is doubtful if they give the guidance desired. After all, in interpreting the words:

[1]Cf. C. J. Cadoux, *Christianity and Catholicism*, 399; J. W. Hunkin, *The Evangelical Doctrine of Holy Communion* (ed. A. J. Macdonald), 14; C. A. Anderson Scott, *Christianity according to St. Paul*, 189; *Foot-Notes to St. Paul*, 115. Anderson Scott recalls Lietzmann's declaration that the rendering 'signifies' or 'represents' 'ought never to have been disputed'.

[2]Cf. Darwell Stone, Art. 'Lord's Supper', *Hastings Dictionary of Christ and the Gospels*, ii. 73.

[3]Cf. W. E. Orchard, *From Faith to Faith*, 280.

[4]Cf. Cadoux, *op. cit.*, 399.

'This is my body,' limited help is afforded by passages about cows, hair, beasts, seeds, fields, rocks, stars, candlesticks, and the mother of Ishmael. In the end the decision turns, not on the copula, but on the subject and the predicate in any particular case. If the bread is a symbol alone, we may well translate: 'This *represents* my body'; but if it is also a means whereby faith appropriates the blessings of Christ's Sacrifice, the least unsatisfactory rendering is: 'This *means* my body.'[1] Since the fraction probably suggests more than a bare symbol, the choice lies between this rendering and the more ambiguous translation: 'This *is* my body,' and for purposes of theology the former is the better.[2]

It is in harmony with the ideas suggested by the rest of the saying that Jesus says: 'Take ye.' The disciples are invited to receive the broken bread in the sense in which it is interpreted by His act and word. Eating is a physical action which on the spiritual side corresponds to the appropriation of life, although the distinction between the material and the spiritual is much clearer to us to-day than it was in the ancient world.[3] The fact that the disciples are directed to eat suggests strongly that the bread is more than an adventitious symbol. Otherwise, it would have been enough to say: 'This is my body'; there would have been no need for the words: 'Take ye,' and no occasion for the Matthaean amplification: 'Take, eat.'[4]

[1]Cf. Moffatt's translation: 'Take this, it means my body.'

[2]For the same reasons Mk. xiv. 24 should be read: 'This means my blood of the covenant, which is shed for many'. Cf. Moffatt: 'This means my *covenant-blood* which is shed for many'.

[3]'And yet even we moderns believe in the close relation of these two; for we hold that with the material elements of the bread and wine spiritual gifts are imparted to the faithful in the Holy Communion,' R. H. Charles, *I.C.C., Revelation*, i. 268.

[4]The Matthaean form merely brings out what is implied in Mk.

If we now have regard to the saying as a whole, it becomes clear that by His action and word Jesus intends the bread to be a means whereby the disciples may participate in the power of His surrendered life.　There is no suggestion of any intention to transform the bread into a quasi-material or mystic 'food of the soul'.　Materially, it is unchanged; spiritually, it becomes a means for the communication of life, because it is invested by Jesus with new meaning and power.　The life is His own, offered for men and made available for them.　As the gift is spiritual, so its appropriation is spiritual, although a broken loaf, among the commonest of material things, is the vehicle of the one and the medium for the other.

If we are right in interpreting the saying in this way, there is no justification for explaining it as a 'community-product' which owes its origin to Hellenistic circles in early Christianity.[1]　This question must obviously receive further consideration when the parallel saying: 'This is my blood of the covenant, which is shed for many,' comes under review, for it is mainly in relation to this saying that the influence of ideas connected with the Mystery-religions has been alleged.　As regards the saying immediately in question several considerations favour its genuineness.　The underlying ideas are fundamentally Jewish.　The practice of symbolic action, the use of the imagery of bread, the idea of eating in connexion with a sacrificial offering, are all found in the Old Testament and were perfectly familiar to Jesus.　Further, what is distinctive in the words bespeaks creative originality, for it

---

[1] Cf. Bultmann, *Die Geschichte der synoptischen Tradition*, 285; Klostermann, *Das Markusevangelium*, 163; Loisy, *Les Évangiles synoptiques*, ii. 541; Dibelius, *From Tradition to Gospel*, 206. Dibelius speaks of the narrative as 'an aetiological tradition of the rite', *op. cit.*, 206, but also says that 'we have every reason to regard one form or another of the story of the Last Supper as old and as a part of the earliest Passion story,' *op. cit.*, 182.

is brought within the orbit of a uniform conception which includes elements derived from the ideas of the Suffering Servant, the Messianic Hope, the Kingdom of God (cf. Mk. xiv. 25), and the ancient usage of the sacred meal. The combination is that of an original thinker, not the product of a community.

The doctrinal significance of the saying is of supreme importance. It suggests that Jesus looked upon His suffering and death as a sacrificial offering of Himself for men. Any conception of His Passion as a martyrdom, or even as a revelation concerning God and sin, is shown to be hopelessly inadequate to His thought. But, more than this, the saying throws light upon the way in which He interpreted His self-offering. In bidding His disciples to receive the broken bread, which He had interpreted as His 'body', Jesus revealed that He did not look upon His sacrifice as a thing apart from men, to be accepted passively as one recognizes an external event. On the contrary, He thought of it as standing in the closest relation to human need, as an experience to be shared and appropriated; and, as a realist, He provided a rite whereby fellowship in His sufferings, and participation in the hallowing power of His sacrifice, might be assured.

(b) 'This is my blood of the covenant, which is shed for many (ὑπὲρ πολλῶν)' (Mk. xiv. 24).

Matthew introduces the saying by the words: 'Drink ye all of it', inserts 'for', changes 'for many' to 'concerning (περί) many', and adds, 'unto remission of sins' (xxvi. 28). Paul records the saying, 'This cup is the new covenant in my blood' (1 Cor. xi. 25). This is repeated almost verbatim in the longer Lukan text, which adds: 'that which is poured out for you (ὑπὲρ ὑμῶν)' (xxii. 20).

The second Markan saying raises critical problems as well as questions of exegesis. In part, these problems

arise from the close similarity of the first half of Mk. xiv.
24 to 1 Cor. xi. 25; in part, they concern the Markan saying itself.   The similarity is at once apparent when the
two passages are closely compared, and the questions for
investigation are whether either is a variant of the other,
whether they are different sayings, or whether they are independent versions of a lost original.   Bound up with
these problems is the further question whether Jesus is
likely to have invited His disciples to drink of the wine as
the symbol of His out-poured blood.

In many theological discussions it is argued that, whatever the original words of institution may have been, the
existing texts show that Jesus spoke of a covenant established in virtue of His blood; and the treatment proceeds
from this point.   This is a strong position, but it is taken
at serious cost.   Such a position may, or may not, be
necessary, but in any case a critical investigation cannot
begin at this stage, but must first consider the claims of the
Markan saying itself.

Complicated as the problems already mentioned are,
two preliminary inquiries must be undertaken.   One of
them concerns the text of Mk. xiv. 24, and the other its
content.   (1) Is the Markan saying a unity?   (2) Is it
intended by Mark as a 'word of institution', defining the
sense in which the cup is to be received, just as the words,
'This is my body', interpret the taking of the bread?

The first question relates to the words: 'which is shed
for many.'   Are they a subsequent addition?   The words
have no parallel in 1 Cor. xi. 25, but they need not, on this
ground, be explained as a gloss.[1]   On the contrary, it is
this phrase which gives distinctiveness to the saying, since

---

[1]See p. 8of.   The longer text in Lk. ends with the phrase: 'even that
which is poured out for you', but this reading may be based on Mk.   See
Lk. xxii. 20.

it defines the statement, 'This is my blood of the covenant.' The genuineness of these words has yet to be considered, but meantime it may be claimed that there is no
sufficient reason to question the originality of the qualify-
ing phrase. It plainly reflects the ideas of Isa. liii.,[1] and,
in the use of the word 'many', is in agreement with Mk.
x. 45; and the earlier discussion has shown how deeply the
Servant-conception influenced the mind of Jesus. The
principal objection on the part of many critics to the
phrase is that it obviously bears a sacrificial meaning, but
our study of the attitude of Jesus to sacrifice has revealed
that this objection is without foundation. If the words
are a later addition, the interpolator is an excellent exegete:
it is better to conclude that they are an integral part of the
saying.

The further Matthaean supplement, 'unto remission of
sins', is probably an interpretative addition made by the
Evangelist. This is suggested, not so much by the content of the phrase, as by the fact that it is Matthew's habit
to expand his Markan source, and because in xxvi. 26-9
there is no sign that he is using any other source. The
words do not imply that forgiveness is impossible apart
from the death of Christ, but that the blood-shedding has
the forgiveness of sins for its purpose. A truer criticism
of the gloss is that it concentrates attention upon a single
element, although an important one, in the purpose of
Christ's self-offering, the establishment of real fellowship
between God and man.[2]

---

[1]Cf. Dalman: 'The "many" to whom the blood of Jesus will be of service, point to the "many" who, in Isa. liii. 11f., are mentioned as those
whom the suffering of the Servant of God will benefit. ... If it were not for
Isa. liii. 12, our Lord would scarcely have used this expression,' *op. cit.*, 171f.

[2]Otto remarks that in Christian teaching forgiveness of sins and expiation
for sins are not the purpose, but the means to the eschatological goal, *op. cit.*,
263, 273.

The second question, whether Mk. xiv. 24 is intended as a 'word of institution', may seem strange, but it is prompted by the Markan narrative itself.   If it is answered in the negative the seriousness of the questions under discussion is diminished; if in the affirmative, the problems are present in their fullest intensity.   It is necessary, therefore, to study Mk. xiv. 24 in relation to its context.

'And as they were eating, he took bread and when he had blessed, he brake it, and gave to them, and said, Take ye: this is my body.   And he took a cup, and when he had given thanks, he gave to them: and they all drank of it.   And he said unto them, *This is my blood of the covenant, which is shed for many.*   Verily I say unto you, I will no more drink of the fruit of the vine, until that day when I drink it new in the kingdom of God.'

It will be seen that the position of the saying is one of much interest.   In the corresponding passage concerning the bread the explanation *accompanies* the distribution, and in view of the significance of the broken loaf, this order is natural.   The fragments are eaten as having a certain meaning; they symbolize the broken Body.   If, in like manner, the wine represents the out-poured blood, it is not unreasonable to expect the same sequence; the wine, one might think, should be received for what it is.   In fact, however, the sequence is inverted in the Markan narrative; the explanation *follows* the statement, 'they all drank of it.'   The wine is drunk and then interpreted.

The strangeness of this arrangement is not a modern discovery.   Matthew, the Churchman, and one of the first commentators on Mark, has observed it clearly.   He recasts his source, turning the statement, 'they all drank of it,' into the command, 'Drink ye all of it,' and inserting 'for' into the explanatory words which follow (cf. xxvi. 27f.).   It is obvious that, in Matthew's view, the explanation should precede the reception. How then are we to account for Mark's arrangement?

Only two theories are possible. Either the arrangement is a mere structural incoherence in Mark's narrative, and, despite its setting, the saying is intended as a 'word of institution'; or it is due to the fact that Mark followed a tradition which did not connect the words about the wine with the giving of the cup. Several considerations favour the latter theory. A description of the cup, or its contents, is certainly natural before the words, 'and they all drank of it.' Mark, moreover, could have recorded his saying at this point, and he was prompted to do so by the manner in which he had introduced the explanation of the bread. He resisted, that is to say, the structural suggestiveness of his own narrative. Again, the words, 'And he said unto them,' which introduce the Markan saying, and the fact that the latter is followed by another saying on drinking 'the fruit of the vine', may indicate that Mark is using a short collection of Supper-sayings, topically arranged as in ii. 21f., iv. 21-5, ix. 41-50. This would be an added reason for thinking that he did not know the words, 'This is my blood,' as a 'word of institution'.

These arguments are far from being conclusive, and there are several considerations to be urged on the other side. In the first place, the arguments all deal with matters of structure, and they require a higher standard of coherence in the Markan narrative than it is reasonable to expect. Mark's style is rough and unpolished, and as a compiler he demonstrably lacks the skill of Matthew.[1] Again, it would be rash to assume that whenever Mark uses the phrase, 'And he said unto them,' he is drawing upon a sayings-collection, and the connexion between the

[1] Cf. Swete, xlvii.ff.; Rawlinson, xxxi.ff.

I

two Markan sayings is not necessarily artificial.   Further, it is possible that his arrangement may be influenced by his eagerness to include the words, 'And they all drank of it,' as a polemical statement in view of existing diversities of practice.[1]   Finally, and most important of all, the form of the saying, 'This is my blood,' strongly suggests that it is intended to be taken as a 'word of institution'.   It is parallel in form to the words, 'This is my body,' which define the sense in which the bread is to be taken, and the presumption is that similarly the words, 'This is my blood,' define the meaning with which the wine is to be received.

These considerations justify us in concluding that the strangeness of the Markan narrative has no special significance, and that Mark intends the words, 'This is my blood,' to express the meaning of the wine as received. In this case, in editing his source, Matthew has brought out its actual implications.

The conclusion just reached increases the urgency of the problems raised by the similarity of Mk. xiv. 24 and 1 Cor. xi. 25 and by the difficulty of the Markan saying as a command of Jesus.   It is not possible to avoid these problems on the plea that Mk. xiv. 24 belongs to a discourse after the Supper, or is otherwise unconnected with the giving of the cup.

The verbal similarity between the two passages is obviously great.   Each passage contains the words 'this', 'is', 'covenant', 'blood', and each, though in different Greek forms, has the phrase 'my blood'.   How close the agreement is appears best when the sayings are set down side by side:

---

[1]Harnack has contended that in certain Jewish-Christian circles water was used instead of wine.   Cf. *Texte und Untersuchungen*, vii. 2, 115ff. See also Otto, *op. cit.*, 237; Klostermann, *Das Markusevangelium*, 164.

Mark: 'This is my blood of the covenant, which is shed for many.'

Paul: 'This cup is the new covenant in my blood.'[1]

The ideas, it is true, are different. The Markan saying interprets the wine as Christ's 'blood of the covenant' shed for many, and is based on Ex. xxiv. 8 and Isa. liii. 12. The Pauline saying interprets the cup as representing the 'new covenant' established by Christ's blood, and rests on a combination of Jer. xxxi. 31 and the ideas illustrated in Ex. xxiv. 1-13. This difference of ideas, however, does not exclude the possibility that one passage is a variant of the other or that both are variants of a lost original. On the contrary, it might account for the origin of the variants. Whether this explanation is probable is the main point for consideration, for, striking as it is, the agreement in vocabulary cannot be considered conclusive in itself.

Is, then, Mk. xiv. 24 a variant of 1 Cor. xi. 25? This view is difficult to sustain, for, in this case, the simpler Pauline form has been replaced by one that is obviously more difficult. The Markan saying is exposed to the serious objection that it offends Jewish scruples, and it may be safely asserted that, as a cult-saying, it could not have come into existence in Jewish-Christian circles.[2] Only in a non-Jewish environment is the transformation conceivable through the infiltration of pagan ideas associated with the Mystery-religions. But this theory, while easily stated, cannot be considered convincing. The language of the entire saying is fragrant with Old Testament

---

[1]The Greek is as follows:

Mark: τοῦτό ἐστιν τὸ αἷμά μου τῆς διαθήκης τὸ ἐκχυννόμενον ὑπὲρ πολλῶν.

Paul: τοῦτο τὸ ποτήριον ἡ καινὴ διαθήκη ἐστὶν ἐν τῷ ἐμῷ αἵματι.

[2]See the opinion of Dibelius quoted on p. 134.

associations, and its ideas, as we have seen, represent a unique combination of the teaching of Ex. xxiv. and Isa. liii. Further, there is a paucity of references to sacred meals[1] in the existing texts which relate to the Mystery-religions, and, whatever may be true of later times,[2] the date to which the evidence belongs renders it improbable that Mystery-influences were operative in the formation of the Gospel tradition during the first generation of Christianity.[3] If, finally, the objections to the genuineness of the saying prove to be wanting in force,[4] there is no reason to resort to this kind of explanation. The evidence, it may be concluded, is unfavourable to the view that Mk. xiv. 24 is a variant of the Pauline saying, provided the exegetical difficulties are not insuperable.

Is, then, 1 Cor. xi. 25 a modification of Mk. xiv. 24? It is in favour of this view that the Pauline passage is much less difficult that the Markan. In it the cup represents the new covenant sealed by Christ's blood; nothing is said of the wine as a symbol of His covenant-blood. Accordingly, it is tempting to argue that the Pauline form has arisen in consequence of the difficulties of the Markan

[1] Cf. H. A. A. Kennedy: 'The evidence regarding Sacramental Meals in the Mystery-Religions is both meagre and difficult to interpret,' *St. Paul and the Mystery-Religions*, 256; C. Clemen, *Primitive Christianity and its Non-Jewish Sources*, 257-66; N. P. Williams, *Essays Catholic and Critical*, 389; A. E. J. Rawlinson, *The New Testament Doctrine of the Christ*, 270-84.

[2] Cf. J. C. Lambert, *The Sacraments in the New Testament*, 418f.

[3] Cf. Kennedy, *op. cit.*, 69, 279. Clemen closes his discussion with the opinion: 'The doctrine which the New Testament really teaches regarding the Lord's Supper cannot be derived, even collaterally or by way of supplement, from pagan sources,' *op. cit.*, 266. T. Wilson recognises that, in the last resort, the Christian sacraments are '*sui generis* in the whole history of the religious life of man,' *St. Paul and Paganism*, 183. See also Rawlinson, *op. cit.*, 279; Goguel, *The Life of Jesus*, 187; Gore, *The Reconstruction of Belief*, 724f.

[4] See pp. 133ff.

saying in Jewish-Christian circles.[1] Such a conclusion, however, is premature, for the theory is no more than a possibility; and it may well be that both passages are authentic or that both represent a lost original. All that we are entitled to conclude from the comparison is that, if the passages are variants, it is probable that Mk. xiv. 24, and not 1 Cor. xi. 25, is the original.

We have now reached the point when it is necessary to examine more closely the difficulty of the Markan saying.

The strongest objection which can be brought against Mk. xiv. 24 is the fact that the Jew regarded the drinking of blood with horror; can Jesus, then, have commanded His disciples to drink wine as the symbol of His blood? From feelings of reverence this difficulty has not received the attention it demands, for there can be no doubt that it is formidable. Writing as a Jew, C. G. Montefiore expresses it temperately when he says: 'I would also venture to suggest how difficult it is to believe that a Palestinian or Galilaean Jew could have suggested that in drinking wine his disciples were, even symbolically, drinking blood. For the horror with which the drinking of blood was regarded by the Jews is well-known.'[2] J. Klausner, also a Jew, makes the point more trenchantly: 'The drinking of blood, even if it was meant symbolically, could only have aroused horror in the minds of such simple Galilaean Jews.'[3] It is not surprising that many continental scholars explain the words as a cult-saying which originated in a non-Jewish environment. Thus, Dibelius

---

[1] Dalman thinks of Greek circles: 'The peculiar equation, not of the wine and the blood, but of the cup and the covenant, may be due to the avoidance of the offence which the other formulation might have given to Hellenic sensibility,' *op. cit.*, 161. He appears to think that the Pauline form presupposes Mk. xiv. 24, but does not discuss the point. See p. 162.

[2] *The Synoptic Gospels*, i. 332.

[3] *Jesus of Nazareth* (Eng. tr.), 329.

writes: 'A Jewish Christian Church with its dread of blood would scarcely have made Jesus say "this is my blood" (in the cup), but rather "this cup means a new covenant which is instituted by my blood, i.e. by my death".'[1]

It is, I think, a fair rejoinder to this argument to say, first, that it is not a question of what 'a Palestinian or Galilaean Jew' would be likely to suggest, but of what might be commanded by a Jew who believed himself to be the Son of Man destined to suffer on behalf of the 'many'.[2] Again, it is a very doubtful canon of authenticity to question words of Jesus on the ground that they would have awakened horror in the minds of Jews. During the first days of His preaching Jesus appeared in the eyes of His family to be 'beside himself' (Mk. iii. 21). To the scribes His claim to forgive sins was blasphemy (Mk. ii. 7). His liberal interpretation of the law of the Sabbath led the Pharisees to take counsel with the Herodians, 'how they might destroy him' (Mk. iii. 6). At His Trial His declaration that His judges would see 'the Son of man sitting at the right hand of power, and coming with the clouds of heaven' so roused the high priest that he rent his clothes, and said: 'What further need have we of witnesses? Ye have heard the blasphemy: what think ye?' (Mk. xiv. 63f.).[3] Further, the men addressed are not

---

[1] *From Tradition to Gospel*, 207.

[2] On the question of the Messianic consciousness of Jesus, Montefiore speaks with the greatest hesitation and reserve. Cf. *The Synoptic Gospels*, i. cxxi.ff. One of the more positive passages is that in vol. ii. p. 20: 'It is, indeed, conceivable that, towards the close of his ministry, Jesus may have realised that his mission was only to succeed, and the Kingdom of God to be inaugurated, by his own suffering and death. . . . His conception of his Messiahship may have been the conception of the Suffering Servant, through whose stripes and death men were healed, rather than that of the righteous and conquering king.'

[3] The Fourth Gospel contains stronger examples, influenced in part by current controversy: cf. vi. 52, viii. 48, 52; ix. 24, x. 20, 33.

just 'simple Galilaean Jews', as Klausner describes them,
but disciples, to whom, though with little success, Jesus
had already imparted the teaching that 'the Son of man
must suffer'.   Difficult as they had found this doctrine to
accept, they would not be likely, in the light of it, to take
the words of Jesus as a bare suggestion that in drinking
wine they were drinking blood symbolically.   Finally, to
interpret the words of Jesus in this way is to put an ambiguous and misleading construction upon them.   Jesus
does not invite His disciples to drink blood, or to drink
blood symbolically, but to drink wine as representing His
life surrendered for many.   The objection under review
has force if the theory of Transubstantiation is accepted;
but there is no probability that Jesus saw any objective
virtues in blood, or implied that His word transformed the
'substance' of wine into the 'substance' of blood.   The
wine remains wine, but wine invested with a new significance and power.   Blood is mentioned in view of the
circumstances, and because of the associations of the term.
The red vintage suggests it, the thought of a violent death
implies it, the well-known Old Testament use of the word
makes it a convenient vehicle of thought; but the term
is misconceived if it is isolated from the ideas it is meant
to suggest.   What Jesus has in mind is a redemptive
activity, not a transformation of 'substance'; He is thinking of His life surrendered for the salvation of many, and
the wine is offered as a symbol of the life and a means
whereby it may be appropriated.

It is not, of course, to be supposed that, at the time, the
disciples understood the full meaning of the words of
Jesus, or the significance of what He invited them to do;
but this fact throws no doubt upon the Markan saying.
Rather is it the manner of Jesus to speak words which
challenge thought and become luminous only in the

course of experience.   His words are 'words of aeonian life'.   The note of challenge, and even of offence, is characteristic of the sayings of One who disdained qualifications, and said: 'Blessed is he, whosoever shall find none occasion of stumbling in me' (Lk. vii. 23).' For these reasons, there is little satisfaction in efforts which trace the Markan saying to an unknown 'community' situate in the back-streets of Rome.   Conceivably, its origin might be such; but every consideration of probability favours the belief that its unstrained allusions, its bold challenge, and its virility of thought have the authentic ring.   The one speaker who is most likely to have used these words is Jesus Himself.[1]

This conclusion has most cogency if it extends to the entire saying, and since there are no adequate reasons for detaching the phrase, 'which was shed for many,' from the rest,[2] it may with justice be claimed for the whole.   If this view is accepted, there is no reason to consider whether Mk. xiv. 24 and 1 Cor. xi. 25 are different versions of a lost original.   Mk. xiv. 24 is original, and 1 Cor. xi. 25 is either a variant of it or is a distinct saying. Which of these alternatives is the more probable may be deferred until the Pauline sayings are examined further.[3]

It remains for us to consider more closely the implications of the Markan saying, and, in particular, the meaning of the phrase, 'my blood of the covenant.'

The idea of a covenant between Yahweh and Israel, which from the side of the people demands obedience, and from the side of Yahweh promises blessings, is deeply inwrought in Old Testament thinking, and the use of the phrase, 'blood of the covenant,' suggests that the ancient story of the institution of the covenant in Ex. xxiv. 1-11

[1]Cf. G. H. C. Macgregor, *Eucharistic Origins*, 64ff.
[2]See p. 126f.   [3]See pp. 203-6.

forms the background of the words of Jesus.   It is necessary, therefore, to examine this story.

The narrative tells that when Moses returns with the
words of Yahweh, the people declare their willingness to
obey.   Next day an altar is built, burnt-offerings are
offered, and peace-offerings are sacrificed to Yahweh.
Half of the blood is then sprinkled on the altar, and when
the book of the covenant is read, the people declare: 'All
that Yahweh hath spoken will we do.'   Blood is then
sprinkled on them, and Moses says: 'Behold the blood
of the covenant, which Yahweh hath made with you concerning all these words.'   Moses and his companions
then ascend into the mount, and it is recorded of them:
'they beheld God, and did eat and drink' (Ex. xxiv. 11).

In this narrative a distinction is drawn between the
blood sprinkled upon the altar and that which is sprinkled
upon the people.   The former is the symbol of the
people's obedience; it is their offering to God, confirmed
by the words: 'All the words which Yahweh hath spoken
will we do.'   The latter, the blood sprinkled upon them,
is dedicated blood which Yahweh has accepted, and the
sprinkling means that the people now share in the blessings and powers which it represents and conveys.   It is this
blood which is described as 'the blood of the covenant'.

It is not easy to determine how far the details of this
story were in the mind of Jesus during the Supper.   Was
He thinking, for example, of this ancient representative
company of men eating and drinking in fellowship with
God, when He took bread for His disciples 'as they were
eating', and, having blessed and broken it, said: 'Take ye:
this is my body'?   Certain it is that the phrase, 'blood of
the covenant,' is taken from the story, and the words, '*my*
blood of the covenant,' suggest reflection on the words of
Moses.   The saying of Jesus strongly suggests the

thought that, as of old dedicated blood was applied in blessing to the people of Israel, so now His life, surrendered to God and accepted by Him, is offered to, and made available for men. Of this life the wine is a symbol: but, since it is given to them to drink, it is more than a symbol. It is a means of blessing, an opportunity for appropriation. It is not transformed into blood, but is a vehicle of the life released for many in the shedding of blood. That the life is conveyed mechanically, *ex opere operato*, is foreign to the outlook and thought of Jesus; but it is true to the meaning of His words at the Supper to say that, in the rite, the life of a fellowship with God is offered to men, so that of them also it may be said : 'they beheld God, and did eat and drink.'

In his recent important brochure, *Die Abendmahlsworte Jesu*, Joachim Jeremias, while recognizing that Ex. xxiv. 8 gives a good meaning for the words: 'This is my blood of the covenant,' finds a nearer interpretation in the thought of the blood of the Passover lamb. He recognizes that the Passover of later times was not an atoning sacrifice, but calls attention to two passages in the Talmudic Literature which speak of the blood of the Passover lamb as 'covenant-blood'.[1] Both passages relate to Zech. ix. 11 : 'As for thee also, because of the blood of thy covenant I have sent forth thy prisoners out of the pit wherein is no water,' and interpret this passage with reference to the deliverance from Egypt. The Passover blood is the blood of the covenant in the power of which the deliverance is accomplished. Jeremias is of the opinion that the thought of Jesus, who during the last days of His Ministry had this chapter of Zechariah in mind (cf. Mt. xxi. 5), is the same; it is the atoning blood of the Passover lamb at the departure from Egypt with which He compares His own 'blood

[1] Targ. Zech. ix. 11; Mekh. Ex. xii. 6.

of the covenant'. He thus describes 'His death as an atoning death which establishes the new and eternal communion of a humanity cleansed from sin with its God —the communion of the Kingdom of God'.[1]

This view seems to me to be less probable than the interpretation which finds the reference, in the words of Jesus, in Ex. xxiv. 8, but the conclusion as to the significance of the words of institution is the same. This is especially clear in the words with which Jeremias closes his essay with reference to the saying on the Messianic feast in the future Kingdom in Mk. xiv. 25: 'As He will there give to them the divine gift of the bread and water of life, so He gives to them now in bread and wine His gift— a share in the reconciling power of His vicarious death. So certainly as they eat the bread which Jesus breaks for them, and drink the wine over which He spoke the word concerning the blood of the covenant, so certainly avails for them the "for you" of His death, and the "with you" of the future Supper-communion in the renewed world.'[2]

(c) *'Verily I say unto you, I will no more drink of the fruit of the vine, until that day when I drink it new in the kingdom of God'* (Mk. xiv. 25).

Matthew's version contains merely stylistic and exegetical variations (xxvi. 29). Luke's version is shorter, and may be independent of Mk. In the second part he has: 'until the kingdom of God shall come' (xxii. 18). See pp. 183ff.

In the third Markan saying Jesus looks beyond the present Supper to the consummation of the Kingdom when He will drink the wine of the Messianic Banquet. The genuineness of the saying needs little discus-

---

[1]*Op. cit.*, 82.

[2]*Op. cit.*, 94. 'His action is a guarantee, is an anticipation of the future Supper-communion established with the Parousia,' *ibid*.

sion.[1] Its ideas are entirely Jewish. The thought of the
Messianic Feast goes back to Isa. xxv. 6,[2] and the phrase,
'the fruit of the vine,' appears in Isa. xxxii. 12 and Hab. iii.
17 (cf. Numb. vi. 4). Moreover, as Montefiore reminds
us, 'the joys of the Kingdom are constantly referred to in
Rabbinical literature under the metaphor of pleasures of
food and drink.'[3] The possibility, therefore, that the
saying is a 'community-product' does not arise.

The saying is closely connected with the preceding
words: 'This is my blood of the covenant, which is shed
for many'; and this is an indication that more was said at
the giving of the cup than the 'words of institution'. The
saying introduces a strong eschatological note into the
account of the Supper, and the question arises how this
element is related to the sacrificial conceptions implied in
the other sayings.

Loisy has argued that the anticipation of the Messianic
Banquet (Mk. xiv. 25) excludes the ideas connected with
the body and the blood (Mk. xiv. 22, 24),[4] but this is a
suggestion which places the various sayings in an unnecessary antagonism. If Jesus Himself drank of the wine,
and this is the opinion of very many commentators,[5] the

[1] Wellhausen thinks that there is no saying of Jesus which gives a greater
impression of authenticity, but he needlessly supposes that Jesus thinks of
Himself simply as a guest, and not the Messiah present or future, *Ev. Marc.*,
115. Cf. Montefiore, *op. cit.*, i. 335; Ed. Meyer, *Ursprung und Anfänge
des Christentums*, i. 179.

[2] 'And in this mountain shall the Lord of hosts make unto all peoples a
feast of fat things, a feast of wines on the lees, of fat things full of marrow, of
wines on the lees well refined.'

[3] *Op. cit.*, i. 334; cf. Strack-Billerbeck, *op. cit.*, i. 992.

[4] *Les Évangiles synoptiques*, ii. 540; cf. Montefiore, *op. cit.*, i. 337.

[5] This view is implied by the Markan words, 'I will no more drink . . .
until . . .', and by the reading of D, οὐ μὴ προσθῶ πεῖν. This reading,
which is supported by 565 a f arm (cf. Legg, *Novum Testamentum
Graece*, in loc.), has an authentic ring. Cf. Lk. xx. 11, and see Moulton,
Grammar of New Testament Greek, ii. 445.

action must have had a different significance for Him from that which it had for the disciples. For them the drinking of the cup foreshadows the approaching death and sacrifice; for Him it heralds the joys of the Kingdom. The disciples themselves are introduced into this aspect of the Supper in the words of Mk. xiv. 25; for them also it is made clear that 'if death is certain, so is reunion'.[1] The eschatological idea, indeed, is indissolubly connected with the Supper in the earliest tradition. It dominates, as we shall see, the Lukan account,[2] and is emphasized by St. Paul in the words: 'For as often as ye eat this bread, and drink the cup, ye proclaim the Lord's death *till he come*' (1 Cor. xi. 26).[3] This thought of the future consummation, however, is distinctively present to the mind of Jesus during the Supper, and is in no way in conflict with the teaching which He gave to the disciples concerning the bread and the cup. With Him they could think of the Supper as an anticipation of the Messianic Feast, but for them in particular it meant also participation in His approaching sacrifice.

Mk. xiv. 25 is of the greatest importance for the insight it gives into the mind of Jesus as He contemplates His death. It shows that the idea of the Kingdom, so central in His Galilaean teaching, was His sure hope and confidence in the very shadow of the cross. He did not renounce His earlier teaching and replace it by the idea of a redemptive sacrifice. On the contrary, He is still sure that the Kingdom will be established; He will yet drink the wine of the Messianic Banquet. The ring of joyful confidence is unmistakable. This hope can only mean that He believed His death to be a necessary step to the establishment of the Kingdom. He must suffer and die,

[1]A. W. F. Blunt, 252.   [2]See pp. 180ff.
[3]Cf. A. Schweitzer, *The Mysticism of Paul the Apostle*, 267.

then the Rule of God can be consummated; this, and nothing less is the implication of His words. When or how the Kingdom will come is not stated, but the atmosphere of the saying, as in Mk. ix. 1 and xiv. 62, is that of a hope whose realization is near.

Important as this thought is in itself, it must not be separated from the Supper with which it is associated; it is the Supper which releases the hope and is the medium of its expression. Much of the discussion in respect of the three Markan sayings has necessarily turned on the meaning of the Supper; but this is no departure from the study of the attitude of Jesus to His death and passion, since it is His own words which bring the death and the Supper into the closest connexion. H. A. W. Meyer shows a just and a true appreciation of the connexion when he says: 'The *atonement* through the death of Jesus is at any rate the necessary *premiss* of even the symbolical interpretation of the Lord's Supper. With every attempt to explain away the *atoning* death, the Supper becomes utterly unintelligible.'[1]

(10) Two Old Testament Quotations; The Stone (Mk. xii. 10f.); The Shepherd (Mk. xiv. 27).

The Acts and the Epistles show that in early Christianity the greatest interest was taken in Old Testament passages which were felt to be illustrated or 'fulfilled' in the life and ministry of Jesus. It is always possible, therefore, that during the oral period such passages were unconsciously read back into His sayings, and this possibility must always seriously be taken into account. On the other hand, it is anything but a critical proceeding to reject in a wholesale manner sayings which contain quotations, for the evidence is overwhelming that Jesus Himself

[1] *The Epistles to the Corinthians,* i. 342n.

read the Old Testament with fresh insight and expressed His thoughts in its familiar language (cf. Mk. vii. 6f., xii. 26, 36; Lk. vii. 27, &c.). The real difficulty arises in particular examples, and in these cases the decision must turn on whether the quotation is well related to its context, whether its use has any distinctive characteristics, and whether its ideas appear elsewhere in the teaching of Jesus. Where these tests are fulfilled, the presumption is that the quotation is original.

> (a) '*The stone which the builders rejected,*
> *The same was made the head of the corner:*
> *This was from the Lord,*
> *And it is marvellous in our eyes*' (Mk. xii. 10f.).

The passage is reproduced verbatim in Mt. xxi. 42, and the first part in Lk. xx. 17.

The quotation is taken from Psa. cxviii. 22f., where it refers to Israel as despised among the nations, but destined in the purpose of God to attain pre-eminence.[1] Some commentators explain it as an addition on the part of the community or the Evangelist,[2] but this view lacks adequate justification. Undoubtedly, the passage was a favourite quotation in early Christian apologetic; it appears in Acts iv. 11; Eph. ii. 20; and 1 Pet. ii. 4-8. Justin Martyr twice speaks of Christ as the 'stone,'[3] and it may well be that the quotation appeared in early Christian collections of *Testimonia* drawn from the Old Testament.[4] But these facts merely raise the question of genuineness; in no way do they preclude the use of the quotation by

---

[1]An alternative explanation (Duhm) refers the passage to the beginnings of the Maccabean House.

[2]So Klostermann, 137; Bousset, *op. cit.*, 69. See also Luce, 310.

[3]*Dial.*, 34, 36.

[4]Cf. J. Rendel Harris, *Testimonies*, i. ii.; D. Plooij, *Studies in the Testimony Book.* See also Bousset, *op. cit.*, 69; Sanday and Headlam, 282.

Jesus.   Although the words introduce a new figure of speech, they are not inapposite as an appendage to the parable of the Vineyard, and the researches of P. Fiebig have shown that quotations from Scripture are found in Rabbinical parables.[1]   In later times there is evidence that the Rabbis gave a Messianic interpretation to the passage,[2] and Jesus who in the parable is thinking in Messianic terms, may well have read it in the same way. J. Jeremias thinks that Jesus is employing the figure of the New Temple, and that He designates Himself as the 'keystone' which brings it to completion.[3]   A parallel idea appears in the saying which lies behind Jn. ii. 19, 'Destroy this temple, and in three days I will raise it up,' which is echoed in the accusation brought against Jesus at His Trial (Mk. xiv. 58)[4] and in the taunts of those who pass by at the Crucifixion (Mk. xv. 29; cf. Acts vi. 14).   Jesus was keenly interested in the fate of the Temple (cf. Mk. xiii. 2), and, accordingly, to believe that He had reflected on an Old Testament passage which, in His view, defined a Messianic function He was destined to fulfil, is historically justifiable, especially in the light of His claim to be the founder of a New Temple 'made without hands' (Mk. xiv. 58).   For these reasons it is unnecessary to trace the passage to the 'community'; it is better interpreted as a quotation of Jesus Himself.[5]

[1]Cf. *Die Gleichnisreden*, 78; *Der Erzählungsstil der Evangelien*, 41, 43.

[2]Cf. Strack-Billerbeck, *Kommentar*, i. 876.

[3]Cf. *Jesus als Weltvollender*, 80.

[4]See the interesting discussion by Goguel in *The Life of Jesus*, 507ff., where Mk. xiv. 58 is claimed as 'a fully authentic saying', with the support of Wrede, J. Weiss, Wellhausen, Loisy, Norden, Bultmann, and Bertram.

[5]The interest of Jesus in passages which speak of the 'Stone' is further illustrated in Lk. xx. 18: 'Every one that falleth on that stone shall be broken to pieces; but on whomsoever it shall fall, it will scatter him as dust' (cf. Isa. viii. 14 and Dan. ii. 44), but this isolated and obscure logion has difficulties of its own.

The use of the quotation is a further proof that Jesus thought of His death, not as a stroke of fate, but as a necessary part of His Mission. The 'stone' is rejected, and by the builders, but this event is not the end. The rejected stone becomes 'the head of the corner'. So God has ordained it, and looking upon the result men confess it marvellous in their eyes. The use of the passage by Jesus implies His obedient acceptance of a divinely appointed *rôle*, and no less His sure conviction of its triumphant issue. For Him rejection is a temporary condition followed by the victory of the divine Will.[1]

(*b*) 'And Jesus saith unto them, *All ye shall be offended: for it is written,*

> *I will smite the shepherd,*
> *And the sheep shall be scattered abroad*' (Mk. xiv. 27).

Matthew has 'the sheep *of the flock*'; Luke omits the section.

This quotation is taken from Zech. xiii. 7, but instead of the future, 'I will smite,' both the Hebrew and the LXX read the imperative, 'Smite the shepherd.' R. H. Kennett,[2] however, suggests that the future should be read in Zechariah as in Mark.

Several commentators explain the future tense as due to the influence of Christian usage or of a collection of *Testimonia*,[3] while others think that the quotation is a later addition prompted by Christian reflection.[4] The following verse, 'Howbeit, after I am raised up, I will go before you into Galilee,' is wanting in the Fayoum Gospel-Fragment,[5]

---

[1] The agreement of this idea with those of Isa. liii. is obvious.

[2] Peake's *Commentary*, 583.

[3] Swete, 338; B.T.D. Smith, 199; Blunt, 252.

[4] Montefiore, *The Synoptic Gospels*, i. 340; Wood, Peake's *Commentary*, 697.

[5] Cf. M. R. James, *The Apocryphal New Testament*, 25.

K

and Holtzmann has argued that verse 29 (Peter's protest: 'Although all shall be offended . . .') follows much better after 27a ('All ye shall be offended'). Montefiore reminds us, however, that J. Weiss takes verse 28 to mean: 'I will go at your head, and will lead you to Galilee,' and that he interprets the verse as the embodiment of 'a very old expectation (or prediction) which was not fulfilled'.[1] The critical objection to the genuineness of the quotation is clearly put by Bertram who sees in the passage an attempt to show that Jesus foresaw His fate, and to prove that what happened was in accord with Old Testament prophecy.[2]

A decision between the alternative explanations is not easy. Bertram's suggestion would account for the genesis of the story, for it relates the narrative to a situation which existed in primitive Christianity. On the other hand, it is just as pertinent to urge that Jesus Himself foresaw His fate, and, as the investigation has already shown, He found its secret in the Old Testament. The passage, therefore, can just as naturally be attributed to Jesus as to the Christian community. Moreover, the quotation is well related to the immediate situation in the story. Few things in the Gospel tradition are more certain than that Jesus foretold the defection of Peter; but Peter's protest, 'Although all shall be offended,' implies the sorrowful observation of Jesus, 'All ye shall be offended' (lit., 'made to stumble'), and in such a connexion the Old Testament words about the scattering of the sheep are very apposite.

The evidence that Jesus used imagery connected with sheep and shepherds is abundant. He saw the people of the land 'as sheep not having a shepherd' (Mk. vi. 34), and spoke of Himself as sent to 'the lost sheep of the house of Israel' (Mt. xv. 24; cf. x. 6). He related His immortal parables of the Lost Sheep (Lk. xv. 3-7) and the Sheep and

---

[1] *Op. cit.*, i. 340f. [2] *Die Leidensgeschichte Jesu und der Christuskult*, 42.

the Goats (Mt. xxv. 31-46).   He bade the 'little flock' of
His disciples not to fear, since it was the Father's good
pleasure to give them the Kingdom (Lk. xii. 32), and in
the Fourth Gospel He speaks of Himself as 'the good
shepherd' that 'layeth down his life for the sheep' (Jn. x.
11).   To use, therefore, Old Testament language, and
prophesy that when He, the shepherd, is smitten, the
sheep will be scattered, is simply to employ His own vocabulary.   Moreover, as J. Jeremias[1] has pointed out, the
figure of the Shepherd is a common designation of the
bringer of Salvation throughout the East, and in the Old
Testament it is used of the Messiah (cf. Mic. v. 4; Ezek.
xxxiv. 23f., xxxvii. 24).

If the quotation is a later insertion due to subsequent
Christian reflection, it has been admirably introduced into
a natural sequence of thought and adapted to the language
of Jesus in the interests, not of doctrine, but of apology.
This is possible, but the presumption, I think, is that the
quotation was made by Jesus.   If this conclusion is accepted, the passage is another illustration of the way in
which the thought of His death absorbed the mind of
Jesus and led Him to ponder the ancient prophecies of
Israel.   If the change from the imperative ('smite') to the
future ('I will smite') is a deliberate modification, and not
caused by early Christian usage, it reveals His conviction
that His suffering and death are not merely events compassed by men, but rather the fulfilment of a purpose deep
in the counsels of God.

(11) THE GETHSEMANE SAYINGS (Mk. xiv. 34, 36, 37f., 41f.,
    48f.).

Rawlinson's view, that the basis of the story of Gethsemane is 'historical and beyond the reach of invention',[2] is

---

[1] *Op. cit.*, 32f.   [2] *St. Mark*, 210.

shared by critics of very different schools.   The opinion,
it is true, is not universally accepted.   Dibelius explains
the story as one which has been built up out of material
supplied by the Old Testament in such a way that it 'became a revelation of Jesus' obedience in opposition to the
inert and dull disciples'.[1]   Bultmann speaks of its 'wholly
legendary character',[2] and Goguel describes it as 'an ad-
mirable allegory' 'which expresses what took place in the
soul of Jesus'.[3]   These views, however, stand opposed to
a consensus of opinion shared by unusual allies.   The
historian, Eduard Meyer, says that this scene and that of
the Denial bear 'the impress of complete authenticity'.[4]
Montefiore, while voicing a warning against pressing the
details of the story, says that 'it may well have a historic
basis', and declares that 'one cannot but marvel at the
wonderful grace and beauty, the exquisite tact and dis-
cretion, which the narrative displays'.[5]   Even more remarkable is the opinion of Joseph Klausner: 'The whole
story bears the hallmark of human truth: only a few details
are dubious.   It must have been transmitted to the Evangelists (or their sources) direct from Peter, James or John,
with such simplicity and conviction that even the ideas or
tendencies of Pauline times could not obscure their memo-
ries.   The sorrow and sufferings of the solitary Son of
man, profound as they are, leave on every sympathetic
heart, be it the heart of the believer or unbeliever, such an
impression as may never be wiped out.'[6]

[1] *From Tradition to Gospel*, 213.

[2] *Die Geschichte der synoptischen Tradition*, 288.

[3] *The Life of Jesus*, 495.

[4] *Ursprung und Anfänge des Christentums*, i. 149.

[5] *The Synoptic Gospels*, i. 342.

[6] *Jesus of Nazareth*, 332.   So much is Montefiore impressed by the sublime words of the prayer that he asks: 'And why should it not, even though
for us Jesus is neither God nor Messiah, give strength to Jewish hearts also?
We must restore this hero to the bead-roll of our heroes,' *op. cit.*, i. 344.

This estimate of the narrative does not, of course, exclude the necessity of considering closely the difficulties, as well as the meaning of the five sayings associated with Gethsemane.[1]

(a) '*My soul is exceeding sorrowful even unto death: abide ye here, and watch*' (Mk. xiv. 34; cf. Mt. xxvi. 38 and Lk. xxii. 40).

Matthew adds, '*with me*'. Luke omits the saying, and has: '*Pray that ye enter not into temptation.*' Cf. xxii. 46 and Mk. xiv. 38.

These words echo the language of Psa. xlii. 5, 11; xliii. 5: 'Why art thou cast down, O my soul?' Once more, they show how inevitably Jesus expressed His deepest feelings in the language of the Old Testament. Mark has attempted to interpret the words when he says that Jesus 'began to be greatly amazed and sore troubled' (xiv. 33).[2] The saying expresses grief and sorrow so deep as to threaten life itself.[3] Something more than shrinking from death is implied. It was not with such feelings that the martyrs faced death,[4] and the only tenable explanation of the words is one which recognizes that it was the prospect of death *as Jesus interpreted it* which tortured His soul in this hour. He saw His sufferings as

[1]It is interesting to recall that even D. F. Strauss recognized as 'an historical kernel', 'the fact, that Jesus on that evening in the garden experienced a violent access of fear, and prayed that his sufferings might be averted, with the reservation nevertheless of an entire submission to the will of God,' *Life of Jesus* (Eng. Tr. by Geo. Eliot, 5th ed., 640).

[2]'To be full of terror and distress' (Weymouth), 'To feel appalled and agitated' (Moffatt).

[3]Cf. Swete, 342; Rawlinson, 211; and see Jon. iv. 9. Klostermann, 168, thinks the idea is that death is to be preferred.

[4]Cf. H. B. Workman, *Persecution in the Early Church*, 303-52. 'The absence of all fear, in fact, is one of the notes of the early Church,' 305. For weeks before the fatal issue, we find the martyrs living in a state of ecstasy,' 321. 'The Christian's contempt of death was remarkable even in an age in which indifference to death formed one of the pleasures of life,' 331.

The prayer, therefore, may be taken as genuine, or, in any case, as representing the mind of Jesus correctly.

The reference to the 'cup' recalls the same expression in Mk. x. 38[1] (cf. Lk. xii. 50), and must be interpreted in the same manner.   The cup is an experience of deep spiritual suffering of which death is the climax.   Martyrdom is included, but it cannot possibly be regarded as the sole ingredient in the cup, in view of the strong consciousness of the fulfilment of a destiny revealed in the prayer itself, in the words, 'but what thou wilt,' and in the reference to the arrival of 'the hour' in xiv. 41 (cf. xiv. 35).   For Jesus the martyrdom has a meaning, and it is the meaning which constitutes the cup.   Those interpretations which speak of it as a 'cup of wrath' are wrong in fact,[2] but not in principle.   It is right to find in it whatever belongs to His Messianic suffering.   The saying does not describe its contents, but if, on other grounds, there is reason to think that Jesus looked on the surrender of His life as an offering for 'the many', the cup can mean nothing less than the bitter experience thereby involved.

There is no contradiction between the prayer and the earlier predictions of death (Mk. viii. 31, and similar sayings).   'It is a natural wish rather than a hope which prompts the prayer: and the very form of it, "Abba Father, all things are possible to thee," suggests that the request is for something beyond human power or expectation (cf. Mk. x. 27).'[3]   Nothing, more than this tension between the acceptance of a destiny and the shrinking of a

---

[1]See pp. 97 ff.

[2]Not to mention other objections, this view is ruled out by the tenderness and confidence in the words. 'Abba, Father,' a bilingualism which may represent the usage of Jesus Himself.   For different interpretations of the phrase see Swete, 344.

[3]H. G. Wood, *op. cit.*, 668.

sensitive spirit, is so eloquent of the realism of the Gospel story.

(c) 'And he cometh, and findeth them sleeping, and saith unto Peter, *Simon, sleepest thou? couldest thou not watch one hour? Watch and pray, that ye enter not into temptation: the spirit indeed is willing, but the flesh is weak*' (Mk. xiv. 37f.; cf. Mt. xxvi. 40f.; Lk. xxii. 45f.).

Matthew omits the reference to Simon, and adds, '*with me*' after 'watch'. Luke's version, which may be independent, says that the disciples were sleeping '*for sorrow*', and records the saying briefly: '*Why sleep ye? rise and pray, that ye enter not into temptation*' (cf. xxii. 40).

These words further illustrate the importance Jesus attached to the presence and sympathy of the disciples. The rebuke is sharp, especially in the case of Peter (cf. xiv. 31), and the command is repeated and extended; they are to watch and pray, and not to enter into temptation.[1] Loisy suggests that the original command was: 'Pray that I enter not into trial';[2] but, while this interpretation does not raise insuperable doctrinal difficulties, it is not required by the infinitive in Lk. xxii. 40, and is excluded by the ἔλθητε in Mk. xiv. 38; Mt. xxvi. 41, and Lk. xxii. 46. The temptation is that of relaxing vigilance, and so of failing to give to Jesus the sympathy and fellowship of which He is in need; it may also be that of proving faithless amid the events which will ensue. Although the rebuke is sharp, the peremptoriness of the command is softened

---

[1] ἵνα c. subj. in Mk. xiv. 38 is used, not of purpose, but either of the content of the prayer (Klostermann, 169), or as a substitute for the imperative (Moulton, *Prolegomena*, 178).

[2] Luce, 337, thinks the conjecture 'natural enough'; Easton, 331, records it with an exclamation mark. Réville similarly conjectured that the saying on the spirit and the flesh was 'obviously spoken by Jesus of Himself'. Cf. Wood, 697.

reflection that the Son of Man is betrayed into the hands of sinful men. Here, every point is significant, the person of the One betrayed, the betrayal itself, the character of those into whose hands He falls. Opposed in every respect to those who surround Him stands the figure of Jesus Himself. Now, as always, He is master of the situation. His 'Arise, let us be going', is not a counsel of flight,[1] but a call to action. He 'goes forth to meet His fate'.[2]

(e) 'And Jesus answered and said unto them, *Are ye come out, as against a robber, with swords and staves to seize me? I was daily with you in the temple teaching, and ye took me not: but (this is done) that the Scriptures might be fulfilled*' (Mk. xiv. 48f.; cf. Mt. xxvi. 55f.; Lk. xxii. 52f.).

Matthew adds at the beginning '*to the multitudes*'. He follows Mark closely, but says, '*All this is come to pass*', and adds '*of the prophets*' after 'Scriptures'. Luke refers to '*the chief priests, and captains of the temple, and elders*' (cf. Mk. xiv. 43). He has '*Ye stretched not forth your hands against me*', and adds, '*But this is your hour, and the power of darkness*'.

The only point to be considered is the phrase, 'that the Scriptures might be fulfilled.' The words are felt by some to be a gloss,[3] but they may well have been spoken by Jesus. As in Mk. ix. 12*b* and xiv. 21 no particular passage is suggested. The point, however, is not of much importance, since, at this stage, it is fully evident that Jesus interpreted His suffering in terms of Old Testament thought.

---

[1]Swete, 349; Gould, 272; Rawlinson, 213; Blunt, 254; Klostermann, 169.

[2]Gould, 272.

[3]Bultmann, *op. cit.*, 305, rejects xiv. 48f.; Ed. Meyer, *op. cit.*, i. 184, regards 48, 49*a* as authentic, but not 49*b*.

(12) THE CRY FROM THE CROSS (Mk. xv. 34; Mt. xxvii. 46).

'And at the ninth hour Jesus cried with a loud voice, *Eloi, Eloi, lama sabachthani?* which is, being interpreted, *My God, my God, why hast thou forsaken me?*'

Matthew has '*about* the ninth hour', and gives the Hebrew form '*Eli, Eli,*' omitting 'being interpreted'. Luke omits the saying.

This saying, together with the reply to the high priest's question (xiv. 62) and the words 'Thou sayest' in answer to Pilate (xv. 2), are the only utterances of Jesus recorded by Mark after the Arrest.[1] The words are a quotation from Psa. xxii., and there is much to be said for the view that they were spoken in Hebrew.[2] Although Codex Bezae and some Old Latin MSS. (c and i) support the reading 'reproached' instead of 'forsaken', it is probable that the common reading is correct. The absence of the saying from Luke and John shows that it raised difficulties at a very early time, and the Western reading is probably a further illustration of this feeling;[3] it is still more obviously present in the *Gospel of Peter* which reads: '*My power, my power,* why hast thou forsaken me?'[4]

The genuineness of the saying is beyond dispute for those who think it expresses feelings of despair. Schmiedel, for example, included it among his nine 'foundation-pillars for a truly scientific life of Jesus',[5] and Arno Neumann described it as bearing, unmistakably, 'the stamp of genuineness'.[6] Other interpretations, however, are possible, and these deeply affect the question.

[1]R. H. Lightfoot observes that this is strong evidence for the general excellence, historically, of St. Mark's passion narrative, *History and Interpretation in the Gospels*, 145.

[2]Cf. Dalman, *Jesus-Jeshua*, 205; Turner, *St. Mark*, 78f.

[3]The Western reading is accepted by Harnack, *Probleme im Texte der Leidensgeschichte Jesu*, 11-5; Turner, *op. cit.*, 79.

[4]V. 19.   [5]*Encyclopaedia Biblica*, col. 1881.   [6]*Jesus*, 162.

It is frequently urged that the saying reveals the interests of primitive Christianity rather than the actual feelings of Jesus. R. H. Lightfoot[1] holds that we must exclude the common supposition that Mark 'in his faithfulness to historical fact . . . allows us to listen to a final and despairing utterance of Jesus, forsaken by both God and man in his extremity'. The Passion Narrative was written for the edification of the Christian communities, and, in the words in question, Jesus is to be regarded as 'claiming as his own a psalm, in which, taken as a whole, more perhaps than in any other passage of the scriptures, to judge by the use which they have made of it, the Christians found revealed to them the meaning and purpose of the passion'.[2] This view stops short of denying the genuineness of the saying, but other interpretations of the kind are clearer in this respect. Loisy, for example, thinks that Psa. xxii. dominates the accounts of the Passion, and that 'nothing was more natural than to place its opening words in the mouth of the dying Christ'.[3] In the opinion of Bultmann the Psalm provided a secondary interpretation of the last cry of Jesus mentioned in xv. 37.[4] The same view is taken by Bertram,[5] and, indeed, nearly thirty years ago it was expressed by B. W. Bacon.[6] This line of interpretation is altogether too doctrinaire to carry conviction, and is too much for an independent observer like Klausner. Jesus, as he sees Him, was 'permeated with the spirit of the Scriptures', and 'it is, on the whole, unlikely that the Church would have put such a verse into the mouth of Jesus if he had not uttered it'.[7] A more positive rejection, however, is fully justified. With the

---

[1] *Op. cit.*, 157-60.   [2] *Op. cit.*, 159.
[3] Cf. Rawlinson, 236.   [4] *Op. cit.*, 304, 342.
[5] *Op. cit.*, 83.   [6] *The Beginnings of Gospel Story*, 223.
[7] *Op. cit.*, 354.

whole Psalm at their disposal, it is incredible that the primitive communities should have passed by its radiant affirmations, and should have selected a verse which proved a rock of offence for later Evangelists, copyists, and writers. It is with a just appreciation of the difficulty of the saying that Goguel says that 'the fact that both Luke and John felt this difficulty constitutes a very strong reason for believing that the cry of dereliction is authentic'.[1] Unfortunately, we do not know precisely how the first Christians interpreted the saying; but it is difficult, if not impossible, to offer any interpretation which, in the absence of historical tradition, would have made it a suitable selection for the exercise of creative activity.

On the assumption of the genuineness of the saying different views have been taken as to its meaning.

We may dismiss at once 'the traditional interpretation', if by this is meant the view that the saying implies that Jesus was abandoned by the Father and, as a substitute for sinners, endured the pains of the lost. This is Luther's interpretation.[2] More cautiously it is expressed by Calvin,[3] with the denial, however, that Jesus endured the divine wrath; and in modern times it has been maintained by Dale.[4] Apart altogether from the ethical and theo-

---

[1] *The Life of Jesus*, 541.

[2] 'Look at Christ, who for thy sake has gone to hell and been abandoned by God as one damned for ever.' Cf. Thomasius, *Christi Person und Werk* (3rd ed.), ii. 177, cited by J. Denney, *The Christian Doctrine of Reconciliation*, 263.

[3] *Institutes*, II. xvi. 10. 'How could He be angry with the beloved Son, with whom His soul was well pleased?'. Cf. Mozley, *The Doctrine of the Atonement*, 145.

[4] *The Atonement*, 61, 360. 'Immediately before His death He was forsaken by God. When we remember the original glory in which He dwelt with the Father, His faultless perfection, and His unbroken communion with the Father during His life on earth, this is a great and awful mystery . . .,' 360.

logical objections, it is enough to say that nothing in the saying requires such an interpretation. It may be that the words imply a feeling of abandonment, and that the suffering has a penal aspect, but abandonment as an actual fact cannot justly be inferred from the cry. On this point Glover's observation is unquestionably true: 'I have sometimes thought there never was an utterance that reveals more amazingly the distance between feeling and fact.'[1]

At the opposite remove from the traditional view is the interpretation which finds in the Cry a final declaration of faith. This view is strongly maintained by J. M'Leod Campbell.[2] The words, he contends, are not a cry of desolation, but an utterance of unbroken trust. This inference is drawn from the character of Psa. xxii. as a whole, and especially verse 24:

'For he hath not despised nor abhorred the affliction of the afflicted;

Neither hath he hid his face from him;
But when he cried unto him, he heard.'

Trust in God, personal trust, it is argued, pervades the Psalm. Accordingly, it is held, the Cry from the Cross does not imply abandonment by the Father, and not even any temporary experience of being forsaken. Substantially, the same view is expressed by Carpenter who speaks of 'this last affirmation of the Kingdom' (cf. Psa. xxii. 28-31) with which Jesus died.[3] Menzies argues that 'he who quotes the first words of a poem may be thinking not of those words only but of some later part of the poem or of its general course of thought'[4]; and the contention is one which has made a wide appeal.[5]

[1] *The Jesus of History*, 192.   [2] *The Nature of the Atonement*, 240f.
[3] *The First Three Gospels*, 393.
[4] *The Earliest Gospel*.   See Rawlinson, 236.
[5] Cf. A. T. Cadoux, *The Sources of the Second Gospel*, 113.

It seems to me that this type of explanation entirely fails to explain the saying.   It is a product of reaction, of recoil from the traditional interpretation; and it is just as 'theological' as the latter.   If the Cry is meant to be a declaration of faith, it is singular, as Strauss observed long ago,[1] that Jesus should quote the verse least adapted to His purpose, and one that is expressive of the deepest misery.   It would indeed be the most tragic irony of history if death prevented the citation of the later affirmations of the Psalm, and it is not convincing to argue that these are implied in words which suggest the opposite.   It must, I think, be allowed that this type of exegesis is no more satisfactory than the former type.   Indeed, if the traditional explanation is stripped of its revolting, and unnecessary features, it is very much nearer the truth.

In contrast with the two kinds of explanation which have been considered, it seems to me best to conclude that the saying expresses a feeling of utter desolation, a sense of abandonment by the Father, an experience of defeat and despair.   If this conclusion does not agree with our theories of the Person and Work of Christ, we ought to adapt these to the implications of the saying, not to explain the latter in terms of the former.   The feeling of desolation is temporary, but it is real, and it is due, so far as it can be explained at all, to preoccupation by Jesus with the fact and burden of sin.   The suffering is not punishment directly inflicted by God, and is penal only in so far as it is a sharing in the sense of desolation and loss which sin brings in its train when it is seen and felt for what it is. Like the explanations already examined, this also is theological, but it differs from these in that it does not begin with theology but with the direct implications of the saying.   When these are accepted, it is legitimate, and neces-

[1]*Life of Jesus* (Eng. Tr. by Geo. Eliot), 5th ed., 688.

ι

sary, to relate them to the fact that Jesus interpreted His death as a suffering for the many, as sacrificial, and as standing in the closest relation to human need. If these conclusions are valid, it appears to be a necessary inference that Jesus so closely identified Himself with sinners, and experienced the horror of sin to such a degree, that for a time the closeness of His communion with the Father was broken, so that His face was obscured and He seemed to be forsaken by Him.

Present-day exposition is reluctant to draw this conclusion and shows a marked tendency to fall back on the view that we do not know exactly what was in the mind of Jesus, and are face to face with 'the supreme mystery of the Saviour's Passion'.[1] Such an attitude breathes a spirit of fine reverence which all must feel who read the saying with sympathy and understanding. Is there not, however, a real danger of reverent agnosticism becoming critical evasion?[2] It is not a question of knowing exactly what the Cry implies, but of saying whether the words: 'My God, my God, why hast thou forsaken me?' imply a sense of abandonment, and it is hard to see how the question can be answered otherwise than by saying that they do involve that inference.

Bishop Gore explained the words by saying that they suggest the agony of a righteous soul, conscious of perfect innocence, and 'finding itself, in a world which it knows to be God's world, exposed to ignominy, failure, outrage, and death, while God remains silent and does nothing'.[3]   He

---

[1]'On the assumption that our Lord really uttered the words it is better to say frankly that we do not know exactly what was in His mind at the time, that we are here face to face with the supreme mystery of the Saviour's Passion,' Rawlinson, 236.

[2]Still more is this danger present when it is explained that the verb in the saying does not mean 'leave alone', but 'leave helpless'.   Cf. Gould, 294.

[3]*The Reconstruction of Belief*, 594.

then observed that it is a cause of profoundest thankful-
ness, for all who feel the like trial in whatever degree, 'that
Christ should have asked the great question—"My God,
my God, why didst thou forsake me?"—and received no
answer'. The only inference which gives meaning to
this very true observation is that the sense of abandonment
was real; but, instead of drawing this conclusion, Gore
went on to say that he saw no reason for believing that
Jesus experienced in His spirit 'the sense of the Father's
alienation from the sinner'. This remark seems to me to
be somewhat beside the point. The desolation is felt
because Jesus loves sinners, and in loving them comes so
near to their plight as to feel in His spirit the shadows of
the Divine judgment upon sin. No doubt the exegesis of
the saying has suffered from well-meaning attempts to say
too much, but it has also suffered from the tendency to say
too little. It does not seem to me that there can be true
progress in a worthy doctrine of the Atonement until we
recognize in the saying the accents of desolation and then
ask, in the light of other sayings and wider indications of
the thought of Jesus, what is implied. The implications
are theological: the desolation is historic fact.

II

THE SAYINGS IN THE L TRADITION

THE sayings in the L tradition are as follows:

(1) The Saying about the Coming Baptism.
(2) The Reply to Herod Antipas.
(3) The Saying about the Suffering of the Son of Man.
(4) The Sayings at the Last Supper.
(5) The Sayings in the Conversations after the Supper.
(6) The Saying at the Arrest about the Power of Darkness.
(7) The Crucifixion Sayings.

It will be seen that these sayings are fewer in number than those in Mark. It must be remembered, however, that the L Source is less than two-thirds the size of Mark, and that, relatively to its size, it is almost as rich as Mark in sayings of the kind. Parallels to the Markan sayings have already been mentioned as they appear, and the question how far the L sayings are independent of Mark will receive constant attention in the discussion.

(1) THE SAYING ABOUT THE COMING BAPTISM (Lk. xii. 49f.).

49. *'I came to cast fire upon the earth;*
And what will I, if it is already kindled?
50. *But I have a baptism to be baptized with;*
And how am I straitened till it be accomplished?'

The passage is followed in Lk. xii. 51-3 by sayings which speak of the sufferings and 'divisions' which are to ensue. To these sayings, but not to Lk. xii. 49f., there

in spite of the verbal similarities; for ix. 22 is Markan,[1] while xvii. 23-37 is from Q, and in the Third Gospel there is no certain example of a Markan insertion in a Q context.[2]   The presumption, therefore, is that Luke derived the saying from L.   If, however, he found xvii. 25 in its present context, an earlier compiler must have taken it from L, since, on this hypothesis, derivation from Mark is even more improbable.   Even if the passage is a comment, rather than a saying, it still reflects a belief, current in a non-Markan circle, that Jesus had spoken of His suffering as the Son of Man.   Whatever, therefore, may be the precise history of xvii. 25, there is good reason to trace the passage to the L tradition.[3]

Among recent writers Otto[4] and Goguel[5] have noted the importance of this saying.

Otto's view of its place in the development of the thought of Jesus in relation to His Messianic suffering has already been indicated in the discussion of Mk. viii. 31, ix. 31, and x. 33f.   In sayings such as Lk. xii. 50; Mk. ix. 12b, ix. 31a, and Lk. xvii. 25, he sees the simplest and most reliable examples of genuine prophetic anticipation.   Of the first of these sayings he declares that no one at a later time would have invented a *vaticinium ex eventu* in such a form.   The formulation is clearer in Mk. ix. 12b, and Lk. xvii. 25, he says, corresponds to it.

In the opinion of Goguel Lk. xvii. 25 falls into a different category from the triple announcement of suffering,

---

[1]Cf. Mk. viii. 31.

[2]Cf. *Behind the Third Gospel*, 161f., and for the view that Mk. is not used in Lk. ix. 51–xviii. 14 see J. C. Hawkins, *Oxford Studies in the Synoptic Problem*, 29-59.

[3]W. Bussmann (*Synoptische Studien*, ii. 92, 131) agrees with B. Weiss (*Die Quellen des Lukasevangeliums*, 86) in tracing the saying to Q, in spite of the absence of a parallel in Mt.

[4]*Reich Gottes und Menschensohn*, 312.   [5]*The Life of Jesus*, 390-2.

death, and resurrection in Mk. viii. 31, ix. 31, x. 33f.   In these passages he sees 'a certain theological basis'; Lk. xvii. 25, on the other hand, makes no mention of death and resurrection, and 'cannot have been invented by tradition'.   Goguel is very much on his guard against any attempt to introduce into the interpretation of the saying later doctrines of redemption.   He describes it as expressing the result of the meditations of Jesus and says that 'all it affirms is that his sufferings will be efficacious'. On his own interpretation of the saying this is a patent understatement, for he says that Jesus 'had the assurance that his sufferings formed part of the plan which God, in his infinite wisdom, had designed for the establishment of his Kingdom', and claims that the sacrifice Jesus accepted 'reinforced the sense of vocation itself'.[1]   'Jesus', he says, 'did not believe that he was the Messiah *although* he had to suffer; he believed that he was the Messiah *because* he had to suffer.   This is the great paradox, the great originality, of his Gospel.'[2]   Obviously, very much more than 'simply a directly religious affirmation' is involved in a saying like Lk. xvii. 25 which voices the necessity of suffering and rejection.   A saying of this kind is dogmatic as well as religious, even if the dogma is not that of later theological systems.   It is dogmatic in the sense that it involves a theory, however broadly it may be expressed, in respect of the conditions under which the Kingdom comes or is established.   One is reminded of the claim of Schweitzer that the resolve to suffer and to die and the prediction of the sufferings 'are dogmatic, and therefore historical; because they find their explanation in eschatological conceptions'.[3]   Whether the conceptions are not more than

---

[1]*Op. cit.*, 391.   [2]*Op. cit.*, 392.
[3]*The Quest of the Historical Jesus*, 385.

eschatological remains to be considered, and certainly they are not expressed in the saying under review.   This particular saying is valuable because, as coming from another source, it broadens the basis for the assertion that Jesus was convinced that He 'must suffer' in fulfilling His strong sense of vocation.

(4) THE SAYINGS CONNECTED WITH THE LAST SUPPER (Lk. xxii. 15f., 17f.).

14. 'And when the hour was come, he sat down, and the apostles
15. with him.   And he said unto them, *With desire I have desired to eat this passover with you before I suffer: for I say*
16. *unto you, I will not eat it, until it be fulfilled in the kingdom of*
17. *God.*   And he received a cup, and when he had given thanks,
18. he said, *Take this, and divide it among yourselves: for I say unto you, I will not drink from henceforth of the fruit of the vine,*
19. *until the kingdom of God shall come.*   And he took bread, and when he had given thanks, he brake it, and gave unto them, saying, *This is my body* [*which is given for you: this do in re-*
20. *membrance of me.*   And the cup in like manner after supper, saying, *This cup is the new covenant in my blood, even that which is poured out for you*].'

Of these sayings 15f. is peculiar to Lk.   There is a parallel to 18 in Mk. xiv. 25, but probably the two are independent versions of the same saying.   To the sayings in 19f. there are close parallels in 1 Cor. xi. 24f. and Mk. xiv. 22, 24.   19*b*, 20 are omitted in D and in the Old Latin MSS., a b e ff² i l.

It is impossible to discuss the Lukan sayings adequately without giving some attention to the narrative as a whole.   From the critical point of view this narrative is of great interest because, to some extent, it is possible to see how a relatively simple story has been developed into a narrative of Institution.   As the textual evidence suggests, 19*b*, 20 is a subsequent scribal addition based almost

entirely on 1 Cor. xi. 24f.[1]   Several critics have also held
that 19a is an interpolation,[2] but no manuscript evidence
favours this view, except the fact that the passage follows
16 in some Old Latin MSS. (b and e) and in the Old
Syriac.[3]   But if 19a is original, it is clear that it has been
derived from Mk. xiv. 22[4] by the Evangelist and that
14-18 represents the original account in the L Source.
The additions made by Luke (19a) and by later copyists
(19b, 20) are successive attempts to bring the narrative in
L into line with the Markan and Pauline stories.

If this critical reconstruction is sound, Lk. xxii. 14-18
is invested with the greatest interest and serious historical
problems are raised.   In this passage there are no words
of institution and there is no reference to the bread, while
the two sayings in 15f. and 18 are eschatological in content.   Is such a narrative conceivable in an early source,
and, if so, what bearing has it upon the parallel accounts
in Mark and 1 Cor. xi. 23-5?

So brief is the original account that it is not surprising
that some scholars have found its continuation in 28-30.
Bacon sees the narrative of Luke's special source in
15-19a, 28-34,[5] and Otto finds the sequel to 19a in
29f.[6]

The effect of Otto's rearrangement is striking, and it
leads to most interesting suggestions.   By bringing the
saying: 'And I appoint unto you a kingdom . . .' (29f.)

---

[1] Cf. Hort, *Introduction*, Appendix, 63f.; Creed, 263f.; Easton, 321f.
Among recent writers Goguel accepts the longer text, on the ground that it
explains the textual variants, *op. cit.*, 447, 458-60. Dibelius explains 19b,
20 as a third variant which has proceeded further than Mk. xiv. and 1 Cor.
in the development of the explanatory words of institution, *op. cit.*, 210.

[2] Cf. Blass, *The Philology of the Gospels*, 179ff.

[3] With additions this arrangement is found in sy[sc]. sy[p] omits 17f.

[4] Cf. *Behind the Third Gospel*, 37.   [5] *The Gospel of Mark*, 178ff.

[6] *Reich Gottes und Menschensohn*, 227-34.

into immediate connexion with the words: 'This is my
body,' he is able to develop the argument that it is, as the
One who is to be 'broken', that Jesus gives to His
disciples the inheritance of the Kingdom.   He does this
because He takes upon Himself the suffering of death and
imparts to them a share in its atoning and consecrating
power.[1]

It may well be that Otto has rightly heard the under-
tones of the great saying in 29f., but it is doubtful if the
critical foundations of his exegesis are sound.   It is entirely justifiable to argue, as Otto does, that the sections
21-3 (The Prediction of the Betrayal) and 24-7 (The Discourse on True Greatness) are inserted by the Evangelist
into his source, for these are self-contained sections which
may well have existed independently of their present connexion,[2] and there is certainly a marked similarity in the
subject-matter of 29f. and 18.   It is also with justice that
Otto rejects Wellhausen's view that 19*a* is a scribal insertion.[3]   But can this passage, which is in almost verbatim
agreement with Mk. xiv. 22, be regarded as anything else
but a Markan insertion made by the Evangelist in his
source?   It is also open to serious question whether Otto
is justified in cancelling 28[4] as a redactional supplement
because the πειρασμοί still lie in the future both for
Jesus and His disciples.   Jesus speaks only of His own
'trials', which without difficulty can be found in His conflicts with the scribes,[5] and as regards His disciples He
says no more than that they have 'continued with' Him.
If therefore the Evangelist has inserted 21-7, it is better
to find the original account of the Supper in 14-8, 28-30;
and indeed there is a natural transition between 18, in

[1]*Op. cit.*, 246.   [2]*Op. cit.*, 228-31.   [3]*Op. cit.*, 227.

[4]*Op. cit.*, 231.   [5]Cf. also Mk. viii. 33 and Lk. iv. 13.

M

which Jesus speaks of Himself, and 28 where He addresses the disciples. All reconstructions of this kind, however, are speculative, and in the present inquiry 28-30 will be treated separately.

However the Lukan account of the Supper is delimited, the problem of its restricted character remains. One possible explanation is that the Evangelist regarded the narrative of institution as an *arcanum fidei*, to be reserved for believers but hidden from profane eyes. This explanation has been put forward by H. N. Bate,[1] and more recently by J. Jeremias[2] who has long held this view. Jeremias argues that the tendency manifest in the Lukan account is further illustrated in the silence of the Epistle to the Hebrews and especially in the Fourth Gospel. He explains the greater detail in the Markan account by tracing the source back to the period before 49-50 A.D. to which the teaching contained in the Pauline narrative of 1 Cor. xi. 23-5 (written in 55 A.D.) belongs. On this theory it remains a difficulty that, even if the source used by Mark was so early, the account was made public in his Gospel when published in 65-70 A.D., and that, with greater detail, it was repeated in the First Gospel some fifteen or twenty years later. This objection is not conclusive, for the practice of secret discipline reserved for the elect need not have been universal. None the less, the explanation cannot be said to be more than a possibility which may be true.

An alternative explanation accounts for the Lukan narrative by the dominance of the eschatological interests which it reveals. It is this aspect of the Supper which specially appealed to the mind of the community in which the account was current, and it is this supreme interest

---

[1] *Journal of Theological Studies*, July, 1927, p. 367f.
[2] *Die Abendmahlsworte Jesu* (1935), 45ff.

which determined the elements in the tradition which were emphasized.   The existing liturgical practice may also have given prominence to the distribution of the wine and to the saying of Jesus which anticipates the joys of the perfected Kingdom.   It is not to be assumed that the tradition relating to the bread, or other words of institution, were unknown to the community; they were taken for granted, and possibly at an early stage in its history their full significance was not appreciated as in other communities.   If the Lukan account is regarded as a narrative of institution and a record of what was said and done, its omissions are serious indeed; but such an assumption is the delusion of an obsolete criticism, least of all to be entertained by *formgeschichtliche* critics, since they trace the origin of narratives to the interests of primitive communities.   Such a narrative as Luke gives must be judged by its contents, and not by its omissions. Elements that are omitted are not thereby compromised, but must be judged in connexion with the narratives which contain them.

Of the alternative explanations given above the second appears to be the better, but, in view of our very limited knowledge of the conditions under which such narratives were formed, either may be true; it is even possible that both the desire for secrecy[1] and the eschatological interests of the community were formative factors.   In any case, it is precarious to set the Lukan narrative over against the Markan and to argue that one is historical and the other is not.   In view of its contents the Lukan narrative is undoubtedly primitive, but it is not a standard by which other accounts are to be judged.

[1] Cf. Dalman: 'It is . . . not incredible that the words in connexion with the wine were *suppressed*, since they might be misunderstood, and lead to accusations against Christ's followers . . .' *Jesus-Jeshua*, 156.

(*a*) 'And he said unto them, *With desire I have desired to eat this passover with you before I suffer: for I say unto you, I will not eat it, until it be fulfilled in the kingdom of God*' (Lk. xxii. 15f.).

The Western reading: 'I will *no longer* eat it' (cf. A.V.) is probably an assimilation to the text of Mk. xiv. 25. So also the reading: 'until it be *eaten new*'.

F. C. Burkitt and A. E. Brooke have argued that the saying implies that the Supper was not the Passover Meal.[1] Jesus has earnestly desired to keep the feast, but He sees that death will prevent Him from doing so; He therefore says that He will not eat the Passover until it be fulfilled in the kingdom of God. This interpretation is also supported by R. H. Kennett[2] and others, and, although it is by no means universally accepted,[3] it seems to me to give the natural sense of the saying.

It is probable that Luke himself identified the Supper with the Passover Meal, since in xxii. 7 he emphasizes the fact that on the day of unleavened bread 'the passover *must be* sacrificed' (cf. Mk. xiv. 12); but it may well be that the saying itself implies that the Supper is not the Passover Meal, since so strong a desire is associated with so emphatic a statement that He will not eat 'until it be fulfilled in the kingdom of God'. In this case, the L Source was in agreement with the Fourth Gospel[4] as regards the date of the Supper;[5] and, in composing his Gos-

---

[1]*The Journal of Theological Studies*, ix. 569-72; xvii. 295.

[2]*The Church of Israel*, 211; W. M. Ramsay, *Expository Times*, xxi. 344.

[3]It is rejected by J. M. Creed, 265, and is not referred to by B. S. Easton.

[4]Cf. Jn. xviii. 28; xix. 14.

[5]Streeter says of Lk. xxii. 15 that the words 'suggest, though they do not quite compel, the view that *in his source* the Last Supper was conceived as taking place on the day before the Passover,' *The Four Gospels*, 423. R. H. Lightfoot says that the words may almost be described as 'the despair of

pel, Luke must have abandoned its representation under the influence of Mark.[1]   In maintaining this view there is no need to suggest that Luke has substituted the word 'Passover' for an original reference to a common meal, for there is every reason to think that Jesus spoke of the Passover.   It is especially in relation to the celebration of a Passover that the strong emotion under which He spoke is intelligible.   Moreover, the Markan story of Preparations for the Passover (Mk. xiv. 12-6) illustrates His intention to partake of this feast.   On this interpretation of Lk. xxii. 15, it is not of the meal which is in progress that Jesus speaks when He says that He 'will not eat', but of the Passover Meal, and the fulfilment to which He looks is that of the Messianic Feast of the Kingdom.

The points discussed above are matters of considerable historical interest, but they do not seriously affect the question of the significance of the Supper.   Even if the Supper is not the Passover Meal, the saying reveals how strongly Paschal associations dominated the mind of Jesus.   For the purposes of our investigation its most important exegetical features are the references to suffering and to the consummation of the Kingdom.

The phrase, 'before I suffer,' in which no object to the verb is expressed, is felt by Dalman to be strange, especially in Aramaic;[2] and it may be that it summarizes, in

commentators'.   'They appear to support the view of the preceding verses that the last supper was a passover, and thus serve to bind the narrative together; but at the same time they certainly suggest that our Lord did not partake of it, and in this way they help to explain the absence of any passover reference in the story of the meal itself,' *History and Interpretation in the Gospels*, 168.

[1] I have treated this point more fully in *Behind the Third Gospel*, 35-40.

[2] *Op. cit.*, 128.   Dalman suggests that one expects: 'Until I suffer *according to all that is written concerning me*' (cf. Lk. xxii. 37).   The critical objections which would be raised against such a text can easily be imagined.

what later came to be conventional language, the actual words of Jesus.   That the thought of His suffering filled His mind at this time, is already clear; the remarkable feature in the saying is the association of this thought with a cry of longing relating to the Passover.   Why does Jesus earnestly desire to eat the Passover before He suffers?   The answer can only be that the Passover has a special significance for Him in connexion with His Passion.   Does this fact suggest that Jeremias is right in maintaining that Jesus interpreted His death by means of ideas connected with the shedding of the blood of the Passover Lamb at the departure from Egypt?[1]   The brevity of the Lukan account does not permit of a decided answer, but it is significant that the question arises in a narrative in which eschatological interests are almost supreme.   The correct conclusion to draw is that if this interpretation is valid in Mk. xiv. 24, where Jesus speaks of His 'blood of the covenant', it is in harmony with the present Lukan saying.   The same inference is supported by the reference to the Messianic Feast in the perfected Kingdom.   This feast is the expression of a consummated fellowship, anticipated by Jesus with a certainty which admits of no doubt.   He expects to eat that feast in company with His disciples, and had desired to celebrate the Passover as, in some sense, its anticipation.   Meantime His sufferings lie near.   The conclusion is irresistible that He regarded His death as an activity making the consummation possible.   This conviction is entirely in agreement with the thought that His blood is covenant-blood.   Whether Jeremias supplies the right foundation for this thought, or whether it is to be sought in Ex. xxiv. 8, remains the secret of Mk. xiv. 24, and to its solution Lk. xxii. 15f. contributes no more than the proof that

[1]See p. 138f and the discussion of Mk. xiv. 24.

Paschal associations filled the mind of Jesus at the Supper.[1]

(*b*) 'And he received a cup, and when he had given thanks, he said, *Take this, and divide it among yourselves:* (18) *for I say unto you, I will not drink from henceforth of the fruit of the vine, until the kingdom of God shall come*' (Lk. xxii. 17f.; cf. Mk. xiv. 25).

The saying in verse 17 occupies the place filled in the Markan account by the words: 'This is my blood of the covenant, which is shed for many.' It is obviously a different saying, but, in narratives which are not reports, there is no reason to infer that the one excludes the other, since more was actually said at the Supper than any one narrative records.

Otto understands the receiving of the cup in the light of Psa. cxvi. 13: 'I will take the cup of salvation, and call on the name of the Lord,' and explains the giving of thanks as the dedication of the cup by the use of the ancient formula: 'Blessed art Thou, Eternal, our God, King of the world, who hast made the fruit of the vine.'[2] It would have been a breach of custom, as observed at the Passover and at other sacred meals, if Jesus Himself had not first drunk of the cup,[3] and although the narrative contains no explicit statement, the fact of participation is probably implied in verse 18.[4]

[1] Otto's suggestion that Lk. xxii. 16 is a redactional assimilation to xxii. 18 is unacceptable because the former saying refers to the Passover and the latter to the Supper itself. There is no reason why an anticipation of the Messianic Feast should not be expressed in both, especially as the anticipation is so strong. Cf. *Reich Gottes und Menschensohn*, 234f.

[2] *Op. cit.*, 242f. Dalman suggests that the traditional words: 'Blessed art Thou who hast created the fruit of the vine', were used, but also says that other benedictions were attached to the wine cup, and, like Otto, refers to Psa. cxvi. 13. Cf. *Jesus-Jeshua*, 150.

[3] Cf. Plummer, 495f.   [4] See below.

The saying in verse 18 is also recorded in Mk. xiv. 25.[1] In spite of natural verbal similarities, it is probable that the two versions are independent,[2] and that of the two the Markan is more original.   The Lukan phrase, 'until the kingdom of God shall come,' appears to ignore the true sense in which Jesus believed the Kingdom to have come already, and seems to be a summary edition of the more original words preserved in Mark: 'until that day when I drink it new in the kingdom of God.'   Some critics[3] think that, in placing the saying at the beginning of the meal, Luke is more original than Mark who records it at the end. This opinion has some justification for certainly the words are loosely appended to Mk. xiv. 24, but the point is not one which can be established.

The meaning of the saying has already been considered in discussing Mk. xiv. 25, but, while it undoubtedly anticipates the joys of the perfected Kingdom, there are special features which emerge in Lk. xxii. 17f.   The word 'for' is interesting, and, if the saying is in its right position, it is significant.   The meaning cannot be: 'Do you share the cup; I will not, until the Messianic Feast,' for no reason is thereby given why He should not drink now.   The antithesis suggested is rather that between the Messianic Feast and the entire action of the present on the part of Jesus and His disciples.   The suggestion is that to drink now is to anticipate the Messianic Banquet, and, for this reason, one must infer that Jesus drank first; otherwise the saying loses its meaning.[4]   But the

[1]See pp. 139ff.

[2]Easton observes that a different Greek wording would hardly have been possible, *St. Luke*, 322f.

[3]Cf. Otto, *op. cit.*, 244; Jeremias, *op. cit.*, 63.

[4]Wellhausen says that to read out of Lk. xxii. 17 that Jesus Himself did not drink is an incredible playing with words (*unglaubliche Wortklauberei*), *Das Evangelium Marci*, 116n.

change to the first person remains to be accounted for:
why does Jesus say so pointedly: 'I will not drink from
henceforth'? The answer can only be that He is thinking
of His approaching death; He can no more share with
them the cup as He is doing now. Thus, the present
fellowship is a farewell meal as well as an anticipation of
the future. The thought lies very near that there had
been other meals of the kind, without the special associations created by the approach of separation and death; and
probably Schweitzer is right in finding the historical basis
of the meals described in Mk. vi. 35-44 and viii. 1-10 in
'eschatological sacraments'.[1] The further suggestion
that, although Jesus would no longer drink with them,
they themselves would continue to keep the feast, is not
excluded; but it is to strain the meaning of the saying un-
warrantably to see in it the equivalent of a command and a
virtual institution of the Christian Eucharist.[2] The explicit command: 'This do, as oft as ye drink it, in remembrance of me,' is attested only by St. Paul,[3] and, of the
Synoptic narratives, all that can be said is that they are not
inconsistent with this tradition and do not exclude it by
their silence. The importance of Lk. xxii. 17f. is the
close association it establishes between the Supper, the
approaching death, and the consummation of the Kingdom in the thought of Jesus. The certainty of the consummation, so quietly assumed, gives urgency to the
command to share the cup now as the expression of a

---

[1] *The Quest of the Historical Jesus*, 374-80.

[2] Cf. N. P. Williams, *Essays Catholic and Critical*, 402-7. The Kingdom of God is not the Christian Church and faith, nor is the Messianic
Banquet the Eucharist. There is no justification for the interpretation:
'The next time that we shall meet together on such an occasion as this, I
shall still be the Host, though present invisibly, and not in tangible form,'
op. cit., 406. See O. C. Quick, *The Christian Sacraments*, 191n.

[3] 1 Cor. xi. 25. See pp. 206ff.

fellowship unmenaced by death. Far from being
threatened by separation, the fellowship is the more intense as death draws near.   But what is the closer relationship between the Supper and the death, the saying
does not disclose, and for this significance it is necessary
to examine other sayings.   What Lk. xxii. 17f. does permit us to say is that the connexion is intimate and that, in
the expression of fellowship, death is faced with uncon-
quered hope and certainty.

(5) SAYINGS IN THE CONVERSATIONS AFTER THE SUPPER (Lk. xxii.
    27, 28-30, 37).

Unlike Mk., the Third Gospel contains the account of
certain conversations between Jesus and His disciples before the departure to the Mount of Olives, and in this
respect it approximates to the arrangement of the Fourth
Gospel (cf. Jn. xiii.-xvi.).   Three sayings are specially
important in view of their bearing upon the attitude of
Jesus to His suffering and death.   These are (a) the saying concerning service (xxii. 27); (b) the words about the
disciples in the New Age (xxii. 28-30); and (c) the application by Jesus to Himself of the words of Isa. liii. 12: 'And
he was reckoned with transgressors' (xxii. 37).

(a) '*I am in the midst of you as he that serveth*' (Lk. xxii. 27; cf. Mk.
    x. 41-5).

This passage claims attention because of its theme and
its position.   Both Lk. xxii. 24-7 and Mk. x. 41-5[1] are
concerned with the subject of service, but it is probable
that they are derived from different sources.[2]   That Luke

[1]See pp. 99ff.

[2]Cf. Wellhausen, *Das Evangelium Lucae*, 123; Creed, 267; Easton, 324;
Streeter, *The Four Gospels*, 210.   Possibly, the reference to a 'contention'

owes the section to Mark is most unlikely, in view of the differences of vocabulary, of substance, and of position. Moreover, its agreement with the Johannine story of the Feetwashing (xiii. 1-17) suggests that, in associating the words with the Supper, Luke is following a definite tradition;[1] for it is hazardous to maintain that Jn. xiii. 1-17 is a free composition based on Lk. xxii. 24-7.

The importance of Lk. xxii. 27 for our investigation is that, while it does not refer to suffering and death, it illustrates the dominating place which the thought of service occupied in the mind of Jesus on the last night of His life. 'Service', however, is a very elastic term, and nothing could be more misleading than to give it some general humanitarian significance, and then to suppose that this is the meaning which Jesus found in His life and death. The words probably echo the ideas of Isa. liii., but of this we cannot be certain.

(b) '*But ye are they which have continued with me in my temptations;* (29) *and I appoint unto you a kingdom, even as my Father appointed unto me,* (30) *that ye may eat and drink at my table in my kingdom; and ye shall sit on thrones judging the twelve tribes of Israel*' (Lk. xxii. 28-30; cf. Mt. xix. 28).

The parallel to vv. 28, 30 in Mt. xix. 28 is inserted in a Markan context as a reply to the words of Peter: 'Lo, we have left all, and have followed thee' (Mk. x. 28).   This position is inferior to that in Lk., since the insertion breaks the excellent connexion between Peter's words and the reply of Jesus: 'Verily I say unto you, There is no man that hath left house . . .' (Mk. x. 29).

(Lk. xxii. 24) is an echo of what is stated in Mk. x. 41 ('And when the ten heard it, they began to be moved with indignation concerning James and John').   In *The Formation of the Gospel Tradition*, 154, I have argued that, in early tradition, there is a tendency for details to pass over from one story to another.

[1]This view is not affected by the possibility that Luke has inserted the passage into its present context.   See p. 177.

As we have already seen, some scholars bring this saying, or part of it, into closer connexion with the giving of the cup.[1]   The suggestion has much in its favour, but, in view of its speculative character, it is best to take the passage as it stands, since, whatever its original position may have been, it is closely associated with the Supper.

It is as a saying strongly influenced by the prospect of death that the words call for notice here; for, although there is no direct reference to death, what is said is spoken in view of its swift approach.   The πειρασμοί, through which the disciples have 'continued with' Jesus, may be the trials preceding the Messianic Age, but are better explained as the conflicts and struggles of His Ministry, especially those connected with the prospect of His Messianic suffering and death.   During these trials the disciples had been far from entering into His mind and purpose, but always He had been able to count on their fidelity.   For this reason He now announces to them the certainty of their part in the perfected Kingdom.

Verse 29 is not easy to interpret.   The common meaning of διατίθεμαι is 'I appoint', or 'assign', but it is probable that in this saying it reflects the use of the Biblical διαθήκη = 'covenant', and should therefore be rendered 'I covenant'.[2]   It is best to find the object of the verb in the clause: 'that ye may eat and drink, . . .' and to reserve βασιλείαν, in the sense of 'lordship' or 'kingly rule,'[3]

---

[1]See pp. 176ff.

[2]Cf. Creed, 269.   Easton, 325, suggests 'appoint'; cf. Moffatt's translation.   Wellhausen, *Das Evangelium Lucae*, 123f., prefers 'bequeath'. Otto, *Reich Gottes und Menschensohn*, 226, points out the advantage of English in the use of the verb 'to covenant'.

[3]As distinct from τῇ βασιλείᾳ, 'the Kingdom,' in 30.   Cf. Wellhausen, *op. cit.*, 124; Klostermann, *Das Lukasevangelium*, 212.

as the object of διέθετο.[1] On this view, the saying may be translated: 'Even as my Father covenanted unto me lordship, I covenant unto you that ye shall eat and drink at my table in my kingdom.'[2] The idea is that, in virtue of the royal power which He has received from His Father, Jesus can guarantee their participation in the joy of the perfected rule of God.

In verse 30 the further promise is made that the disciples will be rulers[3] in the New Age: they will 'sit on thrones judging the twelve tribes of Israel'. Some scholars think that these words are unsuitable in their present position, since the promise is made to the Twelve (cf. Mt. xix. 28). But this is so only in Matthew. Luke may have omitted the reference to 'twelve' thrones, while retaining the phrase 'the twelve tribes', in order 'to soften the awkwardness' of the saying;[4] but it is just as possible, and even more probable, that Matthew has inserted the number.[5] It is fully in keeping with the drift of 29 that in 30 the disciples are invested with authority, and the phrase 'the twelve tribes of Israel' is a conventional expression for the members of the Kingdom. Bultmann's view is that the saying is a formation of the primitive Palestinian community: the speaker is the Risen Christ, and 'in it first were the Twelve regarded as rulers of Israel in the New Aeon'.[6] Neither argument is weighty. The

---

[1]Cf. Creed, 269; Easton, 325. See also the punctuation of WH. Most commentators take the noun with both verbs; cf. Plummer, 502. For the freer use of ἵνα in Hellenistic Greek with the subjunctive, see J. H. Moulton, *Prolegomena*, 206ff.

[2]Codex D, some Old Latin MSS., and the Curetonian Syriac omit 'my' possibly correctly.

[3]Wellhausen remarks : 'κρίνειν is "to rule" as often in the Old Testament,' *Das Evangelium Matthaei*, 99. Cf. Easton, 325.

[4]Montefiore, *The Synoptic Gospels*, ii. 599.

[5]Note the context of Mt. xix. 28.

[6]*Die Geschichte der synoptischen Tradition*, 170f.

first is a mere assumption; the second offers no reason why Jesus is not the speaker. As Luke records them, the words are perfectly relevant to the situation, and, in the absence of forcible objections, their marked Semitic character points to their originality.

The importance of the entire saying is the revelation which it gives of the strong consciousness of authority which Jesus possessed in relation to the Kingdom; He is endowed by the Father with the powers of royal rule. Equally clear is His certainty concerning the consummation of the Kingdom and His right to assign to the disciples the part they are to play in its life; invested with power, He can give them their place and set them their task in the New Age. Few sayings of His breathe such an air of certainty and authority. But the full significance of the words is that they are uttered in the prospect of rejection and death. In the light of this fact no theory is tenable which implies any opposition to be overcome between Himself and God, which interprets His death as defeat, or which limits its meaning to narrowly individual relationships. Jesus goes to death in the assurance that His Father has given Him lordship, that the Kingdom will be perfected, and that His disciples will share in its joys and its duties. That such convictions should be expressed in such an hour is inexplicable unless He believes that His suffering and death manifest His lordship and in some way are necessary to the consummation of the Divine Rule.

(c) '*For I say unto you, that this which is written must be fulfilled in me, And he was reckoned with transgressors: for that which concerneth me hath an end*' (Lk. xxii. 37).

This saying, which is peculiar to Luke, can be studied

with advantage only when it is read in the context in which it appears:

'(35) And he said unto them, When I sent you forth without purse, and wallet, and shoes, lacked ye anything? And they said, Nothing. (36) And he said unto them, But now, he that hath a purse, let him take it, and likewise a wallet: and he that hath none, let him sell his cloke, and buy a sword. (37) *For I say unto you, that this which is written must be fulfilled in me, And he was reckoned with transgressors: for that which concerneth me hath an end.* (38) And they said, Lord, behold, here are two swords. And he said unto them, It is enough.'

Some scholars take the view that this section is an artificial unit. Loisy, for example, as Creed reminds us,[1] suggests that the Evangelist has awkwardly constructed the whole on the simple fact of the resistance recorded in the source of Mark. Wellhausen also connects 38 with 49: 'And when they that were about him saw what would follow, they said, Lord, shall we smite with the sword?'[2] This view carries with it the further inference that 35f. belongs to a different situation when preparations for a dangerous journey were under consideration. Actual resistance, it is suggested, may have been contemplated, or at least defence against attack. 'He hopes', says Johannes Weiss, 'that his disciples will cut their way through.'[3] 'Let us lead the lives of brigands and arm ourselves,' is the interpretation of Goguel.[4] In some of these discussions it is not surprising that 37, or at least 37*a*, is described as an insertion.[5]

There does not appear to be any need for reconstruc-

---

[1] *St. Luke*, 270.   [2] *Das Evangelium Lucae*, 125ff.

[3] See Montefiore, *The Synoptic Gospels*, ii. 603.

[4] *The Life of Jesus*, 454. See also Loisy, *L'Évangile selon Luc*, 521ff.; Ed. Meyer, *Ursprung und Anfänge des Christentums*, i. 182f.

[5] Cf. Creed, 271; Klostermann, *Das Lukasevangelium*, 214.

tions, or for the view that real swords and physical resistance are contemplated. Burkitt gives a true estimate of
the section when he says: 'They are among the saddest
words in the Gospels, and the mournful irony with which
they are pervaded seems to me wholly alien from the kind
of utterance which a Christian Evangelist would invent
for his Master.'[1] 'It is impossible to believe', he observes, 'that the command to buy a sword was meant literally and seriously: it is all a piece of ironical foreboding.'[2]
Every detail in the section is true to the situation in which
Jesus found Himself on the last night of His earthly life
and can readily be understood in relation thereto.

The most probable explanation of the reference to the
buying of a sword is that Jesus is speaking metaphorically.[3] He is thinking of the position in which the
disciples will find themselves after His death. The circumstances will be entirely different from those which obtained when first He sent them forth to announce the good
news of the Kingdom. Then there was no need to provide purse, wallet, and shoes, since normally a friendly
reception might be expected. Now the conditions are
different; He is about to die, and the hostility which faces
Himself may well confront them. His words : 'He that
hath a purse, let him take it, and likewise a wallet: and he
that hath none, let him sell his cloke, and buy a sword,'
are His picturesque way of saying this. He has no
thought of advocating the use of swords or begging-bags.
If this is a correct interpretation, the succeeding reference
to Isa. liii. 12 is entirely apposite. It exactly describes
His own situation and is the clue to His apprehensions for
the Twelve. The manner in which the quotation is intro-

---

[1] *The Gospel History and its Transmission*, 140f.   [2] *Op. cit.*, 141.
[3] Cf. Creed: 'in a general sense as a warning that disaster is coming,' 270;
Easton, 328; Luce, 335.

duced is natural. Jesus does not say as an interpolator might have said: 'This which is written *of me* must be fulfilled,' but: 'This which is written must be fulfilled *in me*'; in other words: 'What is said in Scripture about the Servant must find fulfilment in my case.' It is notable also, as Burkitt has observed,[1] that the quotation does not follow the text of the Septuagint: ἐν τοῖς ἀνόμοις, but reads: μετὰ ἀνόμων. The use of the quotation is even more effective if, as some commentators[2] suggest, the following words: καὶ γὰρ τὸ περὶ ἐμοῦ τέλος ἔχει, are rendered: 'For my life draws to its end.' In this case, Jesus justifies His use of the passage; on the ordinary rendering: 'that which concerneth me hath fulfilment,' or 'an end', the introductory words: 'that which is written must be fulfilled in me,' are only repeated in another form. That Jesus should have been misunderstood by the Twelve is part of the dramatic irony of a tense situation. The cry: 'Lord, behold, here are two swords,' reveals the fact that they have merely caught the surface meaning of His words; and it is the perception of this which draws from Him words which are both a formula of dismissal[3] and an utterance of the deepest sadness: 'It is enough.'[4]

Although this passage is the only express citation from Isa. liii. in the recorded sayings of Jesus, its genuineness ought not to be in doubt: it is naturally related to the context and has every appearance of being a spontaneous utterance. Its presence in the L tradition confirms the

---

[1]*Op. cit.*, 141.

[2]Cf. Klostermann: 'denn mein Lebensgeschick hat (jetzt) sein Ende,' *Das Lukasevangelium*, 214; Luce, 336. See Lk. xxiv. 19, 27; Acts i. 3; xviii. 25; Phil. i. 27, where the article is used in the plural.

[3]Cf. Deut. iii. 26 (LXX).

[4]Cf. Plummer, 507; Creed, 271; Luce, 335.

N

view that Jesus had deeply pondered the description of the Suffering Servant and saw it as a foreshadowing of His own experience of suffering and death.   It is difficult to agree with Burkitt that, in its context, the saying 'suggests that He hardly regarded the passage (Isa. liii. 12) as specifically "Messianic".'[1]   The solemn earnestness with which the words are quoted and the statement that they 'must' be fulfilled in Himself, point to a consciousness of vocation.   In citing the words Jesus has heard the voice of destiny, and the destiny can hardly be other than that of Messiahship as He understood it.   At the same time it must be agreed that the quotation is not an obvious selection from the Servant-poem.   It is certainly not the one which an interpolator would have fixed upon.   Why does Jesus choose just this passage?   The most probable answer is that on this, the very eve of His Passion, Jesus is preoccupied with the thought that He is to be treated by hostile men as a wrong-doer; He will be reckoned with transgressors.   Is there also implied the deeper thought that, in a way unsuspected by men, He is indeed to be reckoned with transgressors since He has taken their side and made Himself one with them ($\mu\epsilon\tau\grave{\alpha}$ $\grave{\alpha}\nu\acute{o}\mu\omega\nu$)? This thought is not explicit in His words, but it is a natural reflection in the mind of one who had pondered the Servant-conception and who quotes a passage immediately followed by the words: 'yet he bare the sin of many, and made intercession for the transgressors' (Isa. liii. 12).[2]   In any case, and however we explain the saying, the use of the quotation is a clear indication that on this last night Jesus was deeply conscious of the menace of evil and of the threat of its apparent triumph in His death.

[1] *Christian Beginnings*, 37.

[2] Cf. Lk. xxiii. 34: 'Father, forgive them: for they know not what they do.'

(6) THE SAYING AT THE ARREST ABOUT THE POWER OF DARKNESS
   (Lk. xxii. 53*b*).

   '*But this is your hour, and the power of darkness.*'

Most commentators note the Johannine ring of this
saying.[1]   In reading the words, it is difficult not to think
of such a passage as Jn. iii. 19f.: 'And this is the judgment, that the light is come into the world, and men loved
the darkness rather than the light; for their works were
evil.   For every one that doeth ill hateth the light, and
cometh not to the light, lest his works should be re-
proved.'   Similar ideas appear also in the description of
the departure of the traitor in Jn. xiii. 30: 'He then having
received the sop went out straightway: and it was night,'
and in 1 Jn. i. 5: 'God is light, and in him is no darkness
at all.'   These parallels in no way throw doubt upon the
genuinenesss of the Lukan saying: on the contrary, the
similarity is an indication that the Johannine teaching is
rooted in the Synoptic tradition.

   The suggestion[2] that Lk. xxii. 53*b* is an editorial adap-
tation of Mk. xiv. 49*b*: 'But this is done that the scriptures
might be fulfilled,' is an opinion without foundation.   It
is much better to conclude that the saying is an excerpt
from the L tradition which the Evangelist has combined
with the question: 'Are ye come out, as against a robber . . .?' derived from Mk. xiv. 48f.

   The phrase 'your hour' stands over against the thought
of 'my hour' or 'the hour': and this contrast may have been
present to the mind of Jesus.   It is one element in the
sense of inevitability or 'predestination' which fills His
thought as He contemplates His Passion.[3]   The hour,

[1]Cf. Creed, 274f.; Easton, 333; Montefiore, ii. 611; Luce, 340.

[2]So Loisy.   See Luce, 340.

[3]Cf. Mk. xiv. 21, 41; Jn. xii. 23, 27, xvii. 1.

however, is one which His enemies have chosen and made
their own.   Here, as always, Jesus is far away from the
idea of a remorseless fate which determines men's actions.
It is in harmony with this point of view that the phrase
'the power of darkness' must be estimated.   No more
than in Col. i. 13, where the same phrase is used, is the
dualism one that is complete.   The power is that which
darkness, a natural metaphor for evil, is permitted to
exercise.   Possibly there is an intended contrast between
the two phrases: 'This is your hour; *and yet*, it is the power
of darkness.'   If so, the saying is an ironic comment upon
the jubilation of those who effect the arrest.   Whether
this is so or not, the words reveal, as an aspect of the
thought of Jesus, the sense of a conflict between evil
powers and Himself.   It is the same idea, though with the
note of victory added, which is expressed in Jn. xii. 31:
'Now is the judgment of this world: now shall the prince
of this world be cast out.'   The Passion-sayings do not
disclose this concept as the main or dominating idea of
Jesus in relation to His death, but they show unmistakably that it is one strand in His thought.

     This is the only saying from this part of Luke which it
is necessary to study in any detail.   The relation of the
sayings in the Lukan account of the Trial before the
Priests (xxii. 66-71) to Mk. xiv. 55-64 is difficult to determine.[1]   If, as most scholars think, the source is Mark,
Lk. xxii. 70 ('*Ye say* that I am') supports the textual evidence in favour of the reading: '*Thou hast* said that I am,'
in Mk. xiv. 62.[2]   In no way can this answer be said to
indicate doubt in the mind of Jesus.   What it reveals is
His sense of the enormous difference between His con-

---

[1]Cf. *Behind the Third Gospel*, 50f.   See also Creed's discussion, 275f.

[2]Cf. Streeter, *The Four Gospels*, 322.

ception of Messiahship and that of the priests.¹   If, as seems to me more probable, Luke derived the section from the L tradition, independent evidence is afforded concerning the Messianic consciousness of Jesus.

The prophecy to the daughters of Jerusalem (Lk. xxiii. 27-31) is peculiar to Luke, but it has no light to throw on the manner in which Jesus regarded His suffering beyond showing how He thought of the need of others in the very shadow of the cross.²   The language is apocalyptic in character, but it is doubtful if the thought is eschatological.   The commentators mention at least three possible interpretations³ of the reference to the green and the dry trees,⁴ but it is quite uncertain whether Jesus is thinking of Romans or Jews.

(7) THE CRUCIFIXION SAYINGS (Lk. xxiii. 34, 43, 46).

(a) 'And Jesus said, *Father, forgive them; for they know not what they do*' (xxiii. 34).

(b) 'And he said, Jesus, remember me when thou comest in thy kingdom.   And he said unto him, *Verily I say unto thee, To-day shalt thou be with me in Paradise*' (xxiii. 42f.).

¹Cf. Moulton, *Prolegomena*, 86.   Note also Lk. xxiii. 3 = Mk. xv. 2, where Pilate's question: 'Art thou the King of the Jews?' receives the answer: 'Thou sayest.'

²Bertram sees the community at work depicting Jesus as the prophet of the destruction of Jerusalem and attempting thereby to solve the mystery of the cross.   Cf. *Die Leidensgeschichte Jesu*, 74.   Montefiore (*The Synoptic Gospels*, ii. 623) says that the passage 'is probably unhistorical, being made up out of a number of Old Testament reminiscences'.   But why should not the reminiscences be those of Jesus Himself?   If, moreover, as Montefiore says, the basis is Zech. xii. 10-4, it is strange that a Christian editor should miss the opportunity of quoting the phrase: 'whom they pierced.'

³Cf. Plummer, 529.

⁴'For if they do these things in the green tree, what shall be done in the dry?' (Lk. xxiii. 31).

(c) 'And when Jesus had cried with a loud voice, he said, *Father*, *into thy hands I commend my spirit:* and having said this, he gave up the ghost' (xxiii. 46).

All these sayings are peculiar to the Third Gospel. The first is omitted by B D W Θ a b sy⁵ and other important authorities. The last is a quotation from Psa. xxxi. 5.

Critical opinion is sharply divided upon the question whether xxiii. 34 belongs to the true text of the Third Gospel, and in view of the many important authorities which omit the passage, this fact is not surprising. It is to be noted, however, that some of the foremost textual critics who reject the passage, hold that it contains a genuine saying of Jesus. Hort, for example, says: 'Few verses of the Gospels bear in themselves a surer witness to the truth of what they record than this first of the Words from the Cross.'[1]   Other writers who cannot agree that the saying is authentic bear witness to its greatness. Thus, Montefiore says that 'it nevertheless is *ben trovato*, both because it breathes the higher spirit of Jesus and because it is based upon the teaching of Jesus'.[2]

For Easton the textual difficulties are decisive.[3]   Creed thinks that 'the omission of a prayer so sublime and so Christ-like seems less probable than its insertion'.[4]   On the other hand, Harnack has strongly maintained that a reason for the omission can be found in the mistaken belief that the words of the prayer for forgiveness referred to Jews.[5]   Streeter has developed a similar argument. He refers to the opinion of Dr. Rendel Harris that the passage

[1] *The New Testament in the Original Greek*, ii. App. 68.
[2] *Op. cit.*, ii. 625.
[3] *St. Luke*, 348.
[4] *St. Luke*, 286.
[5] *Probleme im Texte der Leidensgeschichte Jesu*, 5-11.

was deleted because some second-century Christian found it hard to believe that God could or ought to forgive the Jews, and says: 'One might add, it would have appeared to a second-century Christian that, as a mere matter of fact, God had not forgiven the Jews. Twice within seventy years Jerusalem had been destroyed and hundreds of thousands of Jews massacred and enslaved.'[1] This is a forceful argument, and supported as it is by the impression left by the content of the prayer itself, it is decisive in favour of the genuineness of the passage.

The genuineness of the second saying is bound up with that of the story to which it belongs.   The account of the Penitent Thief (Lk. xxiii. 39-43) is probably Luke's addition to his special Passion Source, and we cannot tell whether it is based on good tradition or whether it is a homiletical development of Mk. xv. 27. Easton says that the didactic motive is obvious and that it is difficult to argue for much historic basis in the section.[2]   Creed suggests that the story comes 'from the same cycle of tradition which told the parable of the Pharisee and the Publican, and the stories of the penitent harlot and the penitent Zacchaeus,' and observes that it is impossible to say how much is to be set down to the Evangelist's own account.[3] These opinions are marked by critical caution, and, if they are not accepted, the only alternative possible rests on an estimate of Luke's value as a historical writer. In this respect it is probable that his reputation has suffered from the excellence of his gifts as a literary artist. It is also worth recalling that on many points criticism has been compelled to revise sceptical judgments.[4]   In these

---

[1] *The Four Gospels,* 138.

[2] *Op. cit.,* 35of.   [3] *Op. cit.,* 285.

[4] The incidental reference to Lysanias (Lk. iii. 1) is a case in point.   Cf. Creed, 307-9.

circumstances, those who continue to accept the special
Lukan narratives as historical have much justification; but
even so, it must always be recognized that our ignorance
of the character of the tradition as Luke found it precludes
dogmatic affirmations.

The same observations are relevant in the case of the
third saying.   In the present state of our knowledge one
common argument seems definitely unfair.   Thus, it is
often said that Luke replaces the Cry of Desolation (Mk.
xv. 34) by the quotation from Psa. xxxi. 5:[1] 'Father, into
thy hands I commend my spirit' (Lk. xxiii. 46).   This
argument is in place only if it can be shown that Mark is
Luke's principal source.   If the L tradition supplied the
Evangelist with his main authority, it falls to the ground,
and it is seriously compromised if it is conceded that he
used a non-Markan source.   This source did not contain
the Cry of Desolation, but probably included the saying
in xxiii. 46; and it is the preference accorded to it by Luke
which explains why the last sayings recorded in the two
Gospels are different.   To suggest that both cries are historical is more than a harmonizing expedient; for the
death of Jesus is not immediately recorded[2] in Mark after
the cry: 'My God, my God, why hast thou forsaken me?'
and it is a credible suggestion that the discord of an unparalleled experience was resolved into the harmony of
habitual confidence and trust.   It is the terrible cry of
Mk. xv. 34 which is the unexpected element in the Passion Story; the saying in Lk. xxiii. 46 is harmonious with
the whole spirit and life of Jesus, and in particular with the
attitude of obedience in which He faced the Cross.

[1] 'Into thine hand I commend my spirit.'
[2] The incident of the sponge full of vinegar follows, and then the words:
'And Jesus uttered a loud voice, and gave up the ghost' (Mk. xv. 37).

III

THE SAYINGS IN THE PAULINE NARRATIVE OF THE LAST SUPPER

IN order to complete our study of the Passion-sayings connected with the story of the Last Supper it is necessary to examine St. Paul's account in 1 Cor. xi. 23-5:

'For I received of the Lord that which also I delivered unto you, how that the Lord Jesus in the night in which he was delivered up took bread; and when he had given thanks, he brake it, and said, This is my body, which is for you: this do in remembrance of me. In like manner also the cup, after supper, saying, This cup is the new covenant in my blood: this do, as oft as ye drink it, in remembrance of me.'

As appearing in a letter written in 55 A.D., this narrative is early; but the phrase, 'which also I delivered unto you,' carries back the tradition to 51 A.D., when St. Paul first visited Corinth. It is probable, however, that the Apostle is thinking of the days immediately after his conversion and of the tradition made known to him at Damascus and Jerusalem. This is the natural interpretation of the words: 'I received of the Lord.' It is most improbable that the phrase, 'from the Lord,' implies a revelation comparable to that mentioned in Gal. i. 12.[1] Neither the terms[2]

---

[1] Cf. Robertson and Plummer, 242f.; Ed. Meyer, *Ursprung und Anfänge des Christentums*, i. 175; Goguel, *The Life of Jesus*, 445.

[2] παραλάμβανειν (cf. 1 Thess. ii. 13; 2 Thess. iii. 6; 1 Cor. xv. 1, 3) and παραδίδοναι (cf. Mk. vii. 13; Lk. i. 2; Acts vi. 14; 1 Cor. xi. 2, xv. 3) are regularly used of the reception and transmission of a tradition.

which are employed nor the contents[1] of xi. 23-5 suggest a revelation, but rather an oral tradition such as the primitive communities were able to give.   St. Paul is recording what he had learnt well within a decade of the death of Christ.

It would, however, be rash to suppose that his narrative must be accepted forthwith in all its details, as superior to the Markan and Lukan accounts of the Supper.   How ancient the Synoptic narratives are, it is impossible to say, but they are certainly very much older than the Gospels in which they stand.   Moreover, it may be that the details of 1 Cor. xi. 23-5 owe something to the effects of St. Paul's sojourn in Antioch and to his subsequent experiences during the Gentile Mission.   No narrative, not even that of an eyewitness, is exempt from the possibility of interpretative modifications, and this danger is increased when, as in the case of xi. 23-5, it is received from intermediaries.   For this reason the sayings in xi. 24f. must be examined with care.

(a) '*This is my body, which is for you: this do in remembrance of me*' (1 Cor. xi. 24).

The first four words appear in every account of the Supper, and their genuineness is beyond dispute.   The phrase, 'which is for you,' is peculiar to St. Paul's account.[2]   Its absence from Mk. xiv. 22 is not in itself a decisive objection, since the idea at least is completely in line with the Markan representation of the self-offering of Jesus in x. 45 and xiv. 24.   Dalman, however, thinks that what is possible in Greek ($\tau\grave{o}$ $\acute{v}\pi\grave{\epsilon}\rho$ $\acute{v}\mu\tilde{\omega}\nu$), appears in Aramaic as a very unusual heaviness', and that the phrase

---

[1]Otto remarks that Christ cannot have revealed: 'The Lord Jesus in the night in which. . . .'   Cf. *Reich Gottes und Menschensohn*, 276.

[2]It is repeated in Lk. xxii. 19*b* in the form: 'which is given for you.'

must be considered 'a hellenisation'.[1]   Probably, as Jeremias suggests,[2] its presence in the Pauline formulation is due to liturgical usage, and to the fact that the parallel expression: 'which is poured out for you', which appears in Mk. xiv. 24, is not suitable in the saying regarding the cup in 1 Cor. xi. 25.   On the whole, it is best to regard the phrase as an interpretative addition which correctly defines the words: 'This is my body.'   The rest of the saying: 'This do in remembrance of me,' is also peculiar to 1 Cor. xi. 24, but as a similar command is found in 1 Cor. xi. 25, both passages may be considered together.[3]

(b) 'This cup is the new covenant in my blood: this do, as oft as ye drink it, in remembrance of me' (1 Cor. xi. 25).

The relation of Mk. xiv. 24: 'This is my blood of the covenant, which is shed for many', to 1 Cor. xi. 25 has already been discussed; and the conclusion reached was that it is not a variant of the Pauline saying.   Is, then, 1 Cor. xi. 25 a variant of Mk. xiv. 24, or are the two independent sayings?

If it is necessary to choose between the two, the Pauline form must be regarded as secondary and derivative.   The phrase, 'This cup,' is easily explained as a closer definition of the indefinite 'This' in the Markan form.   Such a modification might naturally be made in a Gentile environment in order to avoid the difficulties of the bolder Markan saying: 'This is my blood of the covenant.'[4] Once this change is made the rest follows.   It is no longer possible to express the predicate in the words: 'is my blood of the covenant,' since this form is intelligible only if the subject refers to the wine.   The cup is not, of

---

[1] *Jesus-Jeshua*, 144f.   [2] *Die Abendmahlsworte Jesu*, 58.
[3] See pp. 206ff.
[4] Cf. Dalman, *Jesus-Jeshua*, 161; Jeremias, *op. cit.*, 60.

course, thought of apart from its contents, but when it is expressly mentioned as the subject, it becomes necessary to describe it as constituting the covenant made possible by the blood of Christ, and the adjective 'new' is suggested by Jer. xxxi. 31 and by contrast with the covenant of Ex. xxiv. 8. The immediate implication is that the cup is the pledge of the covenant, though how far this idea would have been from satisfying the mind of St. Paul is clear from his impassioned question: 'The cup of blessing which we bless, is it not a communion of the blood of Christ?' (1 Cor. x. 16). In the way suggested, then, it may be contended, the Pauline version came into existence in a form more intelligible to non-Jewish Christians than the challenging words of the Markan tradition.

This argument, it must be allowed, is attractive, and it may represent the facts. It is open, however, to at least two objections. Paul's words do not suggest that he is giving a later form of the saying; he shows no knowledge of any other form and implies that he is recording the original tradition. He may, of course, have been mistaken. Does he not show, in 1 Cor. i. 14-6, a confused recollection of those whom he had baptized? However this may be, in 1 Cor. xi. 23-5, as in 1 Cor. xv. 3-7, he speaks with such deliberation of matters which had been the subject of his teaching that it is difficult to believe that he is reproducing a form of the saying which first became current in a Gentile community. A second objection is that the explanation is not really necessary. 1 Cor. xi. 25 may be as original as Mk. xiv. 24 itself. It has already been suggested that the saying: 'This is my blood of the covenant, which is shed for many,' may not have been fully understood at the time. While this admission is no argument against their genuineness, it suggests the possibility that Jesus may have expounded His own words. Is the saying found in 1 Cor. xi. 25 part of His interpretation? Criticism is rightly on its guard against 'harmonizing expedients'; but when it can be shown that one saying is probably not derived from a second, and that the second need not be a variant of the first, there is matter for reflection. It is especially important to avoid the delusion that different accounts of the Supper are self-contained and mutually exclusive. Form-criticism reminds us that such narratives are merely the rounded residues of earlier stories from which much has fallen away, and that the sayings they contain are those which attracted the interest of the narrators. Similar sayings in different narratives may be, but need not be, identical; on the contrary, they may be original variations on the same theme. How far these principles can be applied in the present case, it may be impossible to decide, but there is certainly as much reason to explain 1 Cor. xi. 25 as an original interpretation of Mk. xiv. 24 as to adopt the hypothesis of secondary modification.

Hesitation to decide between these competing views is disappointing, but the very fact that we are compelled to hesitate adds force to the contention of Jeremias that, essentially, the meaning of 1 Cor. xi. 25 and of Mk. xiv. 24 is the same. 'With τοῦτο τὸ ποτήριον Paul means not the cup, but its contents.' 'Mark and Matthew, as much as Paul, compare the wine with the blood by the shedding of which the new covenant is established.'[1] If this opinion is sound, it matters less whether 1 Cor. xi. 25 is an original utterance, and the practical question is which passage gives the theologian firmest ground for his special work. On this issue there is hardly room for serious doubt: with Jeremias,[2] he is well advised to select the

[1] *Die Abendmahlsworte Jesu*, 59.
[2] *Op. cit.*, 61.

words of Mk. xiv. 24: 'This is my blood of the covenant, which is shed for many.'

Attention must now be given to the command to repeat the rite in 1 Cor. 24f.: 'This do in remembrance of me,' 'This do, as oft as ye drink it, in remembrance of me.'[1] For various reasons, these words are widely regarded as secondary additions. The grounds for this opinion may be summarized as follows: (1) The words are wanting in Mk. and in Mt.; (2) In suggesting the thought of a memorial meal, they introduce a new idea not found in the other accounts; (3) The terminology is that found in ancient formulae used with reference to the commemoration of the dead;[2] (4) The sayings reflect the interests of the primitive communities rather than those of Jesus.[3]

It cannot be said that these arguments are particularly impressive. Enough perhaps has already been said concerning Markan omissions. In reading not a little Synoptic Criticism one has the impression that the critic looks upon Mark as a fellow *Neutestamentler*. Goguel, for example, observes: 'Since the Early Church believed that it was obeying the will of the Lord in celebrating the Communion, the suppression by Mark of a command to repeat the rite which he found in the source would be unintelligible. In introducing it Paul was not conscious that he had altered the tradition.'[4] How much do we know of Mark's source, and would failure to record the command be unintelligible? The fact is, to a modern

---

[1]C. A. Anderson Scott prefers the rendering: 'with a view to recalling me'. Cf. *Christianity According to St. Paul*, 191.

[2]For examples cf. Lietzmann, *An die Korinther* [3], 58, 93f.; Jeremias, *op. cit.*, 58f.

[3]Cf. Wellhausen, *Das Evangelium Marci* 113.

[4]*The Life of Jesus*, 446.

inquirer the question whether Jesus commanded the repetition of the rite is a matter of first importance. Can we suppose that Mark felt the same? If Paul was not conscious that he had altered the tradition by introducing the command, was Mark conscious of the enormity of his offence in omitting it? He may well have taken for granted a command which no one doubted. Again, while a new idea is introduced in the Pauline narrative, it cannot be said to contradict the ideas of the Synoptic accounts; on the contrary, the injunction to recall the presence of Jesus in future celebrations of the Supper is in harmony with the consciousness of a farewell meal reflected in Lk. xxii. 18.[1] Further, the fact that ποιέω and ἀνάμνησις or μνήμη appear in pagan injunctions to commemorate the dead, while interesting, is not surprising, since the words are obvious terms to employ in a very natural request; and, in any case, parallelism is not the same thing as borrowing. Finally, the observation that the sayings are in agreement with the interests of the primitive communities does not exclude the possibility of a definite command of Jesus. Wellhausen's assertion that the sayings assume a custom of celebrating the Supper by the community, which Jesus could not have commanded and the disciples could not have understood,[2] is without adequate foundation. Looking forward, as He did, to the joy of the Messianic Feast in the consummated Kingdom,[3] Jesus might well enjoin the continued celebration of the Supper; and especially if He had attached a new significance to an earlier custom. If, on the night of the Arrest, He desired to associate His disciples with His Messianic suffering, He might well wish that association to be deepened and enriched after His death. It is also

[1] See p. 185.   [2] *Op. cit.*, 113.
[3] Cf. Mk. xiv. 25; Lk. xxii. 18.

too easily assumed that, without any command of His, the Supper would have continued to be celebrated.   To say that St. Paul has made explicit what was already implicit, is greatly facilitated because we know the events which followed the death of Jesus.   Can we be certain that the idea of repetition would have been found to be implicit, if Jesus had not said: 'Do this in remembrance of me'? Without the word, would the custom have arisen?   It may not be possible to answer these questions, but, with some confidence, it may be affirmed that the custom of the primitive Church in breaking bread (cf. Acts. ii. 42) is best understood if it rests on the express word of Jesus. Seductive phrases like 'unconscious aetiological invention', and 'an *ex post facto* legitimation of a custom', have something of the potency of a spell, but they provide a much less credible explanation of the saying: 'Do this in remembrance of me,' than the view that the words are a genuine utterance of Jesus.

Our conclusion, then, is that, in recording the sayings which command the continued observance of the Supper, St. Paul has preserved an original element in the tradition not mentioned by the Synoptists.   If this view is accepted, it enlarges our conception of what Jesus had in mind in instituting the Supper.   He not only intended His disciples to share in the power of His self-offering on the night of the Arrest; He meant them to continue so to do.   In breaking bread and in drinking the cup they were to bring Him and His Messianic work powerfully to mind until He should come with power and great glory.   This is a thought of Jesus which St. Paul has truly expressed when he writes: 'For as often as ye eat this bread, and drink the cup, ye proclaim the Lord's death till he come' (1 Cor. xi. 26).

In view of the importance of St. Paul's account, it is

necessary to examine his interpretation of the significance and meaning of the Supper. Such an inquiry ought to throw light on the question whether his narrative is influenced by his doctrinal views; it ought also to help us to interpret the Supper itself and the meaning it had for Jesus.

There can be no doubt that St. Paul's thought is sacramental in the sense that he regards material things as means for the manifestation and appropriation of spiritual realities. This is true of his doctrine of the Person of Christ, of his conception of the Church as the Body of Christ, and of his description of the individual Christian, and of the Church, as the temple of the Holy Spirit (cf. 1 Cor. iii. 16f., vi. 19f.). But this aspect of his thought is especially evident in his treatment of Baptism and of the Lord's Supper. The fathers of the Jewish Church were 'baptized into Moses' by their experiences in the wilderness and at the Red Sea (1 Cor. x. 2), and the Christian believer is 'baptized into Christ', and therefore 'into his death' (Rom. vi. 3). 'We were buried therefore with him through baptism into death: that like as Christ was raised from the dead through the glory of the Father, so we also might walk in newness of life' (Rom. vi. 4). This teaching does not mean that, as a rite, and apart from moral and spiritual factors, Baptism effects spiritual benefits: such a deduction would be a complete perversion of Pauline thought, with its strong emphasis upon the ethical element in the idea of faith-union with Christ.[1] None the less, it does imply that Baptism is both an opportunity and a means of establishing a spiritual relationship with Christ.

[1]'Neither baptism nor the Lord's Supper is regarded as of magical effect. In every case it is God's grace that is decisive,' A. Deissmann, *St. Paul*, 131.

O

St. Paul's views regarding the Supper can be inferred from 1 Cor. x. 1-4, 14-22, and xi. 20-34.

The first of these passages is one of warning based upon the experiences of the Israelites in the wilderness who, in spite of the highest privileges, became idolators, fornicators, and murmurers against God. It is in this context that he speaks of the manna as 'spiritual meat' and of the water obtained from the rock as 'spiritual drink' (x. 3f); in a mystical sense he can even declare that 'the rock was Christ' (x. 4). There can be no doubt that he is thinking in terms suggested by the Eucharist, and, if this is so, it is natural to infer that he thought of the bread and the wine as spiritual meat and drink, and of the Eucharist as in a true sense mediating Christ to the believer. Just as clearly it must be inferred that he did not think of it as a mechanical means of grace. 'Now these things happened unto them by way of example,' he says of the privileged Israelites, 'and they were written for our admonition, upon whom the ends of the ages are come' (x. 11).

The second section, 1 Cor. x. 14-22, is more explicit. Once more it is a warning against idolatry. St. Paul does not believe that an idol is anything, but he does believe that in eating things sacrificed to idols the Corinthians incur the danger of entering into communion with evil powers. 'I would not', he writes, 'that ye should have communion with demons' (x. 20). Strange as it is to the modern mind, this thought is based on ancient conceptions of sacrifice, and, in particular, upon the idea that to eat of the sacrifice is to share in the sacrificial act itself, and therefore to enter into fellowship with spiritual powers. That this view was held by St. Paul himself is clear from his question: 'Behold Israel after the flesh: have not they which eat the sacrifices communion with the altar?' (x. 18). In these words he is thinking, not so much of the altar itself,[1] but of the God whose altar it is, and of the offering made thereon. Nothing less than this inference does justice to his words.

In itself, the use of this illustration suggests that St. Paul thinks of the Eucharist as a means of entering into communion with Christ and of sharing in His sacrifice. This conclusion, however, is not left to inference, for he writes: 'The cup of blessing which we bless, is it not a communion of the blood of Christ? The bread which we break, is it not a communion of the body of Christ?' (x. 16). The incidental introduction of this question is worthy of note; it merely prepares the way for the plea that to eat meat sacrificed to idols is spiritually dangerous. The implication is that he is assuming a view of the Eucharist shared equally by his readers and himself. It is inadequate to understand 'communion' (κοινωνία) of a fellowship of believers instituted by Christ. This is the secondary idea of the section, suggested in the words: 'seeing that there is one bread, we who are many, are one body' (x. 17, R.V. mg.); but that it is not the main thought is clear when St. Paul sets side by side the Supper and the pagan sacrifice, and says: 'Ye cannot drink the cup of the Lord, and the cup of demons: ye cannot partake of the table of the Lord, and of the table of demons' (x. 21). By communion of the body and blood of Christ St. Paul means a vital relation with Christ Himself as the Crucified Saviour.

The third section, 1 Cor. xi. 20-34, is of even greater interest and importance, because from verses 26-34 it is possible to infer with some confidence what his view of the Eucharist must have been.

When he says: 'As often as ye eat this bread, and drink

---

[1]Some commentators take the view that his meaning is that something of the holiness of the altar passes over to them. Cf. Anderson Scott, *op. cit.*, 185; Howard, *Abingdon Commentary*, 1184.

the cup, ye are proclaiming the Lord's death till he come'
(**xi**. 26), he is thinking of the Eucharist, not merely as
publishing the fact of the death, but as making it known
for what it is, a work, namely, of reconciliation.   He does
not say this, it is true, but, in the light of his treatment as a
whole, it is impossible to believe that his thought is simply
that the acts of eating and drinking recall the circumstances of the original Supper and of the tragic events
which followed.   It is surely the nature of the death that
is in mind and the appropriation of its blessings by men;
and since reconciliation is the fundamental conception
under which he thinks of the work of Christ,[1] it is natural
to suppose that it is under this category that the death is
proclaimed.   The Eucharist, he says, in effect, is an acted
sermon;[2] it is the drama of redemption, in which common
physical acts, eating and drinking, represent and provide
the opportunity for the spiritual appropriation of that
which Christ made possible by His death.

It is just because St. Paul can think so highly of the
Eucharist that he feels so keenly the scandal of the Corinthian celebrations, with their divisions, heresies, and
shameful disorders.   These facts of the situation are in
his mind when he speaks of eating the bread, or drinking
the cup, 'unworthily'.   The disorders ruin the sermon
and destroy the drama, so that the death is no longer proclaimed as a work of reconciliation.   So strong is his
feeling that he declares that 'whosoever shall eat the bread
or drink the cup of the Lord unworthily, shall be guilty of
the body and the blood of the Lord' (xi. 27).   These
words are a rhetorical statement unless, in the Apostle's
thinking, the bread and the wine are, in some sense, the
body and blood of Christ.   So necessary is this inference,

[1]Cf. Rom. v. 1of.; 2 Cor. v. 18-20; Col. i. 20-2.
[2]Cf. Robertson and Plummer, 249.

that reluctance to accept it can only be explained by the fear that one is thereby committed to the view that St. Paul held a doctrine of Transubstantiation. Such a fear is groundless. St. Paul's thinking is poles asunder from the mediaeval belief that the 'substance' of bread and of wine is miraculously transformed into the 'substance' of the body and blood of Christ. What he means is illustrated by his statement that the rock of Kadesh 'was Christ'. The bread and the wine are mystically the body and blood of the Lord, and have this meaning and value because of His word and action (cf. xi. 24f.).

This conception, however, does not represent the whole of St. Paul's thought. He clearly believes that the significance of the Eucharist is ethically conditioned. On the one hand, he does not think that the meaning of the bread and wine is purely a subjective creation on the part of those who participate in the Supper. In his belief, the elements possess a God-given potency. He holds that direct physical ills have fallen upon the Corinthian Christians because they have received them unworthily. 'For this cause many among you are weak and sickly, and not a few sleep' (xi. 30). To the modern mind this is a sub-Christian belief which conceives the Eucharist in magical terms, although few would deny that to participate in the Eucharist unworthily, in a wrong ethical and religious spirit, is to expose oneself to the divine condemnation. We prefer, that is to say, to use abstract expressions, or at least to leave 'the divine judgment' undefined, whereas St. Paul prefers to speak definitely and concretely. Be this as it may, St. Paul's language implies that he did not think the significance of the elements to be one which exists only in the mind of the recipient; their value and meaning are determined by God.

On the other hand, it is equally clear that he cannot

have thought of the bread and the wine as the body and
the blood of Christ, apart from the spiritual attitude and
intellectual apprehension of the participant.   That he
attached the greatest importance to these conditions is
obvious from his solemn exhortation: 'Let a man prove
himself, and so let him eat of the bread, and drink of the
cup' (xi. 28).   The divisions, schisms, and ostentatious
actions of the Corinthian Christians are undoubtedly in
his mind as he writes these words, and it may be inferred
that by a 'worthy' participation he means one that is
marked by the spirit of unity, of humility, and of love.
But the question also arises whether, along with these
spiritual qualities, an intellectual grasp of what the
Eucharist means, must not be included; for St. Paul continues: 'For he that eateth and drinketh, eateth and
drinketh judgment unto himself, if he judge not rightly
the body' ($\mu\grave{\eta}$ $\delta\iota\alpha\kappa\rho\acute{\iota}\nu\omega\nu$ $\tau\grave{o}$ $\sigma\hat{\omega}\mu\alpha$).[1]   Some commentators have supposed that, by 'the body', the Church is
meant,[2] but, in the absence of some clearer indication of a
change of reference, it is much more probable that the
term has the same meaning which it bears in the immediate context in verse 27.   The 'body' is that of the Crucified Lord symbolized by the broken bread.[3]   The words
indicate that the proving, of which verse 28 speaks, has

---

[1]These words are a well-known *crux interpretum*. If by 'he that
eateth, &c.', St. Paul means one who eats 'unworthily', the participle is
causal: '*because* he does not judge rightly the body'; but if, as is more
probable, in view of verse 28, he is speaking generally, it is conditional: '*if*
he does not judge rightly.'   The rendering 'judge rightly' is better than
'discern' or 'discriminate', in the light of the meaning of $\delta\iota\alpha\kappa\rho\acute{\iota}\nu\omega$ in
verse 31.

[2]Cf. Anderson Scott, *op. cit.*, 189.

[3]'. . . the sacred body, into communion with which he enters by partaking of the Supper, and respecting which, therefore, he ought to form a
judgment of the most careful kind, such as may bring him into full and
deep consciousness of its sacredness and saving significance,' H. A. W.
Meyer, 349.

an intellectual as well as a moral character. The man is not only to examine his motives and his conduct, but also whether he has perceived what is involved in eating the bread and in drinking the cup. The implication is that it is upon this kind of self-examination that the opportunity presented to him in the Eucharist depends; only so are the bread and the wine the body and the blood of Christ to him. St. Paul's view is that the blessings of the Eucharist are received, neither *ex opere operato* nor merely by the exercise of faith, but by the power of God under moral and intellectual conditions.

From this study of St. Paul's thought it appears that, if allowance is made for the fact that he is dealing with an actual situation in the course of his ministry, the ideas are, substantially, those which are implicit in the narrative of Mk. xiv. 22-5, where Jesus, both by His actions and His words, institutes the Supper as a means whereby His disciples may share in the power of His surrendered life and anticipate the joy of the perfected Kingdom.[1] It is surprising, in view of his strong eschatological expectations, that St. Paul does not give fuller consideration to the relationship of the Supper to the hope of the Parousia. A reference to this relationship appears in his words: 'Ye proclaim the Lord's death *till he come*' (xi. 26), but it is not developed further. The explanation is doubtless to be found in the fact that he is not directly unfolding his eucharistic beliefs, but is dealing only with the points which concern a definite situation. In his treatment, however, he fixes upon what is most fundamental, the relation, namely, in which the Eucharist stands to the sacrifice of Jesus and to the appropriation of its blessings by the believer. In this vital conception the teaching of Jesus and of St. Paul is the same.

[1] Cf. pp. 124f, 138.

A noteworthy feature of 1 Cor. xi. 23-5 is the objectivity of the account of the Supper. In the three sections which have been examined St. Paul expresses thoughts which can legitimately be based on the narrative, but he does not introduce them into the story itself. How easy it would have been to give a description of the original Supper enriched by his own experience and by that of the Church! In point of fact, he does not do this to any marked degree. If the phrase, 'which is for you,' attached to the words, 'This is my body,' is an expansion, it is, as we have urged, an addition which only brings out what is already implied. We have claimed that the words regarding the repetition of the rite are original; but, even if this view is not accepted, the phrases are not Pauline inventions and only express what already was generally believed. A study, then, of St. Paul's doctrine of the Eucharist throws into strong relief the fidelity with which he records the original tradition.

The character of the narrative bears on the question raised by the frequent assertion that the sacramental element in early Christian tradition is the creation of St. Paul who was deeply influenced by pagan Mystery-conceptions. This issue, however, is of such importance that it must be treated more broadly.

The assertion gains plausibility by exploiting the similarities between the Eucharist and such traces as exist of sacred meals in connexion with the Mystery-religions, and by passing lightly over the distinctive elements in St. Paul's teaching. The well-known invitation: 'Chaeremon requests your company at dinner at the table of the Lord Sarapis in the Serapaeum to-morrow, the 15th, at 9 o'clock,'[1] tells us very little about the character of the feast in question; and this is still more true of the formula

[1] Cf. Moulton and Milligan, *The Vocabulary of the Greek Testament*, 365.

handed down by Firmicus Maternus: 'I have eaten out of the τύμπανον, I have drunk out of the κύμβαλον, I have become an initiate of Attis.'[1]   A credible account of the manner in which the alleged influences can have developed St. Paul's teaching, has yet to be supplied.   Meantime, it is important to observe that to the Apostle the Eucharist is neither an initiation ceremony, nor a rite of deification, nor a simple memorial feast to the departed.   Its closer affinities indeed are Jewish.   It is notable that in 1 Cor. x., xi., all the illustrations, apart from that of eating in an idol's temple, which is prompted by the circumstances of the readers, are drawn from the Old Testament.   Further, St. Paul's teaching throughout moves in personal and spiritual realms.   For him the bread and the wine are not so much 'food for the soul' as media for participating in a redeeming activity.   The end in view is fellowship with a Saviour and a sharing in His sacrifice.   Finally, as we have seen, the ethical and social virtues are strongly emphasized.   Where these are actively present, the Eucharist becomes what it is meant to be: otherwise, it is an instrument of condemnation.   This feature alone is enough to discourage the hypothesis of pagan borrowing. Added to the characteristics already mentioned, it stamps the idea of the rite as a unique and original conception, into the significance of which St. Paul was permitted to see more deeply than any other New Testament writer, but which owes its origin to Jesus Christ Himself.

[1]Cf. H. A. A. Kennedy, *St. Paul and the Mystery-Religions*, 256.

IV

THE JOHANNINE SAYINGS

THE Passion-sayings in the Fourth Gospel must now be examined. However difficult and contentious may be the problems which they raise, these sayings are part of the evidence on which an understanding of the thought of Jesus in relation to His Passion depends.

The most serious problem is the question how the sayings are to be regarded from the historical point of view. It cannot be said, in Great Britain at least, that any common opinion has been reached by New Testament scholars as a whole, although there is a wide and growing conviction that the sayings are not the *ipsissima verba* of Jesus, but words which in some degree owe their form to the Evangelist. This opinion can be expressed in very different ways. In the view of J. E. Carpenter, the members of the Johannine circle represent Jesus in the Fourth Gospel 'as speaking by anticipation in their name'.[1] According to P. Gardner, the Evangelist gives the teaching of Jesus as Plato gives the teaching of Socrates.[2] B. H. Streeter thinks that the original readers would not have supposed the author to mean that the doctrine propounded in the discourses was verbally identical with what Jesus actually taught in Palestine, 'but rather that it was organically related to what Christ taught

[1] *The Johannine Writings*, 225.
[2] *The Ephesian Gospel*, 100ff.; cf. C. J. Cadoux, *Christianity and Catholicism*, 340.

218

in such a way as to be the doctrine which Christ would have taught had he been explicitly dealing with the problems confronting the Church at the time when the Gospel was written.'[1] W. F. Howard holds that 'it is the Evangelist's manner to take a saying of Jesus and render it into an idiom that is rich in meaning for his own contemporaries'.[2] 'He also harps on a word or thought of the Master until it rings through the Gospel. But even more distinctive of the Johannine mind is the way in which he receives a deep saying which has only just found isolated expression in the earlier Gospels, and develops it throughout the Gospel.'[3]

The view that the sayings in the Fourth Gospel are original sayings of Jesus transposed into 'the Johannine idiom', receives strong justification when parallel utterances in the Synoptics are patiently examined; but, in the light of the facts as a whole, it cannot be regarded as a complete explanation. The theory is a very important part of the truth, but it is not the whole truth regarding the sayings. Once it is recognized that original utterances have been pondered and expressed in a new idiom, it is necessary to go further. Can we be sure that the process always begins with an original saying, especially when there is no Synoptic parallel? And in what form were original sayings present to the Evangelist's mind? In some cases he will have been familiar with sayings preserved in Mark, or, possibly, in Q and in some independent collection; but in other cases they would reach him in an oral form already modified in the course of transmission. Moreover, it is not easy to suppose that the process of recasting would invariably begin with a definite

[1] *The Four Gospels*, 371.
[2] *The Fourth Gospel in Recent Criticism and Interpretation*, 221.
[3] *Ibid.*

saying. Could the Evangelist always distinguish with any precision between a saying he had received and an idea which, in his belief, represented the mind of Jesus? Whatever element of uncertainty these possibilities may introduce into questions of exegesis, they are real and must be taken seriously into account; all the more, because the Evangelist was probably conscious of working under the creative impulse of the Spirit who should take of the things of Christ and guide believers into all the truth (cf. Jn. xvi. 13f.). The conclusion, therefore, which we must draw is that no simple formula will carry us through the task of evaluating the Johannine sayings. Many of them are original sayings expressed in another idiom, but others are free productions in which the Evangelist, in the consciousness that he is led by the Spirit, expresses what he believes to be the mind of Christ.

This estimate of the Johannine sayings renders it impossible to present them in quite the same manner as that in which the Synoptic Passion-sayings have been treated. Perhaps the best method is to examine, first, the passages in which the Evangelist clearly speaks in his own person, both in the Gospel and in 1 John, then, the Passion-sayings which he puts into the lips of others than Jesus, and, finally, the Passion-sayings of Jesus Himself. In view of what has already been said these divisions cannot be said to be mutually exclusive; but the method has the advantage of beginning with what is simple and relatively certain and of proceeding thence to what, in the nature of the case, is difficult and more open to debate.

PASSAGES IN WHICH THE FOURTH EVANGELIST SPEAKS IN HIS OWN PERSON

The passages in which the Evangelist himself refers to the Passion are as follows:

ii. 21f.: 'But he spake of the temple of his body. When therefore he was raised from the dead, his disciples remembered that he spake this; and they believed the scripture, and the word which Jesus had said.'

iii. 14f.; 'And as Moses lifted up the serpent in the wilderness, even so must the Son of man be lifted up: that whosoever believeth may in him have eternal life.'

iii. 16: 'For God so loved the world, that he gave his only begotten Son, that whosoever believeth on him should not perish, but have eternal life.'

vii. 30: 'They sought therefore to take him: and no man laid his hand on him, because his hour was not yet come.'

viii. 20: 'These words spake he in the treasury, as he taught in the temple: and no man took him; because his hour was not yet come.'

xi. 51f.: 'Now this he said not of himself: but being high priest that year, he prophesied that Jesus should die for the nation; and not for the nation only, but that he might also gather together into one the children of God that are scattered abroad.'

xii. 33: 'But this he said, signifying by what manner of death he should die.'

xiii. 1-4: 'Now before the feast of the passover, Jesus knowing that his hour was come that he should depart out of this world unto the Father, having loved his own which were in the world, he loved them unto the end. And during supper, the devil having already put into the heart of Judas Iscariot, Simon's son, to betray him, Jesus, knowing that the Father had given all things into his hands, and that he came forth from God, and goeth unto God, riseth from supper, and layeth aside his garments; and he took a towel, and girded himself.'

xviii. 14: 'Now Caiaphas was he which gave counsel to the Jews, that it was expedient that one man should die for the people.'

xviii. 32: 'that the word of Jesus might be fulfilled, which he spake, signifying by what manner of death he should die.'

Most of these passages are 'parenthetic comments', in which, as it were, the Evangelist turns aside and makes reflections on the story he is narrating. Along with other passages of a like tenor (cf. ii. 11, iv. 54, vi. 46, vii. 39, viii. 27), they have often been explained as editorial expansions; but V. H. Stanton is probably right in thinking that 'critics have been tempted to use their knives too hastily by the facility of the operation in these cases'.[1] It is a difficult question to decide whether iii. 14 and 16 ought to be attributed to the Evangelist or classified as sayings of Jesus.   There is considerable agreement that the well-known words: 'God so loved the world . . .' are part of the Evangelist's soliloquy, and probably the words: 'And as Moses lifted up the serpent in the wilderness . . .' should be similarly explained.[2]

The doctrinal ideas in these sayings should be carefully noted.

In the first place, the Evangelist believes that the course of events, including death itself, lay entirely under the sovereign control of Jesus.[3]   Three times he speaks of 'his hour' (vii. 30, viii. 20, xiii. 1), and twice he refers to Jesus as 'signifying by what manner of death he should die' (xii. 33, xviii. 32).   This point is of interest because, in the sayings ascribed to Him, Jesus is also represented as speaking of His 'time' (vii. 6, 8)[4] and of His 'hour' (xii. 23, 27, xvii. 1).   Secondly, the Evangelist thinks of the death of Jesus as a fulfilment of Scripture.   This appears in his statement that after the Resurrection the disciples remembered that Jesus had said: 'Destroy this temple,

---

[1] *The Gospels as Historical Documents*, iii. 58.

[2] Bernard thinks that the Evangelist's comments begin at iii. 16, *I.C.C.*, *St. John*, 112; cf. Lagrange, *Évangile selon Saint Jean*, 86.   Stanton marks the break at iii. 13, *op. cit.*, iii. 62, 171.

[3] 'From the beginning, Jesus, as master of His own fate, has fixed his "hour", and Himself ordains all the conditions that will lead up to it,' E. F. Scott, *The Fourth Gospel: Its Purpose and Theology*, 169.

[4] These two passages, however, probably do not refer to His death.   See p. 234f.

and in three days I will raise it up'; and his comment:
'they believed the scripture, and the word which Jesus had
said' (ii. 22). It is also found in the references to Scripture in connexion with the events of the Crucifixion (cf.
xix. 24, 28, 36). How this belief harmonizes with the
idea that Jesus is the master of His own fate, the Evangelist does not explain. Probably it is an element in current Christian belief which he simply takes over as a piece
of traditional theology. It is noteworthy that he never
introduces the idea of the fulfilment of Scripture into any
of the Passion-sayings of Jesus, apart from the doubtful
exceptions in xiii. 18 and xvii. 12, which refer to the
treachery of Judas, and xv. 25, which speaks of the hatred
of the Jews. In xviii. 8f., 32 he mentions the fulfilment of the word of Jesus Himself.

A third element in the writer's belief is the conviction
that the Only-begotten Son is God's gift, and a demonstration of His love (iii. 16). This thought is not directly
related to the death of Christ, but, in the light of iii. 14,
there can be no doubt that he is thinking of the Cross. In
the same passage the universality of Christ's work is
stated, and it is characteristic of the Evangelist that he
speaks of faith as believing in Christ Himself apart from
any particular theory of the Atonement. The same emphasis on love appears in xiii. 1. Here, however, the love
is that of Jesus Himself: 'Having loved his own which
were in the world, he loved them unto the end.' Beyond
general statements of this kind the Evangelist does not go.
He is content to speak of the death of Jesus as His departure out of the world. The 'hour' which Jesus recognizes
is that in which 'he should depart out of this world unto
the Father'. In the Evangelist's presentation Jesus
knows 'that he came forth from God and goeth unto God'
(xiii. 3). It is therefore true to say, with E. F. Scott, that

for the Evangelist the death 'marks the return of Jesus to the Father, His reinvestment with the glory which He had in the beginning'.[1]

At first sight there is an approach to a theory in the interest which the Evangelist takes in the counsel of Caiaphas: 'it is expedient for you that one man should die for the people' (xi. 50; cf. xviii. 14). When, however, he comments on the words of the high priest, he does not explain the necessity as occasioned by sin, but rather as a means of gathering into one, not only 'the nation', but also 'the children of God that are scattered abroad' (xi. 51f.). This emphasis upon the universality of Christ's work must be regarded as a fourth element in his thought.

Lastly, the Evangelist is strongly conscious of a moral necessity in the death of Christ. It is to this that he refers in iii. 14: 'And as Moses lifted up the serpent in the wilderness, even so must the Son of man be lifted up: that whosoever believeth may in him have eternal life.' The phrase, 'lifted up,' refers to the Cross,[2] as the mention of the action of Moses shows, and the word 'must' implies inward constraint. As in iii. 16 the motive is that of communicating life to believers. How, and in what way, the death of Jesus makes this possible, the Evangelist does not say, and, in the light of his teaching as a whole, we can only infer that it is because in death He is released from the limitations of earthly existence, and enters into the spiritual conditions of His glory.

In general, it may be said that, in the passages under review, the Evangelist shares important beliefs with St.

---

[1] *The Fourth Gospel: Its Purpose and Theology*, 227; cf. *The Literature of the New Testament*, 255. The same feature appears in the sayings ascribed to Jesus. Cf. H. J. Holtzmann: 'An die Stelle seines Geschickes tritt seine Person,' *Neutestamentliche Theologie*, ii. 474.

[2] Cf. Bernard, 112-5; Lagrange, 81f.

Paul and the Synoptists, but that he expresses them differently in terms of his favourite conceptions of life, love, and faith.   He believes that the Cross is the supreme expression of the love of God, that it reveals an inward moral constraint, and that its efficacy is universal; but, in these passages, he does not speak of it in sacrificial terms or as a means of expiation.   It does not therefore follow that sacrificial or expiatory ideas have no place in his thought.   It is necessary, indeed, to consider how far his own ideas are reflected in the sayings which remain to be examined.   The value of the present section is that it illustrates the ideas which he introduces when he is writing most freely.

PASSION-SAYINGS WHICH ARE PUT INTO THE LIPS OF OTHERS THAN JESUS

i. 29: 'Behold, the Lamb of God, which taketh away the sin of the world!'

i. 36: 'Behold, the Lamb of God!'

xi. 50: 'Ye know nothing at all, nor do ye take account that it is expedient for you that one man should die for the people, and that the whole nation perish not.'

Of these passages the last derives its main interest from the Evangelist's suggestion that the words of Caiaphas were an unconscious prophecy, that Jesus should die for the nation and for the children of God scattered abroad throughout the world (xi. 51f.).   It is a mere expression of political expediency: Jesus ought to be put to death in order to avert the dangers of revolution.   'If we let him thus alone, all men will believe on him: and the Romans will come and take away both our place and our nation' (xi. 48).

The first two passages are of the greatest interest and importance.   The words are ascribed to John the Baptist,

P

but there is every reason to think that this is an example of dramatic representation, and that historically the statement is that of the Evangelist.[1]   However the words are interpreted, they express a recognition of Jesus as the Christian Messiah, and it is improbable that this conviction was reached so early by the Baptist, and was expressed in terms which surpass those of Peter at Caesarea Philippi (cf. Mk. viii. 29; Mt. xvi. 16).[2]   There is even stronger reason to take this view if the saying is a confession of Jesus as the Suffering Servant of Isa. liii., for a pre-Christian Messianic use of this conception has not been proved, and it is almost certainly an identification first made by Jesus Himself.[3]

The phrase, 'the Lamb of God,' has been variously explained with reference to (a) the lamb offered at the morning and the evening sacrifice (Ex. xxix. 38-46); (b) Jer. xi. 19: 'But I was like a gentle lamb that is led to the slaughter'; (c) the Paschal Lamb (Ex. xii.); and (d) the Servant of Yahweh, who in Isa. liii. 7 is compared to 'a lamb that is led to the slaughter', and who 'bare the sin of many' (liii. 12).   There is perhaps least to be said for the first of these explanations, since the daily sacrifices were not expiatory in character.[4]   It is also unlikely that the reference is to the gentleness and innocence of a lamb,[5] as in Jer. xi. 19, for, while on this interpretation it is easier to attribute at least the first part of the saying to the Baptist, the words 'which taketh away the sin of the

---

[1]Cf. Bernard, 46.   For a defence of the passage, as an opinion of the Baptist, see Burney, *The Aramaic Origin of the Fourth Gospel*, 104-8.

[2]The narrative of Mk. i. 9-11 implies, when most naturally interpreted, that the words of the divine voice are heard by Jesus alone.

[3]See earlier, pp. 45ff.

[4]Cf. Lagrange, *Évangile selon Saint Jean*, 41.

[5]Cf. Lagrange, *op. cit.*, 40.

world', show that the thought is sacrificial in character. Moreover, the reference is not general, but to a definite and known lamb.   There is much more to be said for the view that the Evangelist is thinking of the Paschal Lamb. As it has often been observed, he shows a special interest in the Passover, and represents Jesus as dying at the time when the Paschal lambs were sacrificed in the Temple.[1] The difficulty of this view is that the Paschal Lamb is not represented in the Old Testament as bearing away sin; its blood is a token which averts the judgment of Yahweh.[2] Perhaps the last interpretation is the best; the Evangelist is thinking of the Servant of Yahweh, for Isa. liii. 7 and 12 easily explain the references to a lamb and to sin-bearing. This identification, however, is not without its difficulties, for αἴρων in i. 29 probably means 'taking away',[3] whereas in the Septuagint φέρειν is used to express the idea of bearing sin,[4] and the picture has points of likeness to the ritual of the Day of Atonement (cf. Lev. xvi. 22).   The dominant conception appears to be that of the Servant, freely used in association with other sacrificial ideas.[5]

E. F. Scott has suggested that in this passage 'we have nothing but a vague concession to the earlier doctrine'.[6]

[1]Cf. Bernard, cvi.   See also Jn. xix. 36 which freely quotes Ex. xii. 46: Neither shall ye break a bone thereof,' *i.e.* of the Paschal Lamb.

[2]Cf. Ex. xii. 13.   Note, however, the opinion of J. Jeremias mentioned on, p. 138f.

[3]So very many modern commentators.   See Bernard, Lagrange, Meyer, *in loc.* Cf. 1 Sam. xv. 25, xxv. 28, and 1 Jn. iii. 5.

[4]Cf. Isa. 12, where ἀναφέρειν is used.

[5]C. J. Ball has suggested that in the original Aramaic *talya*, 'servant', may have carried with it the associations of the Hebrew *tale*, 'lamb'.   He does not, however, bring his suggestion into relation with Isa. liii.   Cf. C. F. Burney, *The Aramaic Origin of the Fourth Gospel*, 107f.; J. Jeremias, *Theologisches Wörterbuch*, i. 185.   H. A. W. Meyer observes: 'The taking away of sins by the Lamb presupposes His taking them upon Himself,' i. 115.

[6]*The Fourth Gospel: its Purpose and Theology*, 219.

It is not quite true, however, to speak of the saying as 'the single text in which Christ is regarded as the great sacrifice for sin', for the ideas implicit in the saying: 'For their sakes I sanctify myself' (xvii. 19), are sacrificial, and the principle of life through death is expressed in the words about a grain of wheat (xii. 24). Moreover, it is not likely that 'a vague concession to the earlier doctrine' would have been expressed at the moment when the Evangelist first brings the historical figure of Jesus before the attention of his readers. It is far better to suppose that the words were of great importance to the Evangelist and that it is for this reason that he thrusts them into the forefront of his Gospel. At the same time the fact remains that the saying stands almost isolated in the Gospel, and that for the most part the other Passion-sayings in it are of a different tenor. The closer parallels are in 1 John. This is a fact of very great interest and importance, and it will be useful at this stage to examine the references to the Atonement in this Epistle. It may well be that in the sayings which are attributed to Jesus, yet to be considered, there are ideas which are distinctively those of the Evangelist. But this is a problem which calls for special consideration, and it is best at this point to compare the statements of the Evangelist, which have been noted as such, with those in the Epistle. This comparison has an important bearing upon the genuineness of the Passion-sayings attributed to Jesus.

PASSAGES WITH REFERENCE TO THE DOCTRINE OF THE ATONEMENT IN 1 JOHN

i. 7: 'If we walk in the light, as he is in the light, we have fellowship one with another, and the blood of Jesus his Son cleanseth us from all sin.'

ii. 1f.: 'And if any man sin, we have an Advocate with the Father,

Jesus Christ the righteous: and he is the propitiation (ἱλασμός) for our sins; and not for ours only, but also for the whole world.'

ii. 12: 'I write unto you, my little children, because your sins are forgiven you for his name's sake.'

iii. 5: 'And ye know that he was manifested to take away sins (ἵνα τὰς ἁμαρτίας ἄρῃ); and in him is no sin.'

iii. 16: 'Hereby we know love, because he laid down his life for us: and we ought to lay down our lives for the brethren.'

iv. 10: 'Herein is love, not that we loved God, but that he loved us, and sent his Son to be the propitiation for our sins.'

iv. 14: 'And we have beheld and bear witness that the Father hath sent the Son to be the Saviour of the world.'

In the present investigation it is not possible to give the same detailed treatment to these passages as in the case of the Passion-sayings. For our purpose it must suffice to summarize the principal ideas they embody. These ideas are:

(1) The belief that the blood, or out-poured life of Jesus, has 'cleansing' power (i. 7);

(2) The close relation between the death of Christ and sin (i. 7, ii. 1f, 12, iii. 5);

(3) The connexion between forgiveness and the 'name' of Christ (ii. 12);

(4) The description of Jesus Christ, 'the righteous', as the 'propitiation' for sins (ii. 2, iv. 10);

(5) The use of the phrase, 'the Saviour of the world' (iv. 14);

(6) The thought that the death of Christ is the supreme revelation of love (iii. 16);

(7) The thought that the coming of the Son to be 'the propitiation for our sins' is grounded in the love of God (iv. 10).

If we compare the several items of this list with the statements of the Gospel, we shall find that some of them are common to the two writings, but that others are either rarely illustrated in, or are absent from, the Gospel.

The last three appear in the Gospel.   Thus, the Samaritans confess Jesus as 'the Saviour of the world' (iv. 42); Jesus declares that a man has no greater love than that he 'lay down his life for his friends' (xv. 13); and the Evangelist pens the immortal word: 'God so loved the world, that he gave his only begotten Son' (iii. 16).

Of the remaining conceptions found in 1 John all that is paralleled in the Gospel is the connexion between the death of Christ and sin in i. 29 and the broad sacrificial ideas implicit in the saying in xii. 24 and xvii. 19.   In the Gospel the Evangelist does not speak of the cleansing power of the blood of Jesus, and in the sayings the nearest approach to this idea is in the words: 'He that eateth my flesh and drinketh my blood hath eternal life' (vi. 54).   Nowhere in the Gospel is forgiveness related to the death or to the 'name' of Christ, and the term, 'propitiation,' or any of its cognate forms, is never employed.   How are those facts to be explained?

A simple answer would be provided if we could say that the Fourth Gospel and 1 John were written by two different writers belonging to the same 'Johannine School', and this view has been taken by some New Testament scholars, including Holtzmann,[1] Schmiedel,[2] Moffatt,[3] Scott,[4]

[1] *Jahrbuch für protestantische Theologie*, 1881, p. 69of.; 1882, pp. 128f., 316f., 460f.

[2] *The Johannine Writings*, 208-11.

[3] *Introduction to the Literature of the New Testament*, 589-93.

[4] *The Fourth Gospel: Its Purpose and Theology*, 88f., 94.   But in his *Literature of the New Testament* (1932), 261, Scott takes the view that the two writings are the work of the same author.

Lord Charnwood,[1] and others.[2]   This critical opinion is based, not only on the references to the work of Christ, but also on differences regarding the Parousia, the use made of the Old Testament, faith, the Logos conception, and the application of the term 'Paraclete'.   It is further supported by certain linguistic peculiarities of 1 John.[3]   It is very doubtful, however, if the differences sustain a theory of diverse authorship.   Moreover, the agreements in vocabularly and syntax are striking.[4] In particular, there does not seem to be any real need to resort to this theory so far as the treatment given to the work of Christ is concerned. As we have seen, the thought that the Cross is grounded in love is distinctive in both writings, and if sin and sacrifice are more prominent conceptions in 1 John, they are not absent from the Gospel. It is probable that the most notable difference, the use of the word 'propitiation' in 1 Jn. ii.2, iv. 10, is exaggerated in the mind because it is commonly understood as suggesting the appeasing of the anger of God. This suggestion, however, is almost certainly mistaken. C. H. Dodd thinks that, with some confidence, we may regard ἱλασμός as based on the sense of καθαρίζειν, 'to purify';[5] and, in substance, a similar view has been taken by J. Moffatt.[6]   We must look, then, to some other explanation of the differences between 1 John and the Gospel.

[1]*According to St. John*, 79.

[2]See the list in Moffatt, *op. cit.*, 589f.   C. H. Dodd has recently argued that 1 John was written by an author who may have been a disciple of the Fourth Evangelist.   See the *Bulletin of the John Rylands Library*, Vol. 21, No. 1, April 1937, pp. 129-56.

[3]Cf. Moffatt, *op. cit.*, 590, and Dodd's article noted above.

[4]Cf. A. E. Brooke, i.-xix.; W. F. Howard, *The Fourth Gospel in Recent Criticism and Interpretation*, 252-7; R. H. Charles, *I.C.C.*, *Revelation*, xxxiv.-vii.

[5]*The Bible and the Greeks*, 94f.   [6]*Love in the New Testament*, 255.

It has been maintained that the differences between the two writings presuppose a considerable time-interval, and that 1 John is the earlier and more primitive work. Holtzmann, indeed, regarded this as a necessary assumption, if identity of authorship is accepted.[1] A. E. Brooke, however, has shown that there is much to be said for the view that the Epistle is the *later* work,[2] and certainly it is not easy to think that the false teaching which is opposed is earlier than the turn of the first century. In this case, the hypothesis that during an interval of, say, twenty or twenty-five years the writer's thought had undergone development to the point represented by the Fourth Gospel, falls to the ground.

The best explanation is to be found in the aim and purpose of the two writings. 1 John is a homily or a series of homilies; the Gospel is influenced throughout by a consistent doctrinal and religious purpose. The Evangelist writes to show that Jesus is the Christ, the Son of God, and to help his readers to obtain life in His name by believing. Such a difference of purpose inevitably affects details of thought and expression, and all the more because in the Gospel the Evangelist's method is definitely selective. No more than any other Evangelist has he any thought of writing a biography; what he uses from the available tradition is deliberately chosen, doubtless with a sovereign hand, because it serves best the end he has in view.

The Fourth Evangelist's principal interest is in the revelation of the Incarnate Word. For this reason we cannot expect his Gospel to contain all his thoughts concerning Christ's death, but only such as are germane to his purpose. The fact, however, that he wrote 1 John is a salutary warning against an over-emphasis of the idea that he wrote with a conscious doctrinal intention. From the com-

[1]Cf. A. E. Brooke, xix.   [2]*Op. cit.*, xix.-xxvii.

parison of the two works we see that he can write with restraint, that he can withstand the temptation to introduce cherished beliefs into his unfolding of the Gospel Story. How this inference is to be related to the evaluation of the Passion-sayings must be considered later. At this point the sayings themselves must be examined, together with the special problems which they raise.

PASSION-SAYINGS ATTRIBUTED TO JESUS HIMSELF IN THE FOURTH GOSPEL

ii. 19: 'Destroy this temple, and in three days I will raise it up.

vi. 51: 'I am the living bread which came down out of heaven: if any man eat of this bread, he shall live for ever: yea and the bread which I will give is my flesh, for the life of the world.'

vi. 53-7: 'Verily, verily I say unto you, Except ye eat the flesh of the Son of man and drink his blood, ye have not life in yourselves. He that eateth my flesh and drinketh my blood hath eternal life; and I will raise him up at the last day. For my flesh is meat indeed, and my blood is drink indeed. He that eateth my flesh and drinketh my blood abideth in me, and I in him. As the living Father sent me, and I live because of the Father; so he that eateth me, he also shall live because of me.'

vii. 6: 'My time is not yet come.'

vii. 8: 'My time is not yet fulfilled.'

viii. 28: 'When ye have lifted up the Son of man, then shall ye know that I am he, and that I do nothing of myself, but as the Father taught me, I speak these things.'

x. 11: 'I am the good shepherd: the good shepherd layeth down his life for the sheep.'

x. 15f.: 'And I lay down my life for the sheep. And other sheep I have, which are not of this fold: them also I must bring, and they shall hear my voice; and they shall become one flock, one shepherd.'

x. 17f.: 'Therefore doth the Father love me, because I lay down my life, that I may take it again. No one taketh it away from me, but I lay it down of myself. I have power to lay it down, and I have power to take it again.   This commandment received I from my Father.'

xii. 7: 'Suffer her to keep it against the day of my burying.'

xii. 23-5: 'The hour is come, that the Son of man should be glorified.   Verily, verily, I say unto you, Except a grain of wheat fall into the earth and die, it abideth by itself alone; but if it die, it beareth much fruit.   He that loveth his life loseth it; and he that hateth his life in this world shall keep it unto life eternal.'

xii. 27f.: 'Now is my soul troubled; and what shall I say? Father, save me from this hour? But for this cause came I unto this hour.   Father, glorify thy name.'

xii. 31f.: 'Now is the judgement of this world: now shall the prince of this world be cast out.   And I, if I be lifted up from the earth, will draw all men unto myself.'

xiii. 21: 'Verily, verily, I say unto you, that one of you shall betray me.'

xiv. 2: 'I go to prepare a place for you.'

xv. 13: 'Greater love hath no man than this, that a man lay down his life for his friends.'

xvi. 7: 'Nevertheless I tell you the truth; It is expedient for you that I go away: for if I go not away, the Comforter will not come unto you; but if I go, I will send him unto you.'

xvii. 1f.: 'Father, the hour is come; glorify thy Son, that the Son may glorify thee: even as thou gavest him authority over all flesh, that whatsoever thou hast given him, to them he should give eternal life.'

xvii. 19: 'And for their sakes I sanctify myself, that they themselves also may be sanctified in truth.'

xix. 26f: 'Woman, behold thy son!'; 'Behold, thy mother'.

xix. 28: 'I thirst'.

xix. 30: 'It is finished.'

Some of the passages in this list have little or no importance for the inquiry.   vii. 6 and 8 probably do not refer to the death of Jesus at all: in view of the words of His brothers in vii. 3f. it is clear that the 'time' of which He speaks

is that of His manifestation as the Messiah. xii. 7 and xiii.
21 are secondary versions of sayings of Jesus connected,
respectively, with the Synoptic stories of the Anointing
and the Prophecy of the Betrayal.[1] The saying: 'Destroy
this temple, and in three days I will raise it up' (ii. 19),
need not detain us; for, whatever these enigmatic words
may imply,[2] it is not probable that they refer to 'the temple
of his body' (ii. 21), unless the Evangelist is thinking of
the 'spiritual house' of Christian believers.[3] In this case,
the main interest of the saying is the further light it throws
on the Evangelist's theology; it would imply the belief
that the death of Jesus is the seed of the Church.

Other passages reveal the want of any distinctive theory
in the Fourth Gospel. Jesus goes 'to prepare a place' for
His own (xiv. 2). He lays down His life that He may
take it again (x. 17). His departure is His glorification
(xii. 23, xvii. 1). Most significant of all is the statement
of xvi. 7. When Jesus says that it is expedient that He
should go away, we seem to be near an explanation of the
purpose of His death; but the reason given is not any explanation of what the death is to achieve, but the observation that, if He does not go away, 'the Paraclete will not
come.' Jesus, that is to say, is represented as preoccupied
with the thought of what will follow His death, not with
the death itself. Apart from the sayings in vi. 51, 53-7,
the only positive implications of purpose are that He lays
down His life on behalf of (ὑπέρ) His followers and others
(x. 11, 15f.), that His action is a proof of love (xv. 13) and

---

[1]See the earlier discussion of Mk. xiv. 8 and 17-21 on pp. 108-14.

[2]In the opinion of Goguel Mk. xv. 29 proves the existence of a tradition
according to which Jesus was said to have been condemned because He
proclaimed that He would destroy the Temple. According to Mk. and
Mt., the charge was recognized as inconsistent and abandoned, while in
Jn. the saying is given an allegorical meaning. Cf. *The Life of Jesus*, 508.

[3]Cf. Bernard, 97.

will provide a centre of universal attraction (xii. 32), that
it is bound up with the judgment of the world (xii. 31), and
that by means of it He Himself is glorified (xii. 23, 28,
xvii. 1) and revealed (viii. 28).

The sayings in vi. 51, 53-7 demand fuller consideration.
There can be little doubt that they are sacramental passages.[1]   The connexion in thought with Mk. xiv. 22, 24:
'Take ye: this is my body;' 'This is my blood of the covenant, which is shed for many,' is unmistakable.   Why
they appear in chapter vi, after the story of the Feeding of
the Five Thousand, and not in xiii, in association with the
account of the Supper, is one of the most difficult questions
connected with the Fourth Gospel.[2]   One of the most
notable features in the sayings is the use of the term 'flesh'
instead of 'body', but Bernard gives the true explanation
when he says that the Evangelist 'prefers σάρξ (cf. i. 14),
probably because he wishes to emphasize the fact of the
Incarnation, as against the nascent Docetism of the age'.[3]
The meaning of the sayings is that by participation in the
Body and Blood of Christ, received in the Eucharist, the
believer obtains 'eternal life' in the Johannine sense of the
term (cf. vi. 54) and mystical fellowship with Christ (cf.
vi. 56).   This startling assertion is protected against the
obvious perils of a materialistic interpretation by the further saying: 'It is the spirit that quickeneth; the flesh pro-
fiteth nothing: the words that I have spoken unto you are
spirit, and are life' (vi. 63). The question of the historical
basis of this teaching is pointedly raised by these sayings,
but for the moment it is necessary to observe its relation to
what is said concerning Christ's self-giving.   This con-

---

[1]Cf. Bernard, clxvii.-xxii.; Howard, op. cit., 211-4.

[2]Cf. Howard, op. cit., 213f.   'The Upper Room was no place for doctrinal polemic,' p. 214.

[3]Op. cit., clxx.

nexion is indicated in the words: 'Yea and the bread which I will give is my flesh, for the life of the world' (vi. 51). Once again, it is the universality of Christ's sacrifice which is the undertone of these words and the belief that it makes possible the communication of life.

It is at once apparent that, substantially, the sayings attributed to Jesus express the same ideas as in the passages where the Evangelist speaks in his own person. Here, as there, it is implied that the issue of His life is under the power and control of Jesus Himself: 'No one taketh it away from me, but I lay it down of myself. I have power to lay it down, and I have power to take it again. This commandment received I from my Father' (x. 18). The Evangelist speaks of the 'hour' of Jesus, and Jesus does the same (xii. 23, 27, xvii. 1). The Evangelist sees God's gift of love in the Only-begotten (iii. 16) and Jesus interprets His death as a proof of love (xv. 13). In each series of passages the universality of Christ's work is asserted (xi. 52, cf. x. 16, xii. 32, xvii. 2); and in each it is described as communicating life (iii. 14f., 16; cf. vi. 51, 53-7). The terminology is also the same, for the phrase 'lifted up' appears both in iii. 14 and in the words of Jesus in viii. 28 and xii. 32. If also we are justified in finding a sacrificial content in the words ascribed to the Baptist in i. 29: 'Behold the Lamb of God, which taketh away the sin of the world!', it is interesting to find a similar passage in the saying: 'For their sakes I sanctify myself, that they themselves also may be sanctified in truth' (xvii. 19; cf. also xii. 24).

The principal differences are that Jesus does not describe His death as an expression of God's love (cf. iii. 16), or as a fulfilment of Scripture (cf. ii. 22, xix. 24, 28, 36), while in His sayings there is a greater emphasis upon the ideas of the sacramental gift of life (vi. 51, 53-7) and of sacrifice (xii. 24). As in Pauline thought, there is also a reference to the shaking effect of His death upon hostile world-powers: 'Now is the judgement of this world: now shall the prince of this world be cast out' (xii. 31).

The question must now be considered: In what sense are the sayings historical? How far can they be relied upon as a basis of knowledge in seeking to understand the attitude of Jesus to His suffering and death? The similarity already noted does not necessarily mean that they are simply the Evangelist's composition, for it is possible that he has assimilated observations of his own to genuine sayings of Jesus, reflected upon and expressed in a new idiom. The difference between the references to the Atonement in 1 John and the Gospel supports this contention. The Fourth Evangelist is not a writer who forces his soteriology upon his material; he is not a theologian bereft of a historical conscience. It is reasonable therefore to infer that, however freely he may reproduce sayings of Jesus, he is controlled by a genuine tradition. This inference, however, does not mean that we can take the Johannine sayings at their face value, and still less that they can be used to discredit sayings of a different kind in the Synoptic Gospels. The Synoptic sayings stand in their own right and cannot be compromised by anything we find in the Fourth Gospel. The Johannine sayings need to be considered in the light of the stylistic peculiarities of the Gospel, the Evangelist's individuality, and the fact that he chooses his material with a purpose.

All the speakers in the Fourth Gospel express themselves in the same style. Thus, it is only the subject-matter of the speech of the Baptist in iii. 27-30 which distinguishes it from a discourse of Jesus; and if, as many critics think, iii. 31-6 no longer stands in its original context, it is significant that the possibility of displacement was unsuspected until modern times. The speech of Jesus in reply to Nicodemus in iii. 10ff. drifts almost imperceptibly into the Evangelist's soliloquy; and the syntax and forms of expression in the Gospel and the Johannine Epistles are surprisingly alike. Despite the inference, already drawn, that the Evangelist's thought is controlled by a genuine tradition, it is beyond question that the sayings are translated into his own idiom.

The Evangelist's individuality is an important factor, not only because he does not hesitate to express the thoughts of Jesus in his own language, but also because he has first passed them through the intellectual moulds of his time. In the Fourth Gospel Jesus speaks as a Jew, but as a Jew of the Dispersion sensitive to Hellenistic influences. At the moment there is a marked tendency to emphasize the Judaic elements in the Gospel. As a corrective to views which treat it as if it were written by a disciple of Philo, this contention is all to the good. Nothing, however, can ever displace the conviction that a Greek air pervades the Gospel. This influence is the work of the Evangelist; it is seen also unmistakably in the way in which he selects, recasts, and employs his material in his endeavour to present Jesus to his Hellenistic readers. The writer's personality is that of a strong, cultured, and sensitive spirit, and to determine its influence in the composition of the Gospel is the most delicate task undertaken by criticism. It is described best as interpretative, and this means that something is brought out of his material and that something is interfused into it; no one can tell where the thoughts of Jesus begin and end. The result of this is that in a historical inquiry we cannot use the Gospel with immediate confidence, and that, just as certainly, we cannot afford to neglect it. The resolution of this dilemma is the problem of the Fourth Gospel.

The method followed by the Evangelist is an added

complication. All recent study of the Gospel emphasizes the fact that from first to last his method is selective. Throughout he is dominated by his desire to present Jesus as the Christ, the Son of God, and the Word made flesh, and the giver of life (cf. i. 14, xx. 31). For this end he chooses his material. The idea that he merely writes to supplement the Synoptic Gospels belongs to the primary department of Gospel criticism. It is not for this purpose that he omits some elements from Christian tradition and supplies others. His supreme motive is dogmatic and religious. What bearing has this fact upon his work?

In the selective method itself there is nothing in the least reprehensible; it is the kind of literary procedure commonly followed by writers who use history as the servant of religion. In their own measure the Synoptists do the same thing; and only the persistent delusion that the Gospels are biographies leads us to think that we must choose between the first three and the fourth. Every writing of the kind must be judged on its own merits.

It is obvious that those who think, from their study of early Christianity, Christian history, and religious experience, that the Fourth Evangelist has correctly interpreted the Person of Christ, will estimate his work at the highest; and that those who do not believe this will remain suspicious. It is therefore vain to imagine that dogmatic interests can be eliminated in the study of the Fourth Gospel. As well cry for the moon! But if such bias cannot be escaped, it can be allowed for by the honest student, and the effort made to apply every objective test before the scales fall. Such objective tests include a careful comparison between the ideas of the Gospel and those of primitive Christianity and contemporary Judaism, and between the Johannine and the Synoptic sayings. An estimate of the amount of agreement between the sayings in the Fourth Gospel and the mind and figure of Jesus as He is known to us from other historical sources, is a less objective, but still not entirely subjective criterion. These tests do not exclude elements which are peculiar to the Fourth Gospel. Moreover, an estimate of sayings capable of direct comparison creates a presumption regarding the value of those which have no close parallel.

An investigation of the relation of the contents of the Fourth Gospel to the thought-world of the first century cannot be undertaken here; and it must be enough to say that such a study has been made in modern times in a series of learned works,[1] with results which strengthen confidence in the broad historical value of the Gospel.

Comparison with the sayings in the Synoptics, or at least with the Synoptic Passion-sayings, is a task of smaller compass. Both in the Fourth Gospel and the Synoptics there is undoubtedly a close connexion between the ideas of death and resurrection. Just as Jesus says that the Son of Man must suffer and rise again (Mk. viii. 31 and parallels), so He declares that He lays down His life that He may take it again (Jn. x. 17) and speaks of His death as His glorifying (Jn. xii. 23, 28, xvii. 1). The language is different but the emphasis on triumph is the same. In the Fourth Gospel, however, the triumph is immediate; there is no reference in the sayings to 'three days', except in the difficult passage: 'Destroy this temple, and in three days I will raise it up' (ii. 19). Common also to all the Gospels is the thought of the Passion as 'the hour' of

---

[1] E. F. Scott, *op. cit.*, *passim*; W. F. Howard, *op. cit.*, 142-244; J. E. Carpenter, *The Johannine Writings*, 254-356; G. H. C. Macgregor, *Jew and Greek*, *passim*; Strack-Billerbeck, *Kommentar zum N.T. aus Talmud und Midrasch*, vol. ii.; H. Odeberg, *The Fourth Gospel Interpreted in its Relation to Contemporaneous Religious Currents*. For further information see the Bibliography in Howard, *op. cit.*, 273-82.

Q

Jesus (Jn. xii. 23, 27, xvii. 1; cf. Mk. xiv. 35, 41; Mt. xxvi. 45; Lk. xxii. 53). The saying about His life: 'No one taketh it away from me, but I lay it down of myself' (Jn. x. 18), is only a fuller expression of that sense of destiny which has impressed all the Evangelists. Common also is the idea that Jesus dies for others. In John He lays down His life 'for the sheep' (x. 11); in Mark He gives His life a ransom 'for many' (x. 45). Sacrificial language is also found both in Jn. xii. 24, xvii. 19 and in Mk. x. 45, xiv. 24, although the sayings are entirely different in content. Finally, in all the Gospels eucharistic ideas stand in the closest association with the sacrifice of Christ (Jn. vi. 51-8; Mk. xiv. 22, 24).

Other sayings remain to be considered; but of those already noticed it may be said that, substantially, the ideas are the same in all the Gospels, although in the Fourth Gospel some of them are more strongly emphasized or are given a somewhat different turn. The latter is especially true of the sayings in Jn. vi. 51-8. In Mk. xiv. 22 and 24 the bread and the wine are spoken of as having a certain value and significance: spiritually, they are the body and blood of Christ, and are means of participating in the sacrificial offering of Christ. In the Johannine sayings, the teaching contained in the words: 'This is my body,' 'This is my blood,' is assumed, but the significance of the actions of eating and drinking is differently expressed. 'He that eateth my flesh and drinketh my blood hath eternal life; and I will raise him up at the last day' (vi. 54). 'He that eateth my flesh and drinketh my blood abideth in me, and I in him' (vi. 56). In these words the imparted gift is not that of a share in Christ's self-offering; it is eternal life and communion with Christ Himself. How is this difference to be explained?

One explanation of the difference is that the Evangelist

has transposed sayings originally spoken at the Supper to
their present position in chapter vi.   This hypothesis enables us to account for their character.   It is not in the
least probable that the Synoptic sayings include all that
was said at the Supper.   Mk. xiv. 22, 24 would hardly
have been intelligible to the disciples without further explanation.   It is significant, therefore, that the sayings in Jn.
vi. 51-8 supply a further unfolding of at least one aspect of
the thought of Jesus.   Participation in His sacrifice and
communion with Himself are not contradictory ideas, but
thoughts intimately related to each other, and it is a natural
transition to pass from one to the other.   The Johannine
sayings, then, may represent the interpretative teachings of
Jesus Himself.   A second possibility is that the sayings
stand in their historical place in Jn. vi, in connexion with
the eschatological sacramental meal which probably lies
behind the account of the Feeding of the Five Thousand.[1]
In this case, however, it is necessary to suppose that the
content of the sayings has been influenced by other sayings
associated with the Last Supper, since in Jn. vi. 51-8 the
suffering and triumph of Jesus are implied.   Such a fu-
sion is by no means unintelligible in a mind like that of the
Evangelist who is far more interested in the significance
of Jesus than in the precise succession of events.   Either
of these views is perferable to a third possibility, namely,
that the sayings have no historical relation to anything that
Jesus said and taught; for to say that the sayings are merely the Evangelist's inventions is not even a plausible explanation of the nature and worth of the Fourth Gospel.

Between the first two explanations it is not possible to
decide.   In either case we must conclude that, to an extent incapable of precise determination, the sayings are
expressed in the Evangelist's language and are influenced

[1] See earlier, p. 185.

by his experience and that of the Church of Ephesus. The use of the term 'flesh' (σάρξ), and perhaps also the use of τρώγω instead of the Synoptic ἐσθίω, are peculiarities of the Evangelist's vocabulary; the emphasis on 'eternal life' and communion with Christ illustrates his spiritual interests and those of the Ephesian community. This conclusion means that in the sayings there is an element of interpretation as well as of recollection. The interpretation, however, begins with words and thoughts of Jesus, and for this reason the results of the process are gain, and not loss, for the historian as well as for the Christian believer.

These sayings have been considered in detail because they represent the point of maximum difficulty. If our conclusion in respect of them is sound, it is reasonable to infer that, as a class, the Johannine Passion-sayings which have Synoptic parallels possess real historical value, not the value of a verbatim report but that of a later version which brings out their meaning in terms of life and Christian experience.

Can this conclusion be extended to those sayings which have no parallel, or no close parallel, in the Synoptic tradition? The examination already made, it may be claimed, sets up a presumption in favour of an affirmative answer, but beyond this point only broad statements of probability are possible. The sayings which invite attention in this connexion are the two which contain sacrificial ideas or images, xii. 24 and xvii. 19; the sayings: 'Greater love' (xv. 13), and: 'Now is the judgement of this world' (xii. 31); the words about the revelation of the Son of Man in viii. 28; and, finally, those which imply the universality of the benefits of Christ's death x. 16, in xii. 32, and xvii. 2.[1]

---

[1] What has been said already concerning vi. 51-8, x. 11, 15f., 17f., xii. 23, 27f., may perhaps be regarded as sufficient.

It was Renan who remarked that the whole of xii. 20-6 is 'exempt from any dogmatical or symbolical design',[1] and only those who doubt the genuineness of all the Johannine sayings will question the originality of the words: 'Except a grain of wheat . . .' (xii. 24). It is less easy to feel certain about the character of the saying: 'For their sakes I sanctify myself' (xvii. 19) because it appears in the long high-priestly prayer, but it is in no way unsuitable to the situation of Jesus or out of harmony with His thoughts. For most people the saying: 'Greater love' (xv. 13), bears its own signature, and Dibelius has ably contended that its form and content suggest that it already formed part of the Evangelist's 'tradition'.[2] The caution of the critic appears when he adds that it cannot be said with certainty that it is a case of the reproduction or recasting of a genuine 'Jesus-word'.[3] The same hesitation must naturally arise in connexion with the saying :'Now is the judgement of this world: now shall the prince of this world be cast out' (xii. 31). The thought at least is harmonious with the idea of deliverance in the 'ransom-passage'(Mk. x. 45) and with the saying in the L tradition: 'This is your hour, and the power of darkness' (Lk. xxii. 53). Jesus undoubtedly regarded His Passion, in one of its aspects, as a conflict with the powers of evil; and the expectation of victory, voiced in the Johannine saying, agrees with the confident hope with which He approached Jerusalem.[4] If this is so, critical hesitation about the precise terms of the Johannine passage is a matter of secondary importance. The same view may also be taken of the saying: 'When ye have lifted up the Son of man, then shall ye know that I am

---

[1] *Life of Jesus*, 13th ed., 297.
[2] *Festgäbe für Adolf Deissmann*, 168-86.
[3] *Op. cit.*, 183.
[4] See p. 186.

he, and that I do nothing of myself, but as the Father taught me, I speak these things' (viii. 28). While there is no express parallel in the Synoptic Gospels, the idea that after His death Jesus will be seen as the Son of Man is found in Mk. xiv. 62 : 'Ye shall see the Son of Man sitting at the right hand of power.' Jesus also may well have said that the future would vindicate His claim to speak in accordance with the Father's revelation to Himself. There is therefore no legitimate objection to the saying as a genuine word of Jesus. Even if the saying is a creation of the Evangelist, it is still true that it represents the mind and thought of Jesus.

In a class by themselves stand the sayings which imply the universality of the effects of the sacrifice of Jesus :

x. 16: 'And other sheep I have, which are not of this fold: them also I must bring, and they shall hear my voice: and they shall become one flock, one shepherd.'

xii. 32: 'And I, if I be lifted up from the earth, will draw all men unto myself.'

xvii. 2: 'Even as thou gavest him authority over all flesh, that whatsoever thou hast given him, to them he should give eternal life.'

To many readers of the Gospel it is a pointed example of the futility of criticism that any one should question the genuineness of sayings so dear to the Christian heart. In reality, the problem cannot be dismissed if the Gospel is read intelligently. The point in debate is not the truth of the sayings, but whether, as they stand, they are likely to have been the words of Jesus. The question might be answered easily were it not for the fact that no saying of Jesus in the Synoptic tradition asserts the universality of the effects of His Passion. Jesus speaks of giving His life and of shedding His covenant-blood 'for many', but He does not say expressly that He dies for all or for the world. It would, of course, be entirely erroneous to infer that He had in mind a limited circle of believers who should be blessed by His sacrifice. Such an idea has only to be stated to be rejected, for it is wholly out of harmony with His spirit. The Johannine sayings under consideration are certainly nearer the truth. It is less evident, however, that they are His actual words.

The silence of the Synoptists on this point of universality is remarkable, when it is remembered how strongly it is emphasized in the Acts and the Pauline Epistles. It is an inescapable inference that, had words of Jesus been known which asserted that He would give His life for the world, they would have been included in the Synoptic Gospels, and in Mark and Luke in particular. As it is, they are not found, except as universalism appears in the outlook and teaching of Jesus.[1] This fact is one of the strongest proofs of the essential trustworthiness of the Synoptic tradition; it is also the justification of the critical view that the Johannine sayings under consideration are the Evangelist's interpretations and not directly the words of Jesus Himself. Why He did not explicitly speak of dying for the world is not difficult to understand. Jesus did not use concepts like 'mankind' or 'humanity', nor does He appear to have dwelt, after the manner of a theologian, upon the more ultimate aspects of His Passion. His interests, as revealed by the Gospels, are supremely personal and religious, and are intimately related to the immediate circumstances of daily life. He speaks of His Passion within the framework presented by Old Testament thought and in relation to His disciples and His immediate followers. Wider horizons are constantly suggested in His teaching, but they are hinted and implied

---

[1] See the important articles of C. J. Cadoux, 'Judaism and Universalism in the Gospels,' *Expository Times*, xxxviii., 55-60, 136-140.

rather than expressed directly. What He says stands against a Judaic background and is directed to the needs of present hearers. Thus, on occasion He speaks of 'the lost sheep of the house of Israel', and of 'the twelve tribes of Israel', and uses language which, if pressed, might suggest, in contradiction to other utterances of His, an attitude of Jewish particularism. It is entirely in harmony with such a habit of mind and of speech that references to the world or to men in general are wanting. The reverse is true of the mind and outlook of the Fourth Evangelist. His standpoint and the circumstances of his Hellenistic environment throw into relief this very question of universalism. In consequence, when he comes to record sayings of Jesus regarding His Passion, he inevitably expresses them in accordance with his own beliefs, without realising, it may even be, that in the form he gives to them he is going beyond what was actually said. In recording such sayings he does not reproduce spoken words of Jesus, but unfolds the ultimate implications of His teaching, and for this reason he is an invaluable interpreter of His mind and thought.

Our conclusion, then, is the same in respect of the sayings without parallel in the Synoptic Gospels as in the case of those already examined, although naturally it cannot be presented as strongly and cogently. An element of interpretation, manifest in some more than in others, enters into all the Johannine Passion-sayings. None the less, contact with original utterances of Jesus is close, with the result that the Evangelist's 'coloured' version, rightly understood, is one that the historian cannot afford to neglect or dismiss.

In the end the difference between the common and the critical view of these sayings is much less than might be supposed. The common view reaches its results at a leap;

the critical method climbs with painful steps and many hesitations.   If it be said; 'Why, then, not leap?' the answer is that a blind leap is not possible for any one who has once perceived the nature of the Johannine problem. Henceforward, he must either lose all confidence in the Fourth Gospel, or win his way by struggle and search.   If he reaches solid ground, as indeed he may, his reward is the consciousness that in his long journey he has not divided intelligence and faith.   His treasure is not a gift passively received, but a possession he has been privileged to win, understood and prized the more because at times he seemed to be within an ace of losing it altogether, but most of all because he now perceives its true nature and value.

PART III
DOCTRINAL

INTRODUCTION

Now that the Old Testament background of the thought of Jesus has been sketched, and the Passion-sayings have been examined, it remains to ask the decisive question: How did Jesus interpret His sufferings and death?

Obviously, the first thing to do is to assemble the leading thoughts which are expressed in the sayings, and to illustrate the amount of evidence on which they rest. This task will be undertaken in Chapter I.

It is naturally to be expected that some of the ideas which must necessarily be included in the summary will raise more ultimate questions than can be answered by the simple expedient of quoting a saying of Jesus. It is also necessary to ask whether there is any unifying principle which binds together the conclusions which directly or indirectly can be based upon the sayings, and which may be regarded as a determinative conception in the mind of Jesus. These broader questions will be treated in Chapter II.

A final question must be considered in Chapter III. Such an investigation as the present is not complete unless it enables us to say how the purpose of Jesus is related to the thought of today. The place of Jesus Christ in the continuous life of the Church, and in Christian experience are facts of life and history; and, if the universe of thought is a rational whole, it must be possible to assign some organic relationship between them and the earliest data of Christian tradition. There is a point at which the interests of criticism, faith, and worship intersect; and, while specialisation must always have its necessary place in the search for truth, nothing less than unification of thought is the final goal of inquiry.

I

THE IMMEDIATE IMPLICATIONS OF THE PASSION-SAYINGS

IN accordance with what has been said in the Introduction, the first task is to assemble the leading thoughts which are implicit in the Passion-sayings examined in Part II. Such a summary, it may be expected, must be both bare and fragmentary. It is important to recognize the reason for this. The investigator of to-day is not in the happy position of having at his disposal all the relevant sayings of Jesus; he cannot even assume that he has more than a few of the more important of them. The study of the formation of the Gospel tradition, absolutely essential to such an inquiry as the present, reveals plainly that the sayings preserved in the Gospels are those which met immediate needs of conduct and belief. Only in part are they those which a historian or a theologian would have collected if Providence had entrusted the preservation of the earliest tradition to such intermediaries.

The late Canon Sanday used to urge that, in estimating the bearing of existing early testimony on the authorship of the Fourth Gospel, we should consider the relation of the extant evidence to the whole body of that which once existed.[1] The reminder is pertinent, and *mutatis mutandis* applies to all historical inquiries. The results, of course, would be injurious if the reminder made it easy to assign to the past only the conceptions which please us;

[1] *The Criticism of the Fourth Gospel*, 40.

but it is all to the good if it delivers us from the assumption that the available evidence is sufficient for dogmatism based on limited knowledge. The evidence presented by the sayings is fragmentary; and the task of the historian is not merely that of building a skeleton of thought, but of clothing it with flesh and blood. If, however, he is wise, he will assemble the fragments first. This is the undertaking of the present chapter. The several sayings have been examined, and the question now is how far they can be articulated.

1. The most fundamental idea which lies behind the Passion-sayings is the steadfast belief of Jesus that the purpose and experiences of His Passion lay deep in the Providence of God. He did not look upon His sufferings as chance events, or as a stroke of fate, or simply as a tragedy compassed by men. On the contrary, His experiences were events determined in the counsels of God. 'How is it written of the Son of man', He asked of His three disciples, 'that he should suffer many things and be set at nought?' (Mk. ix. 12b). The very form of the question suggests a thought long pondered and a lesson vainly taught. The same conviction is expressed in the three Markan sayings which assert that the Son of Man 'must suffer' (Mk. viii. 31, ix. 31, x. 33f.), and in the similar saying in the L tradition: 'But first must he suffer many things and be rejected of this generation' (Lk. xvii. 25). The necessity laid upon Him is an inner constraint independent of the machinations of men. Into the same context of ideas fall His allusions to Old Testament passages. He is 'the stone which the builders rejected', destined by God to become 'the head of the corner' (Mk. xii. 10f). He is 'the shepherd' at whose smiting 'the sheep shall be scattered abroad' (Mk. xiv. 27). It is with especial clearness that His conviction of divine purpose is expressed in His

prophecy of betrayal: 'The Son of man goeth, even as it is written of him' (Mk. xiv. 2 1).   As we have seen, this identification of the Son of Man with the Suffering Servant is so firmly established in the mind of Jesus that He can say of the former what in the Old Testament is said only of the latter.[1]   The same attitude is seen in Gethsemane when Judas draws near, for the words: 'Arise, let us be going' (Mk. xiv. 42), are not a cry of panic but a call to action.[2]   Now as always Jesus is master of the situation.

The Fourth Gospel is at one with the Synoptics in representing this sense of Providential purpose as a conviction of Jesus.   The Passion is 'the hour' of destiny (xii. 2 3, 2 7, xvii. 1). Of His life He says: 'No one taketh it away from me, but I lay it down of myself.   I have power to lay it down, and I have power to take it again. This commandment received I from my Father' (x. 1 8).

2. Closely connected with the foregoing principle is the fact that, in all that concerned His Passion, Jesus looked upon the relationship between Himself and the Father as one of perfect unity.   In no saying of His is there any suggestion of opposition or antagonism; His will and that of the Father are one.   The classic expression of this fact is the prayer in Gethsemane: 'Abba, Father, all things are possible unto thee; remove this cup from me: howbeit not what I will, but what thou wilt' (Mk. xiv. 36).   Here, indeed, is the human shrinking of a sensitive spirit; none the less, the prayer expresses a perfect acceptance of the divine will.   What Jesus does is well-pleasing to the Father, and what the Father wills He does.   A similar thought is implied in the parable of the Vineyard in the words: 'they will reverence my son' (Mk. xii. 6).   Obedience and oneness of aim and purpose are taken for granted.   Jesus comes as God's final envoy; the

[1]Cf. p. 113.   [2]Cf. p. 156.

initiative is divine, and of disharmony or conflict there is no suggestion.

The Fourth Gospel reflects exactly the same attitude. Indeed, it presents it more pointedly, although at the expense of historical realism. In the Johannine counterpart to the prayer of Gethsemane, Jesus is troubled and proposes to Himself the question: 'What shall I say? Father, save me from this hour?'[1] only to reject the suggestion in the words: 'But for this cause came I unto this hour. Father, glorify thy name' (xii. 27f). This conciousness of fulfilling the Father's will is also voiced in the words already quoted in the previous section: 'This commandment received I from my Father' (x. 18).

3. A further point of the greatest importance is the fact that Jesus interpreted His suffering, death, and resurrection positively, as active elements in His Messianic vocation. He did not speak of His Passion as a revelation, however true this aspect of it may be, but rather as a task laid upon Him which it was His mission to accomplish for men. 'I have a baptism to be baptized with,' He says, 'and how am I straitened till it be accomplished!' (Lk. xii. 50). There is a note of urgency in these words and a clear indication that in His death, as in His life, Jesus is seeking to fulfil an end. A further illustration is His declaration that 'the Son of man came not to be served, but to serve, and to give his life a ransom for many' (Mk. x. 45). That an active process is meant, is clear, and the use of the title, Son of Man, shows that Messianic action is contemplated. Jesus is not thinking of service in general, but of definite blessings which He will confer on men by dying. His death is like the ransom by which a slave

---

[1]Probably a question and not a request, since the Markan story is recast under the influence of the Fourth Evangelist's theology. Cf. Macgregor, 266; Lagrange, 332f. See also Jn. xviii. 11b.

R

is set free; it secures for the many the freedom they cannot obtain for themselves.   The 'ransom-saying' does not stand alone in this connexion.   The sayings which declare that the Son of Man 'must suffer' also point to an active Messianic vocation, and the same is probably true of the 'cup' which Jesus is to drink (cf. Mk. x. 38, xiv. 36). Jesus also refers to His death as an event in which He is to be 'perfected' (Lk. xiii. 32), and since immediately before He speaks of going on His way 'to-day and to-morrow', the presumption is that He is to be 'perfected' in the carrying out of His vocation.   All these indications show that to Him His Passion is not only something to be endured; it is an achievement to which His life is dedicated.

It is remarkable how little this aspect of the thought of Jesus finds expression in the sayings of the Fourth Gospel. It is implicit in the words: 'For their sakes I sanctify myself' (Jn. xvii. 19), where Jesus is revealed as one dedicated to a holy purpose, and, as part of the Evangelist's theology, it is expressed in the words assigned to the Baptist: 'Behold the Lamb of God, which taketh away the sin of the world!' (Jn. i. 29); but otherwise it is not found in this Gospel, probably because the Evangelist's main interest is the revelation or manifestation of the Word, not the purpose which Jesus, as the Messiah, came to achieve.

4. The Passion-sayings also imply that, in fulfilling His Messianic vocation, Jesus thought of His Passion as closely connected with the Kingdom of God.   Jesus does not teach that His death is the inauguration of the Kingdom, for already, in Himself and in His Messianic acts, it is present. 'If I by the finger of God cast out devils, then is the kingdom of God come upon you' (Lk. xi. 20).   None the less, His words clearly show that He thinks of His suffering and death as necessary to the establishing of the Divine Rule.   It is characteristic of Him that, strongly

influenced as He is by Isa. liii, He does not describe Himself as the Servant when He speaks of His suffering, but always as the Son of Man. It is as the *Son of Man* that He 'must suffer' (Mk. viii. 31, &c.); as the *Son of Man* that He comes 'to give his life a ransom for many' (Mk. x. 45); as the *Son of Man* that He 'goeth even as it is written of him' (Mk. xiv. 21); as the *Son of Man* that He is 'betrayed into the hands of sinners' (Mk. xiv. 41). In full view of death He declares that the priests will see 'the *Son of Man* sitting at the right hand of power, and coming with the clouds of heaven' (Mk. xiv. 62). This usage indicates how intimately the Kingdom and His death are related in His thinking. Indirectly, as we have seen, the same relationship is suggested when, at the descent from the Mount, He endorses the popular belief that the coming of Elijah is a sign of the End, and thrusts into this context of thought the question: 'And how is it written of the *Son of Man*, that he should suffer many things and be set at nought?' (Mk. ix. 12b). Current conceptions regarding the Messiah and the Kingdom are replaced by a new and original view, which sets at the centre the thought of the necessity of Messianic suffering.

Further evidence is supplied by the sayings at the Supper. Plainly in Mark, and even more clearly in Luke, Jesus interpreted the Supper as, in one of its aspects, an anticipation of the great Messianic Feast (cf. Mk. xiv. 25; Lk. xxii. 18, 29f). Thus it appears that the thought of the Kingdom, so central in the Galilean teaching, glows in the very shadow of the Cross. Jesus both lives and dies absorbed in the thought of the Reign of God.

In the Fourth Gospel, as is well known, this interest is less apparent, although it is not wanting. The phrase, the Kingdom of God, is found twice only, in the story of Nicodemus, and in neither case in connexion with Christ's

death.   It is probable, however, that 'eternal life' is the
Johannine equivalent for the Kingdom of God; and in this
case, in another form, and as denoting life in its richest
expression, the phrase describes what is entailed by the
Rule of God.   This conception is brought in the Fourth
Gospel into association with the Passion when Jesus says:
'He that eateth my flesh and drinketh my blood hath eternal life' (Jn. vi. 54; cf. xvii. 2).   Moreover, in the account
of the trial before Pilate, Jesus says: '*My kingdom* is not of
this world: if *my kingdom* were of this world, then would my
servants fight, that I should not be delivered to the Jews:
but now is *my kingdom* not from hence' (Jn. xviii. 36).
Whatever may be the historical character of the Evangelist's account of this incident, it is clear that he is aware of
the place which the thought of the Kingdom occupied in
the mind of Jesus in the very face of death.

How Jesus understood the connexion between His suf-
ering and the Kingdom of God, is not disclosed in His sayings.   The question is obviously one for consideration
later.   Of the connexion itself there can be no doubt, and
it may well be that material for an answer is supplied in
other aspects of His thought yet to be examined.

5.   One aspect of the thought of Jesus in relation to the
Kingdom is His belief that His death is a victorious
struggle with the powers of evil.   'This is your hour', He
says to those who effect the arrest, 'and the power of darkness' (Lk. xxii. 53b).   The implication is that Jesus is
conscious of the menace of evil powers.   The 'ransom-
saying' also suggests that He thought of men as being in
bondage to evil and of His death as the means of securing
their release: 'The Son of man came . . . to give his life a
ransom for many' (Mk. x. 45).   Indeed, many of the Passion-sayings might be included under this category, such
as, for example, the declarations that the Son of Man 'must

suffer', if there were reason to think of it as the master-principle of His thinking. The presence, however, of other ideas in His sayings shows that it is but a single strand in His thought; it is the dramatic representation of the purpose of His Passion. Aulén is completely justified in maintaining that the idea of the death of Jesus as the conquest of Satan, evil, and death, which for a thousand years was the 'classic view' of the Atonement, is rooted in the Gospel tradition.[1] In the Fourth Gospel it appears in the words: 'Now is the judgement of this world: now shall the prince of this world be cast out' (Jn. xii. 31). Undoubtedly, it is one of the ways in which Jesus related His Passion to the establishment of the Kingdom of God.

6. More central is the belief of Jesus that His Messianic suffering is representative and vicarious. It is borne for men and it avails for them. This belief is implied in the declaration that it is 'for many' that the Son of Man comes to give His life, and in the saying: 'This is my blood of the covenant, which is shed for many' (Mk. xiv. 24). These sayings indicate that the death of Jesus has for its objective the deepest need of man. As we have urged,[2] the first saying must not be watered down to the simple assertion that the service of Jesus in dying is for the advantage of the many. The 'ransom' which He gives is something they are unable to provide, but which He, in the fullness of His grace, supplies in their stead. The saying regarding the covenant implies that, in dying, it is His purpose to make possible a relationship of true fellowship between men and God. The reference to 'blood' is intelligible only as a sacrificial concept; it denotes life freely offered for others. Postponing for further discussion the many questions which the sayings raise, we must boldly conclude that Jesus believed that, as the Messiah, He would suffer as the

[1] Cf. *Christus Victor*.   [2] Cf. p. 100f.

representative of men, on their behalf and in their stead, and that the effect of His death would be to establish that fellowship with God on which His rule depends. The two sayings are complementary. In the 'ransom-saying' the emphasis is upon deliverance; in the words about the covenant it is upon fellowship. Both imply a sundered relationship which is restored by sacrifice.

The same conclusions are suggested by the use which Jesus made of the Servant-conception. This, however, is a point which cannot be directly established by His recorded sayings; it is an inference based on the nature of the Servant-conception and the influence it is likely to have had upon the mind of Jesus when He used it to recast the Messianic idea in relation to Himself and the Kingdom. This question raises wider issues than those which can be considered at present, and must be reserved for discussion in the next chapter.

In the Fourth Gospel Jesus speaks of His death as vicarious when He declares that the bread which He will give is His flesh, 'for the life of the world' (vi. 51), and when He describes Himself as 'the good shepherd' who 'layeth down his life for the sheep' (x. 11). The same truth appears also in the words: 'For their sakes I sanctify myself' (xvii. 19). In this Gospel, however, there is no saying of Jesus which implies that He stands to men in a representative relationship, although it is clear, from i. 29, that this belief was a part of the Evangelist's theology. This fact does not compromise the import of the Synoptic sayings considered above, but, as already argued, is an illustration of the selective method adopted in this Gospel.

7. In addition to the sayings which imply that the suffering of Jesus was representative and vicarious, there are others which point to a close personal relationship between Himself and sinners, and, in consequence, to a poignant

experience of the consequences of sin. Our examination
of the words: 'For I say unto you, that this which is written must be fulfilled in me, And he was reckoned with
transgressors' (Lk. xxii. 37; cf. Isa. liii. 12), suggested
that the saying expresses a sense of Messianic vocation in-
volving self-identification with sinners; but how far this
inference is justified depends on the larger consideration of
the Servant-conception mentioned in the last section.
Certainly, it seems a very inadequate interpretation of the
saying if we say that it implies no more than the prophecy
of Jesus that the Jewish hierarchy would treat Him as a
transgressor. Other sayings, however, point more clearly
to an intimate experience of spiritual suffering. Such
sayings are Mk. x. 38: 'Are ye able to drink the cup
that I drink? or to be baptized with the baptism that I am
baptized with?'; Lk. xii. 50: 'I have a baptism to be baptized with; and how am I straitened till it be accomplished!'; and the prayer in Gethsemane recorded in Mk.
xiv. 36: 'Abba, Father, all things are possible unto thee;
remove this cup from me: howbeit not what I will, but
what thou wilt.' These utterances express spiritual
agony, not simply physical and mental distress. This
impression is deepened when the words: 'My soul is exceeding sorrowful even unto death' (Mk. xiv. 34), are
considered; and most of all by the cry from the Cross: My
God, my God, why hast thou forsaken me?' (Mk. xv. 34).
The conclusion, that in these words the accents of spiritual
desolation are heard, is much easier of acceptance if it is
recognized that Jesus is almost overwhelmed by the knowledge of human sin. The speaker is not the Galilean her-
ald of the Kingdom, but One who has taken upon Himself the Messianic rôle of the Suffering Saviour of men and
has identified Himself with those He represents and serves.

This aspect of the Passion of Jesus is wanting in the

Fourth Gospel, except so far as it is implied in the sayings which describe the death as vicarious.   This deficiency is due to the Evangelist's preoccupation with the thought of Christ as the Divine Word and Son of God.   It is here more than anywhere else that one gains the impression that the Prologue (Jn. i. 1-18), if it does not dominate the Gospel throughout, certainly focuses its leading ideas. It is in keeping with the Johannine delineation that, through believing, men enter into union with Christ as the branches are related to the vine; but it is foreign to its presentation that the Son should identify Himself with sinners and enter into an experience of the night of sin.   As depicted in the Fourth Gospel Christ is indeed the Saviour (cf. iv. 42), but as the Revealer of God, not the Redeemer of men.[1]

Since the Fourth Evangelist's failure to present this aspect of the Messianic suffering of Jesus is explicable in the light of his doctrinal and religious purpose, it has no bearing at all upon the historical character of the Synoptic sayings instanced above.   In themselves, these are enough to authenticate the keen spiritual suffering of Jesus, in the pursuance of His vocation, as an essential part of the Gospel tradition.   What is involved in this suffering, its character and significance, are questions answered by none of the sayings which have been preserved.   These problems, however, are matters which the historian, as well as the theologian, must consider in connexion with the sayings and the wider indications of the thought of Jesus regarding the Kingdom, the Messianic Hope, the Suffering Servant, and the doctrine of sacrifice.   The fact directly attested by the Synoptic sayings is an intense

---

[1]In view of Jn. i. 29 and of 1 Jn. i. 7, ii. 1f., iii. 5, iv. 10, the restraint shown in the Evangelist's fidelity to this representation is the most remarkable example of religious portraiture in literature.

spiritual agony endured by Jesus in the fulfilment of His vocation for men.

8. Thus far our attention has been limited to those aspects of the suffering and death of Jesus which concern His personal relationships with the Father and with men; the vocation is one which He Himself must fulfil. This, however, is not the whole of His teaching; there are sayings which show that He intended men to participate in His self-offering and to appropriate the power of His surrendered life. His redemptive service is not intended to be a work wrought apart from men; it is rather a work into which they are permitted to enter, in such a way that what He does on their behalf becomes a vital factor in their approach to God.

This is a side of the thought of Jesus to which insufficient attention has often been given, in consequence of the tendency to think of the Atonement as a 'finished work' which man has simply to accept as a gift of grace. Everything has been done by Christ; man has only to receive the benefits of His death! The extent to which this idea is rooted in the teaching of Jesus is evident; it is a reflection of the tremendous emphasis in the sayings already considered upon the unique character of His Messianic vocation. The redemption He provides and the fellowship He makes possible are utterly beyond the power of man. Such is the unmistakable assumption reflected by the words and attitude of Jesus.

It does not necessarily follow, however, from this view of the redemptive work of Jesus that man's attitude thereto is entirely passive; and there is clear evidence in the Passion-sayings that this was not His thought. On the contrary, the attitude for which He looks is essentially active; men are to share in the power of His self-offering and make it their sacrifice before God. And they are to do this, not merely by pleading the merits of something external to themselves, but by relating themselves so intimately to Christ's achievement that, without adding to it anything of their own devising, it becomes an essential element in their personal dealings with God.

I have conjectured that the rudiments of such an attitude as this are discernible in the part which Jesus expected His three intimate disciples to play during the Agony of Gethsemane.[1]   The reiterated demand that they should watch and pray is not a cry for protection, but a demand for sympathy and understanding in the hour of His Messianic suffering.   It is an appeal for that attitude of mind and spirit which gives meaning to what He does.   There is, however, too much that is mysterious in this story for any interpreter to speak with certainty or to press his views upon the acceptance of others.   All that can be asserted definitely is that the central features in this episode are the need of Jesus and the failure of the disciples.   That He looked for them to play a human part in His Messianic activity, is an inference which requires further evidence.

The proof that Jesus intended men to participate in the power of His self-offering is supplied by the Supper-sayings.   These sayings are absolutely vital to an understanding of the attitude of Jesus to His death.   In Part II they have been examined in detail,[2] and the attempt must now be made to relate the results there reached to the problem as a whole.   It was argued that, when Jesus bade His disciples eat the bread and drink the wine, He was inviting them to share in the life which He was offering on their behalf.   The metaphorical expressions in the sayings: 'This is my body,' 'This is my blood of the covenant, which is shed for many' (Mk. xiv. 22, 24), are the terms 'body' and 'blood', which signify in different ways the life

[1]Cf. pp. 150f, 155f.   [2]See pp. 118-39.

of Jesus given for men. To eat, therefore, the bread and to drink the wine, is to participate in the surrendered life and to appropriate its consecrating power. The elements are both symbols and media and derive this significance from the word of Jesus Himself. The bearing of this conception upon the Messianic activity of Jesus, as He conceived it, is clear. Jesus did not regard His service as accomplished apart from, and independent of, men; it was a sacrifice consummated only as men entered into it and made it their spiritual possession.

It is beside the point to argue that, since the death of Jesus was still to be accomplished, the Supper was provisional and anticipatory.[1] Rather must it be maintained that at the Supper Jesus thought of His Messianic work as a present reality of which death, followed by resurrection, would be the culmination. There is no hint in the Synoptic sayings of a spiritual food available only after death. Indeed, the bread and the wine are not primarily indicated as food, but as means for participating in a redemptive activity.

In the Fourth Gospel there is nothing corresponding to this conception. As we have seen,[2] its sacramental sayings do not imply any relationship between men and the sacrificial ministry of Jesus, but speak rather of the gift of 'eternal life' and of communion with Christ as conveyed to the believer. Once more, this difference is due to the Evangelist's selective purpose and to his predominating emphasis upon the death of Christ as a revelation of love.

Many problems are raised by the relationship between

---

[1]Cf. N. P. Williams, *Essays Catholic and Critical*, 406, 423. 'Their first real and sacramental Communion in the body and blood of Christ can only have been made after that body and blood had been glorified and freed from spatial limitations by the resurrection,' *ibid.*, 423.

[2]See p. 242.

the Eucharist and the suffering and death of Jesus, and, in particular, the whole question of faith. These points, however, are matters for consideration in the following chapter, inasmuch as the answers cannot be drawn from explicit utterances of Jesus. For the present it is enough to note the positive inference, supported by the Supper-sayings, that Jesus did not regard His Messianic suffering as an automatic or self-acting work, but as an activity which is completed in a human relationship thereto. This principle is of the greatest ethical importance, for it stamps at once any conception of Christ's death as an external means of salvation as entirely foreign to His thought.

9. Finally, it is the paradox of the teaching of Jesus that, although His vocation of Messianic suffering is unique, He none the less interprets it as an activity which, in some measure, men are to reproduce. Thus, He assures the sons of Zebedee that they shall indeed participate in the cup of His suffering. 'The cup that I drink ye shall drink' (Mk. x. 39). If we believe that for Jesus the 'cup' was a symbol of more than martyrdom, we must draw the same conclusion in respect of His declaration regarding James and John. Suffering in the service of the King-dom is the least interpretation of which His words are capable. What is meant is a suffering which in some sense is representative and vicarious, and which has for its end the realisation of the Reign of God. The same in-ference is probably justified in the case of the saying: 'If any man would come after me, let him deny himself, and take up his cross, and follow me' (Mk. viii. 34). Some-thing more than a general exhortation to manifest the spirit of self-sacrifice is meant by these words; they imply that Jesus believed that what He was doing as the Messiah, in like manner His followers were called upon to do. It is impossible to suppose, with the Passion-sayings before us,

that Jesus thought that in this matter He and His follow-
ers stood on the same plane, as fellow-sufferers in a com-
mon redemptive service; the sense of a unique vocation in
His words is too strong for such a view to be entertained.
But it is also impossible to conclude that He looked upon
His suffering as utterly solitary, without parallel or ana-
logue in the experience of men. The Cross was supremely
His, but just because of this He could see it everywhere.

The Fourth Gospel does not contain sayings fully comparable to those cited above, but it does speak of parallel
sufferings which disciples of Jesus are called to undergo,
including hatred by the world (xv. 19), persecution (xv.
20), tribulation (xvi. 33), and death (xvi. 2). Twice it
declares that 'a servant is not greater than his lord' (xiii.
16, xv. 20), and the implication is that what Jesus does or
suffers is a pattern or example which, to the extent of their
power, His followers are to copy. That this Gospel does
not contain sayings which demand more than fidelity to
the example of Christ, is in harmony with its representation of His death as mainly a manifestation of divine love.

The principal ideas which are implicit in the Passion-
sayings have now been indicated, and it remains to consider
them as a whole.

The comparison of the Synoptic sayings with those of
the Fourth Gospel is instructive. It confirms the conclusion already apparent in Part II,[1] that the witness of
this Gospel to the meaning of Christ's death is limited in
range, owing to the Evangelist's predilections and the
purpose he had in view in writing his Gospel. Summarily
stated, the implications of the Johannine Passion-sayings
ascribed to Jesus are that a deep-seated necessity lay
behind His death, which was entirely under His control
and in accordance with the Father's will, and which was

[1] See pp. 232, 238ff.

vicarious without being representative and expiatory.
The death is a supreme expression of love, and is conceived,
in the main, as a departure from the limitations of earthly
existence so that the life of the Exalted Christ can be appropriated by the believer in faith and in sacramental
communion.

The conclusion is inescapable that, important as this representation is for religious and devotional purposes, it is
of little value to the historian who seeks to discover how
Jesus contemplated His suffering and death. Equally
for the theologian the gain is small. By restricting his
construction within the limits set by the Fourth Gospel he
obtains a theory which is easy to state and which offends
the susceptibilities of no one, but he gains it by ignoring
half the problems of the doctrine and by neglecting or explaining away striking sayings in the Synoptic tradition.
To say this is not to deny the value of the Fourth Gospel
which lies elsewhere, especially in connexion with the doctrine of the Incarnate Word; it is rather to place the Johannine representation regarding the suffering and death of
Jesus in its true place, as secondary and subordinate to the
evidence afforded by the Synoptic Gospels. The sound-
est procedure for the investigator is to concentrate attention on the Synoptic sayings, noting where they are confirmed by the Johannine sayings but making no discount
in cases where the testimony of the Fourth Gospel is
wanting.

Adopting this method, it will be useful to assemble the
several results already gained from our study of the Passion-sayings. These may be stated briefly as follows.

Jesus looked upon His suffering and death as the fulfilment of a divine purpose, in which His will was at one
with that of the Father, and in virtue of which He accepted
an active vocation connected with the Rule of God. He

thought of His death as a victorious struggle with the powers of evil, and interpreted His suffering, in relation to men, as representative and vicarious in a sacrificial ministry which involved participation in the consequences of human sin. So far, however, was He from thinking of His Messianic work as automatic and self-acting in its results that He provided a rite whereby men should be able to share in the power of His surrendered life and make His offering their own. He also called upon men to reproduce an experience of cross-bearing in their lives.

This summary should not be regarded as a complete statement of the way in which Jesus regarded His suffering and death. It is merely a convenient articulation of the several inferences which have been drawn from the Passion-sayings in the course of the present chapter. Many questions are raised which require further consideration and must be examined in the following chapter. One point of the utmost importance, however, may be made now. The summary reveals the outlines of an intelligible attitude to the Cross. It may, therefore, prove misleading to say that Jesus had no theory of atonement in respect of His death. If by this common opinion it is meant that He formulated no doctrinal theory such as can be found in the works of Christian theologians in later times, the statement is true; but if it is meant that He had no convictions of His own about the purpose of His sufferings, the end they were to fulfil, and the manner in which they would prove effective, a view is held which is not only improbable in itself, but is directly opposed by His sayings regarding His Passion. To these considerations must be added the urgency with which He approached Jerusalem, and His experience in the Garden and on the Cross. His words and acts are those of One who knows what He must do and why He does it. The atti-

tude is one of intelligent and conscious decision.   For
these reasons it must be inferred that Jesus had a very definite 'theory' of atonement.   To Him the Cross was not
an enigma, but the highway of conscious Messianic purpose.

The question whether there is an ineluctable doctrinal
element in the sayings of Jesus is so important, that it is
advisable to consider it carefully before proceeding further.   Is this element really present?   Or, on the contrary, is the hesitation of critics to admit its presence justifiable?

It is easy to see how the critical hesitation has arisen.
Many 'Lives of Christ' exist in which the method of
approach is theological.   In these works theology is read into the Story of Jesus; nothing is said which is inconsistent
with it, and by its aid gaps in the record are cleverly filled,
with the result that the Life is not a historical work, but a
contribution to Apologetics.   It was only to be expected
that, with the growth of criticism, such works would fall
under the deepest suspicion.   No critic with a reputation
to lose would dream of writing such a Life.   From them
he turns away with the conviction that here he has nothing
to learn.   Unfortunately, this healthy scepticism can en-
danger research.   It is one thing to impose a theology
upon a historical study; it is quite another thing to imagine
that a historical investigation of the words of Jesus can be
made without discovering an implicit theology.   Not the
least benefit which Schweitzer has conferred upon us
is his perception of a dogmatic element in the Story of
Jesus, and his claim stands even when it is admitted that
his exclusive reliance upon Eschatology, as the master-key
of the Gospel tradition, is mistaken.   The truth slowly
emerges that a study of the life of Jesus which does not find
in it a theology in solution, is self-condemned.   This is

the lesson of the failure of the Liberal-Critical School to estimate the Person of Jesus. The resultant picture is a lay-figure totally incapable of initiating the Christian Movement. The same lesson is taught by the successive attempts to bridge the gulf between the Rabbi of Nazareth and historical Christianity, by over-emphasizing the creative influence of St. Paul. These splendid constructions lie in ruins, and it only remains for research to retrace its steps in estimating the place of theology in relation to history. It will be necessary to admit that in the mind of Jesus there were doctrinal concepts, which are not compromised because they stand in a traceable relation to later developments in New Testament teaching. I am not thinking, of course, of systematized theology, but of those thoughts about God, man and sin, which are its foundation material. Translated into its simplest terms, the question whether there is a dogmatic element in the thought of Jesus, is the inquiry whether He knew what He meant to achieve for men by His Messianic ministry of suffering and death. This question, it is here maintained, should be answered in the affirmative.

II

ULTIMATE QUESTIONS RAISED BY
THE PASSION-SAYINGS

As we have seen, besides the immediate inferences which can be drawn from the Passion-sayings, ultimate questions are raised which cannot be answered directly by appealing to the recorded words of Jesus, but to which answers are necessary if we are to understand His attitude to His suffering and death. These questions include such points as the relation of His suffering to the perfecting of the Reign of God; the sense in which His suffering is representative and vicarious, and the bearing of the Servant-conception on this issue; the penal aspects of the Passion; the relation between sacramental communion and faith-union with Christ; the nature of the fellowship of men with His sufferings. These problems must now be considered.

Although the Passion-sayings do not supply an immediate answer to any of the questions noted above, there is reason to think that material for answers exists.

The nature of the existing Passion-sayings encourages this hope. As we have argued, these sayings are not a collected summary of the utterances of Jesus relative to His Passion, chosen for the purpose of doctrinal discussion; they are survivals preserved by practical needs. It is all the more remarkable, therefore, that the sayings are found to be organically related; they reveal a connected order of thought. At the beginning of the last chapter reference

was made to the necessity of clothing with flesh and blood
the skeleton provided by the fragmentary sayings of Jesus,
but it is now seen that this metaphor is inadequate.   If a
spatial simile is admissible, it is found best in the objects
revealed at the coming of morning light.   Hills, farm-
steads, rocks, woods, trees, roads, and streams stand out
against a background obscured by mist and cloud; but
from the broken outline it is possible to imagine the general configuration of the whole landscape.   Somewhat
similar is the illumination made possible by the existing
Passion-sayings; they not only convey their immediate
suggestions, but hint at the thoughts and beliefs of the
Speaker from whom they come.   But it is even better to
think of the Passion-sayings as organically related, for they
express the living thoughts of an active and original mind.
The Fourth Evangelist expresses this conviction in the
saying of Jesus: 'The words that I have spoken unto you
are spirit, and are life' (vi. 63).   Du Bose puts the same
thought in another way when he writes: 'I hold that the
Gospel of Jesus Christ is so true and so living in every part
that he who truly possesses and truly uses any broken fragment of it may find in that fragment something—just so
much—of gospel for his soul and of salvation for his life.'[1]
This religious truth has an intellectual counterpart.   No
historical method is more mistaken than one which merely
adds together the implications of isolated Passion-sayings.

But there is more material at our disposal than the existing Passion-sayings.   As a corrective against the dangers of a subjective construction, the investigation of the
attitude of Jesus to the Kingdom of God, the Messianic
Hope, the Son of Man, the Son, the Servant of Yahweh,
and Sacrifice, made in Part I, is essential.   However incomplete its results may be, such a study reveals the hin-

[1] *The Gospel in the Gospels*, 4.

terland of thought out of which the sayings emerge.   It is
not, therefore, a forlorn hope to attempt to discuss the ultimate problems.   Everything we know of Jesus is a light
upon their darkness.   Nothing that is inconsistent with
His environment of thought can safely be credited to Him,
but what is harmonious with His mind may be historically
true if it fills out the meaning of His words.

It is certain that the application of these principles
leaves much to the insight of the investigator.   None the
less he has room to advance.   Whether his results are objective can be judged only by those who are prepared to retrace his steps and to ask if he has reached conclusions
which are consistent with our knowledge of the Jesus of
history.

1. There is no need to investigate further the view that
Jesus believed that His Passion was an experience which
came to Him in the Providence of God, or the claim that in
respect of His suffering His mind and that of the Father
were at one.   There is, however, an important implication, not expressed in the recorded words of Jesus, which
needs to be emphasized in view of later theological constructions.   The perfect unity of purpose which existed
between Jesus and His Father excludes all theories of vindictive punishment.   Upon the words: 'Not what I will,
but what thou wilt' (Mk. xiv. 36), all such theories of the
Atonement, implying the punishment of the compassion-
ate Son by an angry Father, irrevocably founder.   What
Jesus does is an act well-pleasing to the Father; and for
this reason every theory worthy of the name must embody
the idea of the perfect obedience of Jesus to the Father's
will.

This New Testament thought has never entirely disap-
peared from the mind and teaching of the Church, but it is
common knowledge that it has frequently been obscured

and sometimes almost forgotten. No one perhaps has impressed it more deeply upon the Christian consciousness of to-day than J. M'Leod Campbell. 'Let my reader endeavour to realize the thought,' he writes, 'The *sufferer suffers* what he suffers *just through seeing sin and sinners with God's eyes, and feeling in reference to them with God's heart*. Is *such* suffering a *punishment?* Is God, in causing such a divine experience in humanity, inflicting a punishment? There can be but one answer. . . . I find myself shut up to the conclusion, that while Christ suffered for our sins as an atoning sacrifice, what He suffered was not—because from its nature it could not be—a punishment.'[1] In these burning words all theories of vindictive punishment are utterly consumed; they have no validity, either in the words of Jesus or in His thoughts about God.

While, however, this conviction cannot be too strongly stated, there is reason to think that the anger which such theories incite has clouded the judgment of many theologians, and it may be that the words of Campbell, so often quoted, are partly responsible for this result. In destroying error, it is easy to compromise truth; and it is improbable that such theories would ever have gained currency unless men had felt that a truth of some kind was at stake. R. C. Moberly pointed out that 'punishment' need not mean retributive vengeance, and that, while it is one thing to deny that Christ's sufferings were penal in this sense, 'it is another and more doubtful matter, to deny that they can be called penal in any sense at all.'[2] This question obviously calls for careful and dispassionate inquiry, but it is best to postpone it until the representative and vicarious aspect of Christ's sufferings has been further examined.

[1] *The Nature of the Atonement*, 4th ed., 101. The italics are his.
[2] *Atonement and Personality*, 398.

The immediate conclusion to draw is that the sufferings are not 'penal' in any sense which is in contradiction to that attitude of perfect filial obedience manifest in the acceptance by Jesus of a ministry of suffering and death.

2. That Jesus thought of His Passion as the fulfilment of an active Messianic vocation closely related to the Kingdom, may now be taken for granted; but it is desirable more fully to examine the implications of this statement. Jesus, we have seen, did not speak of His suffering as a revelation, but as a task to be accomplished. That He made such a revelation, both in His life and death, is one of the most precious truths in the Christian Faith. It must also be recognized that the revelation is both active and objective. In revealing God, Jesus not only brings certain truths to light, He also embodies them in Himself so that in His life and work they find living and visible expression. When, however, all this has been said, we are far from doing justice to the nature of His redemptive work. What He accomplishes are specific Messianic acts on which the realisation of the Rule of God depends.

It is for this reason that all forms of the 'Moral' Theory of the Atonement prove wanting. Born in a spirit of recoil from harsh theories, they are halting-places in the search for a truer theology. To this fact witness is given in the successive attempts to supply their deficiencies. In the work of H. Rashdall this is apparent in the attempt to see, beyond an act of self-sacrifice[1] in the death of Jesus, a 'symbolical expression' of the fact that God suffers.[2] And this view, which H. Bushnell so powerfully advocated,[3] has been strongly argued by C. A. Dinsmore[4] and H. M.

---

[1] *The Idea of Atonement*, 45.   [2] *Op. cit.*, 453f.

[3] Cf. *The Vicarious Sacrifice*, 35: 'Nay, there is a cross in God before the wood is seen upon Calvary; hid in God's own virtue itself. . . .'

[4] Cf. *The Atonement in Literature and Life*, 232f.

Hughes.[1] Development is also noticeable in the Dale Lectures of R. S. Franks, who prefers the term 'Experiential Theory' and interprets the sacrifice offered by Jesus as meaning that He gave Himself up to the Father to be the personal instrument of His love for men.[2] These and other indications[3] show how far the 'Moral' Theory has been modified from the form in which it is contended that the Incarnation and the Atonement are one.[4]

The nature of Christ's redemptive activity is determined by His conception of the Kingdom as the Rule of God. This means that it is concerned supremely with the moral and spiritual needs of men. The Kingdom of God, as He saw it, is not a community of men engaged in the common pursuit of an ethical ideal; it is the fellowship of those among whom the Divine Rule is exercised; it is the Reign of God among men. It is reasonable, therefore, to infer that the Messianic work of Jesus is that of establishing the moral conditions in which the Rule of God can be perfected. That Rule is a sovereignty which can be fully exercised only over willing and obedient hearts in unclouded fellowship with God. The obstacle to such a relationship is human sin; and, in consequence, the Messianic activity must concern the situation thus created. It is redemptive action necessitated by sin. The suffering, death, and resurrection of Jesus are successive acts in a victorious conflict with evil powers and in a sacrificial ministry which He fulfils for sinners.

It must be freely granted that this view of the Messianic

---

[1]Cf. *What is the Atonement?* 86-105. 'The passion of God found its highest expression in the incarnation, life and death of His Son, in and through whom He resisted sin even unto death, and travailed for man's redemption,' *op. cit.*, 95.

[2]Cf. *The Atonement*, 186-191.

[3]Cf. W. R. Maltby, *Christ and His Cross*, 155-9.

[4]Cf. J. M. Wilson, *The Gospel of the Atonement*, 88f.

activity of Jesus cannot be demonstrated by an appeal
to His recorded words, although it may with justice
be claimed that it is supported by His references to 'the
power of darkness' (Lk. xxii. 53), to 'the ransom for many'
(Mk. x. 45), and to 'the blood of the covenant, which is
shed for many' (Mk. xiv. 24).   In the end, it is a conclusion which must depend upon His words and deeds as a
whole.   But besides the sayings mentioned above, two
other contributary considerations need to be taken into
account.   One of these is the increasing preoccupation of
Jesus with the fact of sin as the Passion draws nearer.   It
cannot have been long before the day near Caesarea
Philippi that He spoke so plainly about 'the things which
proceed out of the man' and defile him (Mk. vii. 15).
When the seventy returned from their mission He said: 'I
beheld Satan fall as lightning from heaven' (Lk. x. 18).
Immediately after Peter's confession, when Peter rebuked
Him because of His words about the necessity of suffering
and death, He said: 'Get thee behind me, Satan: for thou
mindest not the things of God, but the things of men' (Mk.
viii. 33).   And in His parables, of which the Lost Son
(Lk. xv. 11-32), the Unforgiving Servant (Mt. xviii. 23-
35), and the Wicked Husbandmen (Mk. xii. 1-11) may
serve as examples, Jesus showed how deeply the reality of
sin pressed itself upon His imagination.   Indeed, at the
very beginning of His public ministry, His words: 'Repent ye, and believe in the good news' (Mk. i. 15), reveal
how clearly He saw it as an effective barrier to the Reign of
God.   Jesus did not describe sin in the manner of St. Paul
in Rom. v. 12-21, vii. 7-25 or discuss the origin of the evil
yetzer as the Rabbis did, but in its concrete manifestations
He recognized how destructive it is.   Inevitably, therefore, one thinks of His Messianic work in relation to the
Kingdom as intimately concerned with sin.   The other

consideration referred to above is the representative and vicarious character of His suffering. It is right to introduce this point here, even if its implications require further discussion, for we have good reason to assume that the thought of Jesus is a unity. If, then, he believed that, as the Son of Man, He stood in a representative relationship to men, we can infer that His work was the removal of obstacles created by sin between them and their heritage in the Reign of God.

3. It is now necessary to examine more fully the representative and vicarious element in the suffering of Jesus which has already been found in His sayings. But a task left over from the last chapter must first be undertaken. Although there is little doubt that Jesus interpreted His suffering and death in the light of the Servant-conception, we cannot infer the substance of His interpretation directly from His reported sayings. All the probabilities, however, favour the view that He interpreted the Servant's work as consisting in representative and vicarious suffering. The theme of the Suffering Servant was treated in Part I. Here it is sufficient to recall that the Servant's destiny is that of one who is 'pierced' through the rebellions of others, 'crushed' through their sins, whose 'chastisement' wins men's peace, and by whose 'stripes' they are healed. Such is his suffering that men are led to cry:

> 'We had all gone astray like sheep,
> We had turned each his own way,
> And Yahweh made to light on him
> The sin of us all.'

It is incredible that Jesus can have viewed His own suffering in the light of this sublime poem without at the same time interpreting it as representative and vicarious suffering. All the more certain is this, if Jesus read Isa. liii. in the belief that He was the Messiah: and the claim that He approached the poem with this conviction, is strongly supported by the fact that He reinterpreted the idea of the Son of Man in terms of the Suffering Servant, not the Servant-conception in terms of the Son of Man.[1]   It is because of Isa. liii that Jesus completely recast the doctrine of the Son of Man.   The Son of Man, in whom He saw Himself, is a new figure clothed with the marred form of the Servant.   To say this is really to confess that Jesus interpreted His destiny as that of the Suffering Redeemer, as the representative of the many whose supreme need is reconciliation to God.   Our knowledge that language of this kind can be exploited in the interests of crude theories of the Atonement must not be allowed to prevent us from drawing this vital inference.   Rather is it necessary to examine more closely the nature of representative action and to consider in what way Jesus is likely to have viewed His suffering within this category.

The representative activity of Jesus is wrongly conceived if it is looked upon as imputed to men on the ground of belief.   Such an idea is not only wanting in the Passion-sayings of Jesus, but is also out of harmony with His teaching as a whole.   It treats His suffering as if it were a transaction the benefits of which can be transferred to the account of another.   There is undoubtedly a substitutionary aspect in the suffering of Jesus, in the sense that He did for men what they have no power to do for themselves; but the thought of redemptive service is thrown entirely out of focus unless faith-union between men and Christ is so intimate that His offering becomes increasingly their own.   Not more satisfactory are theories which explain the representative activity of Jesus by saying that He suffered as Man, and that in Him Humanity was reconciled

[1]See pp. 32, 48, 113, 259.

to God. Irenaeus wrote that 'in the Second Adam we were reconciled, becoming obedient unto death',[1] and similar ideas can be found in the writings of modern theologians.[2] So long as language of this kind is that of epigram, it expresses the truth of Christ's Priesthood; but, if it is pressed, it leads to abstract conceptions which lose touch with life and to unethical reactions in conduct and belief.

The truer view of the representative activity of Jesus is one which recognizes that in His suffering and death He has expressed and effected that which no individual man has the power or the spirituality to achieve, but into which, in virtue of an ever-deepening fellowship with Him, men can progressively enter so that it becomes their offering to God. The language of M'Leod Campbell is that of an older day, but he powerfully presents this point of view when he writes: 'Our faith is, in truth, the Amen of our individual spirits, to that deep, multiform, all-embracing, harmonious Amen of humanity, in the person of the Son of God, to the mind and heart of the Father in relation to man—the divine wrath and the divine mercy, which is the atonement.'[3] In this view the suffering of Jesus is indeed representative and vicarious, but, in relation to men, it is neither crudely substitutionary nor automatic in its action, but something which is to be owned and appropriated.

Thus far, our discussion has centred upon the relationship of men to the redemptive suffering of Jesus, but,

---

[1] *Adv. Haer.*, v. 16. 3.

[2] Cf. Du Bose: 'As humanity had fallen in Adam, and by his act or its own act in him, so humanity threw off its sin and death in Christ, and by His act or by its own act in His Person,' *The Gospel in the Gospels*, 157. Cf. Moberly: 'He was not generically, but inclusively, man', *Atonement and Personality*, 86. Moberly, however, denies that there can be such a thing as 'impersonal humanity', *op. cit.*, 93.

[3] *The Nature of the Atonement*, 194.

obviously, something more must be said of the representative activity itself.   In what way, it may be asked, did Jesus find a representative character in His suffering? His sayings and His use of the Servant-conception imply that He assigned this significance to His Passion: is it possible to apprehend its nature?

The clue, so far as we can speak of a clue, is probably to be found in the Old Testament conception of corporate personality.[1]   When the Psalmist says:

'But I am a worm, and no man;
A reproach of men, and despised of the people' (Psa. xxii. 6),

he is not merely describing himself nor the community he represents, but both.   There is a recurring alternation in the point of reference throughout the whole Psalm.   The personality revealed is that of one who is the living embodiment of the community.   The same complex relationship is visible in the Servant-poems, in Isa. l. 6: 'I gave my back to the smiters, and my cheeks to them that plucked off the hair: I hid not my face from shame and spitting'; and still more notably in Isa. liii. 12: 'He bare the sin of many, and made intercession for the transgressors.'   The mysterious bonds which separate one person from another are here broken down.   Without the loss of self-identity, the personality revealed is at once individual and corporate.

In the sacred literature, then, which He pondered, there was a basis for the representative and vicarious character which Jesus found in His suffering.   While, however, the idea lay ready to hand, it was not appropriated by Him apart from the living experience out of which it springs. Its deepest roots are love for men and an unshaken conviction concerning the purposes of God.   The relationship

[1]Cf. H. Wheeler Robinson, *The Cross of the Servant*, 32-6.

is best described as one of self-identification with sinners. It is wrongly conceived if it is looked upon as a state in which there is a loss of personal distinctions. On the contrary, and paradoxical as it may seem, it is possible only so long as the difference between 'thou' and 'I' is preserved. True self-identification with others is the supreme act of love whereby, in the most intimate manner, they are regarded as oneself, seen in the pure light of God, as they are not able to see themselves; it is to enter at once into their joys and their sorrows, but especially to share the gloom and darkness of their sin, to be conscious of its weight and to feel its shame, so that the sin-bearing becomes a redemptive activity both in itself and in the lives of men. Such a relationship may exist between one individual and another, but in the personality of Jesus, conscious as He was of a unique vocation in relation to men, the self-identification exists not only between Himself and particular individuals, but between Himself and mankind; it is a communal relationship in which there is a consciousness of representing men before God. It is in this large sense that we must interpret the representative and vicarious element in His suffering. What the experience involves, so far as one can interpret it at all, can be described only by considering more fully the character of His suffering consequent upon His exposure to the consequences of sin.

4. We have seen that the Passion-sayings reveal on the part of Jesus an intimate knowledge and experience of the consequences of sin; and it is necessary now to consider the nature of this experience so far as it is capable of analysis. In particular, the question must be asked whether the intense spiritual agony endured by Jesus in the fulfilment of His Messianic vocation is rightly described as 'penal'. It has already been observed that the rejection of theories of the Atonement which imply vindictive or sub-

stitutionary punishment does not foreclose this question; it still remains a matter for careful inquiry whether the sufferings of Jesus are penal in character.

Two observations of general interest are worth making in this connexion. Not a few works and essays could be cited, written in some cases by theologians of repute, in which the distinction referred to above is ignored. It seems to be assumed that the rejection of a few popular beliefs, more ancient than modern, as for example, that punishment can be transferred, or that God's attitude to sinners can be changed, or that His justice has to be satisfied before He will forgive sinners, is enough to settle the question once for all. It does not appear to be realized that the refutation of these errors merely clears the ground for discussion. The other point for notice is that in most of the classical discussions of the Atonement in modern times the penal character of the sufferings of Jesus is affirmed, in spite of the popular objections noted above.[1] These facts cannot, of course, be allowed to coerce the

---

[1] R. W. Dale, for example, stigmatizes the idea that sin was imputed to Christ as 'a legal fiction' (*The Atonement*, Preface to seventh ed., lxiii.), and rejects the statement that a ransom was paid by the Divine mercy to the Divine justice as 'mere rhetoric' (*op. cit.*, 357); yet his contention is that Christ 'endured the penalties of sin, and so made an actual submission to the authority and righteousness of the principle which those penalties express' (*op. cit.*, 423). J. Scott Lidgett also maintains that 'His relationship to the human race, and His consequent Incarnation, enabled Him, and Him alone, to *give complete expression*, under our penal conditions, to the submission of mankind to God, to make reparation to His law, and to put away sin from man' (*The Spiritual Principle of the Atonement*, 378). P. T. Forsyth affirms that 'Christ, by the deep intimacy of His sympathy with men, entered deeply into the blight and judgment which was entailed by man's sin, and which must be entailed by man's sin if God is a holy and therefore a judging God'. 'You can therefore say', he continues, 'that although Christ was not punished by God, He bore God's penalty upon sin. That penalty was not lifted even when the Son of God passed through' (*The Work of Christ*, 147). Cf. J. Denney, *The Christian Doctrine of Reconciliation*, 273. It is noteworthy also that J. K. Mozley, after illustrating fully the history of the doctrine of the Atonement, says, 'I do

critical judgment, but they certainly emphasize the need for careful thought in a field where strong feeling easily clouds the issue.

Much depends on whether we believe that sin carries with it penal consequences which in the last analysis must be traced to the will of a Holy God. That consequences, which serve both as a deterrent and a discipline, do follow sin, is too plain to be denied. But if this is true, a further inference must be drawn. It is only as punishment is felt to be *deserved* that it is accepted as discipline and welcomed as a deterrent. Thus, the retributive aspect of punishment is fundamental to its nature, although it is not the only aspect in which it presents itself to the mind. Many Christian thinkers who recognize this truth hesitate to describe the retributive principle as the expression of the Divine Will, largely, I believe, because they fear that they are committed, or will be thought to be committed, to a sub-Christian belief in a passionate and tyrannical God. Instead of seeing the penal consequences of sin as the action and attitude of God, they prefer to speak of an inevitable process of cause and effect in a moral universe. But this is merely a descriptive phrase; it explains nothing, and comes perilously near to a naturalistic account of ethical relationships. The God of historical Christianity is the Living God and cannot be bowed out of His universe. It is not necessary, of course, to think of every ill

not therefore think that we need shrink from saying that Christ bore penal suffering for us and in our stead' (*The Doctrine of the Atonement*, 216). And, finally, in his *Mediator* E. Brunner contends that 'the Cross, conceived as the expiatory penal sacrifice of the Son of God, is the fulfilment of the scriptural revelation of God, in its most paradoxical incomprehensible guise' (*op. cit.*, 473). Brunner, it should be added, thinks that if the forensic aspect of the Atonement is stressed exclusively, the doctrine tends to become one-sided and crudely objective. Hence, he finds room for what he calls 'the ritual idea', that is for the conception of the Atonement as an expiatory sacrifice (*op. cit.*, 475).

consequence as the direct result of a special Divine voli-
tion; but it is necessary, if Christian values are to be con-
served, to think of penal suffering as the reaction of the
holiness and love of God in a world of moral realities.   If
this is so, penal suffering is not the expression of a legal
principle, but an ethical and spiritual manifestation of the
Divine activity.   It is a hasty and incomplete generalisa-
tion to trace its operation to some particular attribute of
God, as, for example, to His justice; its final ground is
His nature and being, and, in the last analysis, His love.

Nothing is more needed in modern theology than a
resolute endeavour to think seriously about the love of
God.   It is so easy to degrade the idea until it becomes
weak and sentimental.   The love of God calls for all that
is best in man; and this means that, as a being subject to
growth and development, he cannot be insured against
the consequences of sin or denied their painful discipline.
The greatest love is a love which in endurance permits
man to win his soul.   All this, together with the out-
flowings of the healing ministries of grace, is the mark of
perfect love, and therefore of the love of God Himself.
It is for the same reason that God requires a sacrifice: not
that He may be placated, but because His love can be
satisfied with nothing less than a perfect response from man.

Our conception of penal suffering must vitally affect our
estimate of its place in the experience of one who loves
wrong-doers so intensely as to identify himself with them.
Obviously, it cannot simply be transferred from one to
another, so that, since it has been borne by a benefactor,
the sinner is acquitted and may go scot free.   Such a
theology attempts to deal with moral relationships on the
basis of a patent illegality,[1] whereas, as we have seen, penal

---

[1]David Smith supplies two excellent illustrations of this in his book, *The
Atonement in the Light of History and the Modern Spirit*, 108ff.

suffering is not a legal, but an ethical category. Like forgiveness itself, it is a mark of God's redemptive dealings with men. In consequence, the idea of one accepting penal suffering instead of another, and of offering it to God as a means of reconciliation, is completely mistaken. The penal element in the suffering of a lover of sinners is something quite different. It is not a burden which he takes over, and bears in the place of another; it is an experience into which he *enters* in virtue of his love.

Just because he loves sinners, he feels their shame, and experiences by sympathy and intuition the penalty of their sin to a degree which is impossible for them until they know a true religious awakening. For love's sake he enters into a night of gloom and darkness where sin works itself out in the consuming fires of Holy Love. This is the experience of 'sin-bearing' which, however we describe it, and whether we deny it or not, is a fact of common daily life, illustrated a hundred times in the complex relationships of the home, the family, the nation, and the wider life of mankind.[1] It is the incalculable secret of great and enduring love. It may well be that we require another word than 'penal' in order to describe suffering of this kind. By all means let us find it if we can, for usage has so tarnished the word 'penal' that mental effort is required in order to do justice to its meaning. Thus far, a better term has not been found. Indeed, it may be doubted if it is likely to be found, since the word 'penal' exactly expresses the required idea, namely, that of a suffering which is caused by the inevitable consequences of sin in a world ruled by God.

The answer to the question raised at the beginning of this section admits by now of little doubt. It is impossible to think of the suffering of Jesus Himself as any-

---

[1] Cf. W. R. Maltby, *Christ and His Cross*, 77f, 94f, 165.

T

thing else but penal suffering.   Were He no more than a
teacher or a prophet, it would be necessary so to describe
that intense spiritual agony which is implied by His sayings.   All the more must we take this view in consequence of that representative relationship to men which
is so marked an aspect of His Messianic consciousness;
and most of all if terms like 'Messiah' and 'Son of Man'
are the self-chosen, but inadequate designations of a sinless and more-than-human personality.   The conclusion
to be drawn, even if no sayings require it, is that by reason
of His relationship to sinners Jesus entered into the blight
and judgment which rest upon sin, and bore its shame and
desolation upon His heart.   Because He loved men so
greatly He became one with them, entering into the
situation in which they stood, sharing the pain of their
disobedience, and feeling the pressure of their sins.   Such
suffering is penal because it is the fruit of the judgment
which rests on sin; it is accepted, not by way of barter or
exchange, but because it is part of the moral situation of
those who are loved.   It is the cost of the redemptive
passion of the lover who enters into the penal suffering of
the beloved, and bears it upon his heart because there is
nothing less that love can do.   Its significance in the work
of redemptive service is not that it changes God, or delivers men from the pain of penal suffering; but that it
constitutes the one who bears it a Mediator and a Saviour,
in and through whom they can draw nigh to God.

5. A question of quite a different kind arises in connexion with the problem of man's relationship to the redemptive work of Christ.   What is the place of faith in
this relationship?   Is the communion made possible in
the Eucharist different in kind from that experience of
faith-union with Christ of which St. Paul speaks when he
writes: 'I have been crucified with Christ: and it is no

longer I that live, but Christ liveth in me' (Gal. ii. 20), or when he speaks of Christ as set forth by God as a means of atonement 'through faith' (Rom. iii. 25)?

It is a challenging fact that there is no saying of Jesus, either in the Synoptics or in the Fourth Gospel, which mentions faith in connexion with His death.[1]   Jesus asks for faith in God (Mk. xi. 22), welcomes its presence in men (Mt. viii. 10), depends upon its presence in His works of healing (Mk. v. 34, vi. 5f.; Mt. xv. 28), and emphasizes its necessity in the life of His disciples (Mt. xvii. 20); but in no recorded saying of His does He ask for faith in Himself as Redeemer and Saviour.   This negative statement is true, but it may easily prove misleading.   It would be quite unwarranted to conclude, on the basis of this evidence, that Apostolic teaching on this theme, and in particular Jn. iii. 16, has no foundation in the thought of Jesus.   In the first place, several sayings support the contention of M. Goguel that, after Peter's Confession (Mk. viii. 29), Jesus 'now asks for attachment to his person, and not only for the acceptance of his message'.[2]   Thus it is that He calls upon His disciples to deny themselves, to take up their cross, and follow Him (Mk. viii. 34), and declares that whosoever shall lose his life for His sake shall save it (Mk. viii. 35).   'What doth it profit a man', He asks, 'to gain the whole world, and forfeit his life?' (Mk. viii. 36).   To be ashamed of Him and of His words in this adulterous and sinful generation is to incur the shame of the Son of Man when He comes 'in the glory of his Father with the holy angels' (Mk. viii. 38).   And there are other sayings which cannot be precisely dated in which He speaks of the divisions brought about by Himself and His ministry within families (Lk.

[1] Jn. iii. 15f. is almost certainly part of the Evangelist's soliloquy.
[2] *The Life of Jesus*, 385.

xii. 51-3), and claims a decisive and unparalleled relationship to Himself. 'If any man cometh unto me, and hateth not his own father, and mother, and wife, and children, and brethren, and sisters, yea, and his own life also, he cannot be my disciple' (Lk. xiv. 26). Primitive Christianity was only describing this attitude of self-committal to Jesus by means of another terminology when it began to speak of faith in Christ; and if it is said that, in the sayings quoted above, the attitude is one directed to Jesus Himself rather than to His work, it is fair to reply that the distinction is artificial since, at the time Jesus spoke, His Messianic work was an all absorbing thought.

Secondly, it is impossible to differentiate in absolute terms between the ultimate nature of sacramental communion and the concept of faith in Christ. That there is a distinction is obvious, since faith-union with Christ can be experienced apart from any conscious sacramental relationship. There is nothing to indicate that sacramental ideas are in St. Paul's mind when he declares that he has been crucified with Christ, and that his present life is a life lived by faith in the Son of God, who loved him and gave Himself up for him (Gal. ii. 20). And there have been, and are, not a few among Christians of all ages capable of using such language along with imperfect and even erroneous conceptions of the Eucharistic gift. For such men, faith in Christ is an immediate and direct experience which reveals no obvious need of outward ritual expression beyond that of language or of song. On the other hand, when sacramental communion is considered, its essential nature is seen to be just that intimate experience of fellowship with Christ which is described in St. Paul's words; it is faith in action by the use of a symbolism which gives it peculiar strength and vitality. We must therefore infer that, although Jesus did not, in so many words, speak of faith as defining the relation of men to His redemptive work, in effect He indicated it as such in His institution of the Eucharist; and that later Christian teaching was only interpreting His mind in its declaration that salvation is by faith in Him.

Lastly, the reproduction of the spirit of Messianic suffering, to which Jesus called men, is itself rooted in the faith-relationship. It was to men standing in close attachment to Himself that He spoke of drinking the cup (Mk. x. 38), and of taking up the cross (Mk. viii. 34). And the same is true of St. Paul when he writes: 'I fill up on my part that which is lacking of the afflictions of Christ in my flesh for his body's sake, which is the church' (Col. i. 24). The discussion whether in these words 'the afflictions of Christ' are *satisfactoriae* or *aedificatoriae* may easily obscure the vital consideration that in any case the action springs out of a believing relationship to Christ, and is unintelligible without it. This fact is well illustrated in the famous paraphrase of J. B. Lightfoot: 'Yes, I Paul the persecutor, I Paul the feeble and sinful, am permitted to supplement—I do not shrink from the word—to supplement the afflictions of Christ. Despite all that He underwent, He the Master has left something still for me the servant to undergo. And so my flesh is privileged to suffer for His body—His spiritual body, the Church.'[1] The experience here described is clearly derivative; it is founded in a prior believing relationship to Christ and to His redemptive work. Nor is it out of place to say that is exactly true to the Christian experience. It is by filling up 'that which remains over of the afflictions of Christ' that men enter more fully into the meaning of His sacrifice, and the last thing they can claim is that their service

[1] *The Epistle to the Colossians*, 162.

stands in any comparable relationship to the achievement of Christ.   It appears, then, that the summons of Jesus to cross-bearing is the summons to a life of faith in action determined ultimately by a relationship to Himself.   It was, therefore, a natural step when Christian teachers used boldly the language of faith-union with Christ; it is not the language of Jesus Himself, but it is directly rooted in His historical teaching.

Why Jesus instituted the Eucharist and called men to cross-bearing rather than laying down as a primary necessity the demand for faith in Himself, is a very interesting and important question.   Probably, the answer is to be found in a point of view which preferred the concrete to the apparently abstract, and which found it natural to think of faith as expressed mediately and in action.   In such an outlook Jesus was true to the deepest needs of human nature, for while Christianity is justified in calling men directly to exercise faith in Christ, it has succeeded best when it has associated its evangelical appeal with Eucharistic worship and practical Christian endeavour.

6. The last point for consideration in the present chapter is whether there is any unifying principle which binds together the several ideas which are implicit in the Passion-sayings.   It is not a credible suggestion, that these ideas can have been held by Jesus in isolation one from another; the presumption is that they are inter-related and fall within a framework of thought.

The most probable view is that the bond which unites these ideas is the sacrificial principle.   So long as sacrifice is interpreted as a means of appeasing an angry God, this perception is hidden from us; but immediately its highest expression is found in a representative offering which the worshipper makes his own in seeking renewed fellowship with God, its relevancy is complete.   That Jesus was sympathetic to this principle, has already been argued,[1] and it has also been maintained that it is implied in His use of the 'ransom-passage' and in the words: 'This is my blood of the covenant, which is shed for many.'[2] It is a substantial confirmation of these opinions, that every important aspect of the sacrificial principle can be found in the thoughts of Jesus concerning His Passion. The aim of sacrifice is a restored fellowship; its medium is a representative offering; its spiritual condition is the attitude of the worshipper; its rationale is the offering of life; its culmination is sharing in the life offered by means of the sacred meal. These ideas form a natural background against which the Passion-sayings can be readily understood.

In view of what has been said it is permissible to speak of 'the Sacrifice of Jesus'; but, in using this phrase, it is necessary to observe that in at least two respects every other expression of the sacrificial principle is transcended. On the one hand, His Sacrifice has a moral and spiritual value which has no parallel elsewhere, inasmuch as His self-offering is the active expression of conscious purpose. He wills what He does, and the whole force of His personality is in His achievement. On the other hand, the significance of His Person raises His action into a new category of sacrifice. What He is determines what He does to such a degree that His Sacrifice is limited in no way in respect of time or place. Historical as an event in time, it is not chained to the circumstances and conditions of nineteen centuries ago; it has the marks of universality and perfection.

It is important to notice the manner in which the sacrificial principle is implicit in the redemptive work of Jesus. There is no warrant for supposing that it was the sacri-

[1]See pp. 67-75.   [2]See pp. 74f, 103-5, 136-9.

ficial system of Judaism which determined His thinking in respect of His Passion. His attitude to the cultus would not have been as detached as the Gospels show it to have been, and His sayings would be more explicit than they are, if the sacrifices of the Temple had deeply influenced His thought. So far from looking to the existing sacrificial system as a determining element in His thought, we should rather interpret the cultus as a partial and imperfect expression of a principle which is completely manifested in His Sacrifice; and it may well have been His perception of this relationship which influenced His respect for a system which He felt to be wanting in spiritual and religious worth. The source of His indebtedness should be found, not so much in the cultus, as in that sublimated expression of the sacrificial principle which is found in the description of the Suffering Servant. Here supremely is to be discerned that portraiture of a sacrificial ministry which led Him radically to transform current conceptions of the Messianic office as realized and fulfilled in Himself. If this observation is true, it is beside the point to object that prevailing notions in Judaism about the meaning of sacrifice were along the lines of the gift theory rather than along those of Robertson Smith's communion theory.[1] Whether this opinion is true, is a point about which experts will continue to differ, and, as we have previously observed, it is doubtful if either principle can be asserted to the exclusion of the other.[2] The vital question, however, whether there is a sacrificial idea at the root of the thinking of Jesus, is not to be settled by discussions regarding the origins of sacrifice, but by interpreting His sayings and Old Testament repre-

---

[1] This is one of the objections brought by R. S. Franks against Bishop Hicks' *Fullness of Sacrifice*. Cf. *The Atonement*, xiii.

[2] See p. 50.

sentations of sacrificial life and worship. These investigations, it is here submitted, justify us in speaking of the Messianic work of Jesus as His Sacrifice.

The advantages of seeing the work of Jesus in the light of sacrifice are great. Light is thrown upon dark problems in the doctrine of the Atonement and safeguards are provided against perils of statement abundantly illustrated in the history of doctrine.

One answer at least is suggested to the question, why we do not find clearer and more explicit statements in the sayings of Jesus regarding the purpose of His Passion. The answer is only partially to be found in the plea that He did not think after the manner of a systematic theologian, for, as we have urged, it is improbable that He can have approached, and even sought, death without a clear understanding of what He meant to achieve. It is more naturally found in the fact that the sacrificial principle contains an implicit rather than an explicit theology. It is a complex of religious assumptions, mysterious doubtless to those to whom it is strange, luminous to those for whom it is an accepted mode of thought. No one builds a theory out of accepted assumptions unless they are challenged; there is no need to elucidate the familiar. This fact goes far to explain why Jesus does not define the nature of His Sacrifice. Indeed, the presence of explanatory statements in His sayings would be highly suspicious, suggesting later interpretation instead of the reflections of an original mind. Thus, the sacrificial principle not only explains the nature of His oblation, but also accounts for His silence concerning it.

A second merit of the sacrificial principle is that it enables us to meet the ethical difficulties raised by objective theories of the Atonement. The difficulty of such theories has always been that they tend to look for the ground for reconciliation with God *outside* man. Something is done for him in virtue of which he can draw near to God. As against such views it is almost an axiom of the religious consciousness that reconciliation depends on man's *personal* attitude to God. Man is not saved by appropriating the merits of another; he has no peace by substituting the sacrifice of another for his own. The sacrificial principle provides release from this dilemma. It does this because it reminds us that the sacrifice is more than the offering, that it is not complete apart from the worshipper on whose attitude and spirit its ethical value depends. Thus, we are led to distinguish between the offering of Jesus and the sacrifice He made possible. The nature of His self-offering remains to be defined. Here it is enough to say that, while it is perfect, it is not a counter in some process of celestial arithmetic. It is rather the vehicle of man's aspiration, the centre of his hope, the wings of his prayer. In a word, it is the 'one true, pure, immortal sacrifice' only as it is appropriated by personal faith, in corporate worship, and in sacrificial living. A mode of approach which has this character makes it possible to describe the Sacrifice of Jesus in a manner free from harassing ethical objections. Man himself approaches God by a way the stones of which he has not cut; he finds access to the Father through the self-offering of Jesus.

III

THE ATONEMENT

IN accordance with what was said in the Introduction to Part III, it is necessary to inquire what view of the Atonement is in harmony with the results reached in the present investigation. In what form may the doctrine be stated when the theological implications in the sayings of Jesus are worked out? This question is not only interesting and important in itself, but is also necessary to the investigation, since the problem of Gospel Origins is injuriously isolated unless it is related to the end as well as to the beginnings. It should be emphasized that in order to justify a theory of the Atonement, a much broader basis is necessary than that which is afforded by the sayings of Jesus, and in what follows it is not pretended that the sayings demand the theory which is presented. What is claimed is that the views set forth are in harmony with the results of the preceding investigation.

I

Perhaps the commonest presentation of the Atonement in the Christian teaching and preaching of to-day is some form of the Abelardian theory that 'Christ reconciles men to God by revealing the love of God in His life and still more in His death, so bringing them to trust and love Him in return'.[1]   Naturally, this central conception is capable of being presented in a variety of ways, and, as we have seen, of being enriched by developments which make it more vital and objective.   To the protean forms of the theory there is no need to refer at length, nor to the individual writers who have presented them.   It is enough to say that the possible variations are many, from views which present the death of Christ as little more than a martyrdom to those which see in it the suffering love of God Himself objectively manifested on the plane of history.

The central truth in this theory is an essential element in any doctrine of the Atonement worthy of the name. Indeed, it may be said that any theory has lost its base unless it is continually in touch with the statement of St. Paul: 'God commendeth his own love toward us, in that, while we were yet sinners, Christ died for us' (Rom. v. 8). Whether it is an adequate theory is another matter.   For purposes of discussion the barer forms of the theory may well be left untouched.   It is better to consider it in the form preferred by those who urge that the love of God is not only manifested in the death of Christ, but is definitely objective, since it persists in spite of all that sin can do, and has for its end nothing less than the reconciliation of sinful men with God in the harmony of a restored mutual love.

The objections most commonly brought against this view are that it is vague and indeterminative, that it gives no satisfactory account of the suffering and death of Jesus, and that it is inadequate to human need, especially the

---

[1]R. S. Franks, *The Atonement*, 2.   Cf. Peter the Lombard: 'So great a pledge of love having been given us, we are both moved and kindled to love God who did such great things for us; and by this we are justified, that is, being loosed from our sins we are made just.   The death of Christ therefore justifies us, inasmuch as through it charity is stirred up in our hearts,' quoted by H. Rashdall, *The Idea of Atonement*, 438.

need of those who are conscious of the reality and power
of sin.

It is difficult to see how these objections can be met.
The last is particularly pressing.   As a moral condition
to forgiveness, and therefore to reconciliation with God,
penitence is essential.   No man can find peace with God
until he cries: 'I have sinned before heaven and in thy
sight.'   But any one who looks into his own heart is
appalled to find how fitful, incomplete, and individualistic
his penitence can be.   It comes and goes, quickened by
the revelation of divine love in the Cross, but speedily lost
again in the whirl of life.   Again, it is limited by our
knowledge of God and of our own inner experience.   If
we think meanly of God, our penitence cannot be deep;
and if we think lightly of sin, it cannot be real; if sins are
buried and forgotten, it cannot exist at all.   Further,
penitence is almost incurably individualistic.   If we feel
the weight of our own sins, we are more complacent about
social sins in which none the less we share, sins of neglect,
of national pride and passion, of social cruelty and oppres-
sion.

It is undoubtedly true that, as a manifestation of divine
love, the Cross will deepen penitence.   When it fades the
Cross will quicken it, when it is complacent it will rebuke
it, when it is self-centred it will enlarge its range.   It will
expose our sin as sin against love and convince us that
forgiveness is costly.   These are great gifts, but they do
not match the depth of human need.   Such a penitence is
still compassed with imperfection; it is hedged about by
all the limitations of the finite, never constant, never complete, never invested with the note of universality.   It is a
penitence restricted by sin and constrained by creature-
hood.   It does not become the poignant Amen of the
soul to a representative penitence perfect, constant, and

inclusive, ever presented before the throne of God as a cry into which man can enter, a sorrow he can feel, a confession in which he can participate. How can such a penitence be fitting in the eyes of a Holy God who is 'of purer eyes than to behold evil' and cannot 'look on perverseness'?

In addition, it cannot escape notice how greatly the concept of salvation is altered. Salvation follows from a discovery about God; it is the consequence of a perception! It is indeed an amazing discovery, since we learn that God loves us unto suffering and death; but its stupendous character does not alter its nature as something perceived. In consequence, salvation becomes response to the revelation; it is the re-orientation of the soul after confession and trust. The logical end is a God-mysticism in which the soul closes with the One who is made known in Jesus.

The claim that the Abelardian theory does not give a satisfactory account of the suffering and death of Jesus, is strongly supported by the present investigation. Among the Passion-sayings of Jesus there is none in which He declares that He dies to reveal, or to express, or to embody the love of God. The idea of a suffering God is unknown to His sayings. In all that He said and taught there is nothing to suggest that His object in dying was so to confront men with the untiring love of God that through penitence and contrition they should be brought to trust and love Him in return. It is even doubtful if He thought of these things; they are the beliefs we read into the mind of a Jesus seen with the eyes of the imagination, not the Jesus of history. All this, however challenging it may be, cannot be said too emphatically.

This argument does not mean that the ideas mentioned above have no contact with the teaching of Jesus. On the contrary, all that the theory asserts is true, and the reason why this can be said is easily seen. The Christian of to-day sees the love of God, and even the suffering love of God, in the Cross of Jesus because he views it in the light of history and experience. His theory is a valuation of the Cross, not an unfolding of its purpose and meaning. Jesus, however, looked forward: what He had to say concerning His death was not its significance in the history of revelation, but its meaning for Himself in the fulfilment of His Messianic purpose. That is why the Abelardian theory can be true and at the same time fundamentally incorrect as an interpretation of the mind of Jesus. The truth is that the so-called 'cruder' theories of the Atonement have a closer affiliation with His thought, provided we eliminate from them all that is inconsistent with His fundamental convictions regarding God and man. The thoughts of Jesus in relation to the Cross are 'objective' in the older sense in which this term was used in theories of the Atonement; that is to say, it is a principle cardinal to His thinking that, as the Son of Man, He fulfils a ministry for men before God.

If this claim is valid, it is necessary to accept all that is true and beautiful in the best forms of the 'Moral Theory' as an introduction or preface to a theory of the Atonement more in harmony with the sayings of the historical Jesus. The theory itself is still to seek.

II

The peculiar difficulty of the doctrine of the Atonement is that of seeing it as a whole. For purposes of thought parts of the doctrine have to be considered in themselves, with the result that they are easily seen out of focus; and it is to this fact that many of the most serious problems are due.   Strictly speaking, there is no Atonement apart from the whole process by which sinners are reconciled to God; and this includes the passion of God expressed in the Cross, the life and death of Christ Himself, and the relation of men to Him and His atoning work.   All this, and nothing less, is the Atonement. Two points of special importance are the self-identification of Christ with sinners and the union of believers with Him; and to dissociate the two is perilous.   Indeed, it may be truly said that nearly all the popular objections to the doctrine can be traced to pre-occupation with some aspect of the Atonement which is isolated from the rest.   None the less, for purposes of exposition, the danger has to be incurred, although it is greatly diminished if one recognizes that it exists.

In this section the work of Christ in its Godward aspect will be considered in itself, apart from the relationship of men thereto.   What is the theological counterpart to the conviction of Jesus, that His Messianic service is the self-offering of Himself for men?

Many theologians give no consideration to this question in the belief that God neither requires nor desires a sacrificial offering.   This view, I suggest, not only leads to an unsatisfactory doctrine of the Atonement, but is inconsistent with the attitude of Jesus to His suffering and the meaning of some of His most important sayings, not to speak of the teaching of the Epistles, the repeated emergence of objective theories, and the witness of Christian experience regarding penitence, forgiveness, and fellowship with God.   Only if we think of sacrifice as a means of appeasing God is the conception out of place.   As a means by which men may approach God and find recon-

ciliation with Him the idea of a sacrificial offering is in
harmony with the highest conception of the love and holiness of God in the doctrine of the divine Fatherhood.   In
the work of Christ the offering is made representatively, in
the name of men, and with the intention that they should
participate therein.

It is obvious that no modern presentation of this doctrine is possible unless the representative ministry of
Christ rests on a firm religious basis.   Is this true in point
of fact?   Can modern Christianity speak of Christ as
man's representative before God?   Clearly, this is a question of vital significance.

An affirmative answer to this question is not capable of
demonstration; it is an utterance of faith based upon
reason in the light of relevant facts.   Of these facts one
of the most important is the close connexion between the
idea of a present representative ministry and the strong
conviction of Jesus regarding His Messianic office as the
Son of Man.   Our investigation has revealed this conviction as a fundamental element in His thought.   He lives
and He dies as the suffering Son of Man.   It is, however,
in no sense contradictory to this assertion to say that He
accepted the concept of Messiahship with marked uneasiness.   When He is challenged by Caiaphas whether he is
the Christ, His reply is in effect: 'Yes, if you care to use
that name'; and to this attitude corresponds His avoidance
of the term 'Christ', and His preference for the title 'Son
of Man'.   This attitude, we have seen, is not one of doubt
or uncertainty; it is the point of view of one who is forced
to use names and concepts which are felt to be utterly
inadequate to express His relationship to men.   If this is
a just historical inference, we have reason to discard Messianic terminology in our modern theology, and to replace
it by language which lies nearer to the heart of the thought
u

of Jesus Himself. If in the Resurrection He conquered death and all its powers, we are justified in thinking and speaking of Him as our 'kinsman now', or, in the more sober language of theology, as man's representative before God. Whether we use such a terminology depends upon our estimate of His Person, our agreement with the witness of the historic Church, our reading of history and of personal Christian experience. The choice is the decision of faith faced by the 'Either-Or' of the Christian challenge.

Only is this the case, if a worthy meaning is put into the word 'representative'. In the sense in which it is used in this discussion, it does not indicate one whose activity lies apart from ourselves, or serves instead of our own, but one whose service leaves in our hands the decisive word in the affirmation of faith. Christ is our representative because in His self-offering He performs a work necessary to our approach to God.

What, then, is the nature of His self-offering? At this point theology is confronted by the fact that no word of Jesus reveals His answer to this question. He speaks of 'the blood of the covenant, which is shed for many', but He does not explain how His out-poured life is a sacrificial work for men. Some justification for this silence has already been suggested in the nature of the sacrificial concept; but this suggestion only indicates more fully the task of Christian theology as that of hearing the silence of Jesus.[1]

The best answer which theology can give is one that is in harmony with the sacrificial principle and with the sayings of Jesus. In making its answer, it does not pretend to give a historical account of the mind of Jesus

---

[1] Cf. Ignatius, 'He that hath the word of Jesus truly can hear His silence also,' *Eph.* 15.

Himself, since, as we have seen, the materials for such an account have not been preserved. What theology can do is to express in its own language a view of the self-offering of Jesus which rests on the data of Gospel history and tradition, and interprets them in the light of subsequent thought and experience. From this point of view a threefold answer may be given.

(1) In the first place, the self-offering of Jesus is His perfect obedience to the Father's will. The obedience is His own, but since He presents it as the Son of Man, it is also representative obedience; it is the obedience which men ought to offer to God, and which they would offer if they fulfilled the obligations of their sonship. As representing men, Christ in His suffering offers that obedience, truly embodied in Himself, in their name and for their sake, not by way of barter or exchange, but with the intention that they should identify themselves with it and so offer it themselves. The writer of the Epistle to the Hebrews gives expression to this aspect of the sacrifice of Jesus when he quotes the words of Psa. xl. 7 : 'Lo, I am come ... to do thy will, O God,' and then writes: 'By which will we have been sanctified through the offering of the body of Jesus Christ once for all' (x. 10). The relation of this conception to human need is of the closest, since it offers the possibility of a true obedience to the will of God which can be achieved in no other way. It is also based on that sense of Providential purpose and of unity with the Father's will which governed the whole life of Jesus and is perfectly expressed in His death for men.

(2) Secondly, the self-offering of Jesus is His perfect submission to the judgment of God upon sin. This is the living truth behind the long history of the successive attempts to find a penal element in the sufferings of Christ, attempts which are by no means limited to older state-

ments of the doctrine of the Atonement, but which can be seen in the most notable discussions of the last fifty years. However hard it may be to recognize the fact, there is in this conception a truth intimately concerned with human need.   In a worthy doctrine of Reconciliation those consequences which in point of fact follow upon sin, and which in the last analysis must be traced to the judgment of God, cannot be ignored.   Man's attitude to them must undoubtedly be a factor of great importance.   So long as he views penal suffering with resentment he cannot know the meaning of fellowship with God; only when he accepts it as just, and therefore as the discipline of the soul, is the upward path open to him.   Readily, however, as one may assent to this truth, a journey of struggle and often unavailing effort is projected, from which few travellers return except with tales of defeat.   What is needed is the vision of a perfect submission with which man may identify himself.   No offer of penal suffering as a substitute for his own will meet his need, but a submission presented by his Representative before God becomes the foundation of a new hope.   And once more the assertion that such is part at least of the self-offering of Christ is closely related to His teaching and experience as the Suffering Son of Man.   Of His bitter suffering by reason of human sin there can be no doubt, and that He entered in love into the penal suffering of men we have found ground to infer.   If, then, His representative relationship rests upon fact, it is right to see in His suffering an offering of submission which man can make his own.   In the stately language of another generation the basis of this formulation is expressed in the words: 'His relationship to the human race, and His consequent Incarnation, enabled Him, and Him alone, to *give complete expression*, under our penal conditions, to the submission of mankind to God, to make reparation to His law, and to put away sin from man.'[1]

(3) Thirdly, the self-offering of Jesus is the expression of His perfect penitence for the sins of men. This is a view with which J. M'Leod Campbell[2] and R. C. Moberly[3] have made us familiar. In Campbell's words, Christ made 'a perfect confession of our sins'; in the phrase of Moberly, He 'offered the sacrifice of supreme penitence'. This conception made a great appeal to a generation which could no longer tolerate crude theories of penal substitution, but in large measure it has failed to win wide acceptance on the ground that it replaces a legal by a moral fiction. No one, it is said, can confess sins but the sinner; no one can be penitent in his stead. These objections probably rest on an obsolete atomistic conception of personality, and completely ignore the true relationship between men and the offering of Christ. Campbell pointed out to an acute reviewer that he had no thought of suggesting a *substituted* repentance,[4] and in his *Nature of the Atonement* he strongly maintains that Christ's offering was accepted by the Father entirely with the prospective purpose that it is to be reproduced in us.[5] Moberly himself denies that Christ consummated penitence in the sense that men are not to repent, or to regard His penitence as a substitute for their own;[6] and he seeks to provide a link between believers and the work of Christ by the doctrine of the Holy Spirit, which is the Spirit of Christ, at work in the hearts of men, and by his exposition of the meaning of the Church and the Sacraments. So far

---

[1] J. Scott Lidgett, *The Spiritual Principle of the Atonement*, 378. The italics are his.

[2] *The Nature of the Atonement.*

[3] *Atonement and Personality.*

[4] *Op. cit.* (4th ed.), 340.

[5] *Op. cit.*, Chapter vii.

[6] *Op. cit.*, 283.

as the view outlined in this chapter is concerned, this particular difficulty does not arise; for while the self-offering of Christ is perfect, it is the Godward side of a process of reconciliation which is completed in the human response. The offering avails for individual men so far as they participate in its redemptive power through union with Christ.

The more difficult question is how Christ can make an offering of penitence for others, especially in view of His sinlessness.

Unparalleled as this aspect of the representative work of Christ must always be, it is not without human analogies. Of course, if we take the hardshell view of the nature of human personality, no progress along this line is possible. In theology and ethics few errors are so costly as the habit of thinking of persons as separate entities like the pebbles on a sea shore. But such a view is not true to human experience, and it breaks down hopelessly once the expansive power of love in human relationships is recognized. Even apart from experiences founded on love, this fact can be seen. Men of probity when forced into contact with sin feel themselves imprisoned in its clinging folds; its weight falls upon their spirit and humiliates them by its shame. If they have a developed communal self, they may even be conscious of the guilt of wrongs they have not committed and become the 'conscience' of a community. Infinitely more true is this when the heart is filled with love. Moberly has given us a classical example in his picture of the love of a mother who makes the shame of a child her own.[1] One can only say that in some mysterious manner the sins of others become an intensely personal concern. In love we pass beyond the confines of individuality and are united with them in a

[1] *Op. cit.*, 122ff.

union which is not the loss of identity but the enrich-
ment of life. But if the sin of others can be felt, it
can also be confessed, not indeed as our own, but as
that of those who are loved. We can feel the penitence
they ought to feel and voice it before God. This experience is too real to be dismissed; the examples of it
come from the highest and holiest planes of human life,
and it is the vantage ground from which we catch
glimpses of a representative penitence in the self-offering
of Christ.

Such a ministry might be attributed to Christ on the
sole ground of His love for men. In this case the argument would be from the less to the greater, from the fact
of representative penitence in men to its exercise by Him.
But there is another foundation for affirming this belief:
to do so is only to extend what is already implied in His
self-identification with sinners. Self-identification of
this kind is much more than the patient endurance of the
penalties of sin; it also includes a sense of the horror of
sin, a sorrow for its presence in those who are loved, and a
longing for their reconciliation with God. Must it not
also entail the voicing of the better mind and aspirations
of men? The strong representative element in the Messianic consciousness of Jesus is a decisive reason for
believing this to be true of His self-offering, and therefore
of finding in it the expression of representative penitence
for the sins of men.

But is sinlessness a fatal bar to the exercise of such a
ministry? Can representative penitence be expressed
by one 'who did no sin, neither was guile found in his
mouth'? The analogies already drawn from human experience have much to teach in answer to this question.
Similar ministries among men are indeed exercised by
those who confess themselves to be sinners, but they can-

not be fulfilled by those who love sin. The celebrants are those whose endeavour it is to put sin beneath their feet and whose eyes are on the goal of Perfect Love. This fact is important. It is impossible to argue that, if they reached that goal either here or hereafter, they would thereby be debarred from the service of representative penitence, for to suppose this is to hold that the condition of the holiest of activities is sin. So far, indeed, is this from being true that it is actually sin in men which makes their offering imperfect; they are held back from the exercise of representative penitence because they are sinners. The bearing of this argument upon the self-offering of Christ is manifest: His sinlessness is the necessary condition of His oblation. Moberly is undoubtedly right when he contends that sin blunts the edge and dims the power of penitence, and that, in the perfectness of its full meaning, penitence 'is not even conceivably possible, except it be to the personally sinless'.[1]

We have reason, then, to find this element in the self-offering of Christ. Doubtless, when all has been said, it remains the very mystery of love, that the sinless should voice the penitence of sinners. Human analogies help us up to a point, but it is no matter for wonder if they do not take us all the way. 'How are we', asks Althaus, 'who as sinners cannot know what perfect love is, to understand what complete solidarity may be achieved by perfect love?'[2]

III

Thus far, with full recognition of the dangers of a one-sided emphasis, an attempt has been made to isolate the

[1]*Op. cit.*, 117.　　　[2]*Mysterium Christi*, 210.

central element in the doctrine of the Atonement, namely, the offering, which Christ, as the representative of man, presents to the Father on his behalf. It is now necessary to examine the complementary aspect of the doctrine, in other words, the way in which this offering becomes a fundamental element in man's approach to God. Once more, this is a doctrinal, and not a historical theme. From its nature historical criticism knows nothing of a Living or Exalted Christ, except so far as the idea appears in the New Testament writings. This idea, as a truth of Christian experience, belongs to religion, and therefore to theology. As already explained, however, it is necessary to envisage the historical inquiry in the light of its doctrinal development. For this reason, therefore, the subject treated in the present section is man's relation to the work of Christ.

The historical roots of the inquiry lie in the repeated attempts of Jesus to associate men, and in particular His disciples, with His Messianic suffering and death: His promise to James and John that they should drink His cup, His words about cross-bearing, His attitude to His three disciples in the Garden, and, above all, His institution of the Supper. All these, in different ways, are indications that Jesus did not view His suffering as a work accomplished apart from the response of men. The Supper is a means whereby His disciples may participate in the power of His self-offering, since by His word the bread which they are bidden to receive is interpreted by Him as His body, and the wine as His covenant-blood shed for many.

Naturally, the question whether the Supper is meant to be a permanent means of fellowship in the redemptive activity of Christ is of vital importance for such an inquiry as the present. Historically, as we have seen, the question is not capable of a categorical answer, since the words: 'This do in remembrance of me' (1 Cor. xi. 24f.), are reported only by St. Paul. Short of proof, however, the question should be answered in the affirmative, since criticism runs into the teeth of its own evaluation of the Synoptic narratives if it builds on the silence of stories which are not reports, but answers to primitive needs. The immediate observance of the Supper in primitive Christianity, attested by the Acts of the Apostles,[1] shows that reassurance regarding the continued observance of the Supper was not required; and, in these circumstances, the command for repetition in the Pauline tradition is sufficient in itself, either as a valid historical saying, or as an indication of how the original disciples had understood the intention of Jesus on the last night of His earthly life. Theology, therefore, does not build on an uncertain foundation when it finds in the Eucharist a permanent means whereby men may participate in the self-offering of Jesus.

In view of the teaching of Jesus, it goes without saying that there is nothing magical in the operation of the Eucharist, and that its efficacy does not depend on the mere performance of the rite. As we have maintained, it is a means by which effect is given to the experience of faith-union with Christ in His redeeming work, and it is this experience which is primary and fundamental. It is faith-union which provides the nexus between men and the self-offering of Jesus; it is in virtue of this relationship that all that He offers in His death is available for man in his access to God. This is the justification for the strong emphasis which the New Testament lays upon faith in connection with the death of Christ, for the faith mentioned is not only belief, but also, and especially in the

[1]Cf. ii. 42, 46, xx. 7, 11, xxvii. 35.

Pauline Epistles,[1] a mystical and personal relationship between the believer and Christ.

It is necessary to consider this relationship established by faith-union with Christ more fully. Ultimately, it is a unique relationship, and yet in human life it is not without parallels. It has some resemblance to the abandon with which a scientist greets a truth which facts force upon his attention. It is more like the act by which we make a poet's thought our own. We may reflect, for example, that death is not extinction, but our experience is altogether different when we read Shelley's lines:[2]

> 'Peace, peace! he is not dead, he doth not sleep—
> He hath awakened from the dream of life—
> 'Tis we, who lost in stormy visions, keep
> With phantoms an unprofitable strife.'

If we accept this thought, we give ourselves up to it; the words are no more Shelley's alone, but the vehicle of our own belief. For many people music provides the better analogy. When we listen to Brahms' *Requiem*, or to one of Beethoven's symphonies, we surrender ourselves to the wonder of the inexpressible; something in our personality is unloosed, and thoughts and feelings for which words are too poor find release and interpretation. The experience is sacramental, and life is full of such experiences.

Faith in Christ is a much more intimate experience because it is a relationship established between ourselves and a Living Person; it is 'recumbency upon Him as our atonement and our life, *as given for us*, and *living in us*; and, in consequence hereof, a closing with Him, and cleaving to

---

[1]'According to St. Paul this union of heart and will, an ethical union of personalities, was, no less than justification, an immediate result of the act of faith in Christ, or in God in Christ,' C. A. Anderson Scott, *Foot-Notes to St. Paul*, 38.

[2]*Adonais.*

Him'.[1]   This, of course, is the language of religion, but
it is the only language that is at all adequate, if the religious experience is real.   When faith of this kind is exercised, it is as if the eyes of the soul were opened and the
bond of the tongue loosed.   It is like entering into the
sunshine from a dark cold room.   The personality is
transfigured because it is surrendered to a love which en-
folds it and to a life on which it feeds.   Such a faith can become so intimate and immediate that it is only to be expressed in the words: 'It is no longer I that live, but Christ
liveth in me: and that life which I now live in the flesh I live
in faith, the faith which is in the Son of God, who loved
me, and gave himself up for me' (Gal. ii. 20).   Its effect
is such that His death becomes our sacrifice.   'That which
Christ uttered to God in His death, we by faith utter in
Him.   All that the cross meant of surrender to God, of
honour to the law of righteousness, of repudiation of
transgression, becomes by our faith the object to which our
repentance and consecration are joined, and in which they
are perfectly expressed to God.'[2]   'We become one with
Him in His submission and self-oblation; one with Him,
also, in His high-priestly acts.   The result is our growing
share, according to the completeness of our union with
Christ, in the spirit manifest in His death, our entrance
into fellowship with the spiritual principle of His Atonement.'[3]   This is precisely the position implied in the
words of Campbell, already quoted,[4] in which he speaks
of faith as 'the Amen of our individual spirits to that
deep, multiform, all-embracing, harmonious Amen of

---

[1]John Wesley, *Works*, v. 9.   The italics are his.

[2]J. Scott Lidgett, *The Spiritual Principle of the Atonement*, 407f.

[3]*Ibid.*

[4]See p. 283.

humanity, in the person of the Son of God, to the mind and heart of the Father in relation to man'.

In the light of this conception, man's relationship to the offering of Christ described in the last section is clear. In faith he participates in

> 'That only offering perfect in Thine eyes,
> The one true, pure, immortal sacrifice.'

Neither the obedience, nor the submission, nor the penitence of Christ is accepted as a substitute for his offering; but each becomes a vehicle for his own approach. When he comes into the presence of God, it is not as a naked soul, carrying poor gifts of his own devising; he comes as one whose gifts are transfigured and caught up into something greater. The poverty of his obedience, the weakness of his submission, and the frailty of his penitence pass into strength and power in virtue of his union with Christ by faith and love. A gratitude is created which is too deep for words, and a sense of obligation which brooks neither denial nor delay.

All theories of the Atonement find room for the exercise of faith, but it may be doubted if any of them supplies so full an opportunity for its ethical and devotional expression as one founded on the sacrificial principle, just because it is of its essence that the worshipper should identify himself with that which he offers to God.

Thus far we have limited the inquiry to the relation of the individual believer to the work of Christ, but it is also necessary to consider his relationship as a member of a worshipping community. This point is especially germane to an attempt to study the Atonement in the light of sacrifice, since frequently, and perhaps normally, sacrificial worship is offered by the worshipper, not simply as an individual, but as a member within a community. It is also required because the communal relationship is prominent in the attitude of Jesus to His suffering and death. This fact is one of the reasons why the teaching of Jesus, in relation to man, centres in the Supper rather than the attitude of direct personal faith.

The importance of worship in connexion with the appropriation of the work of Christ is that in itself it implies a Godward relationship: it is 'the response of the creature to the Eternal.'[1]   If this is its nature, worship may well be expected to contribute to the perfecting of man's relation to the self-offering of Jesus in His suffering and death. The different elements in worship each serve this end. Preaching, which is a true part of worship,[2] brings home to the worshipper the truth and glory of Christ's redemptive work and draws from him the response of faith. It does this as much by teaching as by exhortation. Only as God is known can He be worshipped: even the worship of 'an Unknown God' implies a half-suspected secret, a mystery not yet made known. In the same way man's attitude to the work of Christ depends on knowledge. The individual can win knowledge for himself by study and research, but even he, as a worshipper, needs to hear in company with others the proclamation of the Word. In this lies the supreme opportunity of preaching. Because it is so great it can descend to the pedestrian essay; but it can also rise to heights which transcend anything which can be given by the printed page or learned discussion, since it is the good news proclaimed by the Church and not simply the word of the preacher. For this purpose the discussion of theories is not necessary, but preaching may

---

[1] E. Underhill, *Worship*, 3.

[2] 'The Word is for Evangelical worship something as objective, holy, and given, as the Blessed Sacrament is for Roman Catholic worship. Indeed, it is a sacrament; the sensible garment in which the supra-sensible Presence is clothed,' E. Underhill, *Worship*, 278.

with advantage supply constructive teaching and seek to remove patent errors and misunderstandings. Its range, indeed, is enormous. Any preaching which makes Christ and His work known, in relation to the Divine Rule, forgiveness, reconciliation, and faith; or which presents Him to the understanding as the healer, the sin-bearer, and the restorer of man; or which describes His priestly ministry and His call for sacrificial living; makes possible an intelligent and whole-hearted response to all that He has done for man.

Praise and adoration serve the same end, especially if they are offered as the spontaneous tribute of man without thought of result or gain. Faith rises on the wings of praise because unsuspected powers of human personality are released in response to a richer insight of the infinite grace of God in Christ, and an attitude of the soul is expressed which, temporary as it is, can become the basis of a steady and permanent relationship. Here lies the justification for the anthem and the hymn. So long as the temptation to judge a hymn as if it were a scientific statement is resisted, its words bring home powerfully to the mind the wonder of Christ's suffering and death, while the act of singing defines and directs an attitude of adoration and faith.

Silence and meditation also provide a necessary discipline. One of the more notable features in present-day interest in questions of worship is the perception that this method of the soul's approach to God can be corporate as well as private. The value of meditation in respect of the work of Christ is that it is contemplated by an exercise of the whole personality. The activity of the intellect is not in abeyance, but it is not isolated from other human relationships. The thought of Christ ever presenting Himself before God and calling man to fellowship with Himself in His redeeming activity can be embraced in the full exercise of thought, feeling and will, in a spirit analogous to that in which one contemplates a scene in nature, a matchless work of art, or the mystery of perfect music.   A passage of Scripture may form the starting-point for this silent meditation, as, for example, the majestic words in which the writer of the Epistle to the Hebrews describes the entrance of Christ 'not into a holy place made with hands, like in pattern to the true; but into heaven itself, now to appear before the face of God for us' (ix. 24); or again it may begin with some sacred picture or emblem or act of ritual which brings home vividly to the mind the surpassing worth and dignity of the work of Christ.

Prayer necessarily plays an important part in perfecting man's relationship to the work of Christ.   It does this because in prayer longing is expressed for more perfect obedience, submission and penitence, and because the spirit of loving devotion, which is the foundation for the experience of union with Christ, is deepened and enriched. All this, of course, is true of private prayer, but it is also true of the prayers we utter in fellowship with others with whom we have common relationships and responsibilities. Especially is prayer the communal act in which we confess that Christ's self-offering is our offering with which in contrition and faith we seek to identify ourselves.

References to worship, preaching, adoration, meditation, and prayer may seem to some to be out of place in a scientific study of the doctrine of the Atonement; and, indeed, in most discussions they are conspicuously wanting. There is, of course, justification for the exclusion of such themes when it is a question of deciding technical points, like the use of words, the history of ideas, the genuineness of sayings; but if, as here, there is a desire to study the attitude of Jesus to His death, there can be no just appreciation of the results that are reached until they are seen in the light of Christian life and worship.

The act of worship which bears most closely on man's corporate approach to God in Christ is the sacrament of Holy Communion, and it is from this standpoint that its importance is most clearly seen. Indeed, it will generally be found that neglect of the sacrament accompanies an over-emphasis upon the individual and personal aspect of man's relationship to the work of Christ. So long as attention is limited to this aspect, it is natural to feel that the rite is not of central importance. The immediate need is to establish the personal faith-relationship! How can the celebration of a rite be compared with this paramount necessity? This attitude is logical, and cannot be effectively challenged, so long as the initial assumption is held. The position is entirely altered once it is recognized that reconciliation is a process realized in the lives of those who are members of a community. As such, the individual must perforce approach God by means of a rite, just because it is an act of communal worship, a means whereby one man in association with other men can draw near to God.

It is some dim perception of this truth which must be held to account for that growing appreciation of the necessity and value of sacramental worship which is one of the facts of the present religious situation. The tendency of modern thought is to stress the communal elements in human life, even to the loss, and, it may be feared, the serious loss of its individual aspects. The change is an inevitable redressing of the balance from the unhealthy individualism of the nineteenth century, and it must be confessed that, in spite of its perils, it is a much needed adjustment, a step on the way to a better understanding of man's true place in life. Christian thought cannot but be in-

x

fluenced by the force of the contemporary current; it is compelled to study man's approach to God from the standpoint of his communal relationships. This is the reason why, in so much present-day thinking and writing, there is a new and sustained interest in sacramental worship. It is not a question of imitation, or of unhealthy concentration upon external things, to the neglect of spiritual realities; it is the urge of the perception that man is a social being first, last and always, and that he must approach God as one who has fundamental responsibilities to his fellows. Once this truth is grasped, the Eucharist is seen from a new angle; it cannot lie at the circumference of Christian worship, but must stand at the centre, as a means whereby man approaches God and appropriates the blessings of Christ's self-offering.

These reflections throw light upon the act of Jesus in instituting the Supper in close connexion with His Messianic suffering. It is no longer matter for surprise that He invited His disciples to partake in a rite instead of speaking to them about personal faith-union with Himself. The latter, we have seen, is included in the former, but the rite is that which is needed in a corporate relationship. When, in addition to the original disciples, one thinks of the unnumbered multitudes of men who through sacramental worship have entered into fellowship with Christ, the perfect suitability of the Eucharist to human need is especially evident. This perception means that no modern presentation of the doctrine of the Atonement is likely to be satisfactory which ignores, or deals imperfectly with, the doctrine of the Eucharist. The Eucharist falls within the orbit of the Atonement alike by reason of the teaching of Jesus and of the life and experience of the Church. Clearly as this fact is being recognized to-day, it is no new discovery. Before the Oxford Movement of the last century, it was recognized by John and Charles Wesley, as their collection of *Hymns on the Lord's Supper*[1] shows. The lines of Charles Wesley:

> 'This eucharistic feast
> Our every want supplies;
> And still we by His death are blessed,
> And share His sacrifice',

exactly express the doctrine commended in these pages.

Wherein, it may be asked, does the communal aspect of the Eucharist differ from that which it presents to the worshipper as an individual? Simply in this: that, whereas the individual may find the taking of consecrated bread and wine the means by which he enters into the power of the offering they represent, in the worship of the community he does this with a clear sense of the relationships in which he stands to others. He is a member of the community, wide as earth and inclusive of heaven, for which Christ died. It is in this consciousness that he approaches God, conscious not only of personal sins, but also of the sin of the world, its blindness, cruelty, and hardness of heart. In this sin he is enmeshed, whatever his individual contribution to it may be, because he is a child of man, a member of a sinful community. It is not to be wondered at, that, in this conviction, he sees a deeper significance in the self-offering of Christ than can be gained in any other way. Within him sound the words: 'Behold the Lamb of God, that taketh away the sin of the world!' and the Amen of his spirit to Christ's offering of obedience, submission, and penitence, attains its deepest intensity. In

[1]The Preface, taken from Dr. Brevint's *The Christian Sacrament and Sacrifice*, was sometimes published separately. 'Wesley taught his people by precept and his own practice the importance of frequent communion. The Sacrament of the Lord's Supper was administered to the Societies in London every Sabbath Day,' R. Green, *Wesley Bibliography*, 44.

this way the Eucharist offers its supreme opportunity for participation in the Sacrifice of Christ.

In conclusion, it is important to insist on the necessity of combining the personal and the communal aspects of man's approach to God in Christ. In itself, the individual relationship is too narrow, and too much dependent upon the accidents of temperament, to be satisfactory; while the danger of the communal approach is that it may become formal and lifeless. 'Sacramental communion', writes Moberly, 'is vainly material after all, if it is not conceived of mainly as an aspiration and growing on towards oneness—not mechanically, so much, of flesh, as inherently of character and of spirit, with the Crucified.'[1] Such a conception rightly combines both sides of man's relationship to the self-offering of Jesus. Especially necessary is it further to combine both aspects with obedience to Christ's call to sacrificial living in His words about cross-bearing and the drinking of His cup. The more we shoulder the responsibilities of others, and drink the cup of their sins and sorrows, the more fully we discover the incomparable greatness of Christ's work for men. As we tread the *via dolorosa* we learn that it begins, as it ends in the heart of God, that the Sacrifice of Jesus is the expression in history and in time of what is eternally true, that for all men there is an abiding High Priest of whom we can say:

'He pleads His passion on the tree,
He shows Himself to God for me.'

[1]*Atonement and Personality*, 271.

INDEX OF SCRIPTURE REFERENCES

INDEX OF SUBJECTS

INDEX OF PROPER NAMES

PRINTED IN GREAT BRITAIN BY ROBERT MACLEHOSE AND CO. LTD.
THE UNIVERSITY PRESS, GLASGOW